FACILITATING DEVELOPMENTAL ATTACHMENT

The Road to Emotional Recovery and Behavioral Change in Foster and Adopted Children

DANIEL A. HUGHES, PH.D.

JASON ARONSON INC.
NORTHVALE, NEW JERSEY
LONDON

Director of Editorial Production: Robert D. Hack

This book was set in 11 pt. Bell by Alabama Book Composition of Deatsville, Alabama and printed and bound by Book-mart Press of North Bergen, New Jersey.

Library of Congress Cataloging-in-Publication Data

Hughes, Daniel A.
    Facilitating developmental attachment : the road to emotional
recovery and behavioral change in foster and adopted children /
Daniel A. Hughes.
        p.   cm.
    Includes bibliographical references and index.
    ISBN 0-7657-0038-7
    1. Attachment behavior in children.   2. Foster children — Family
relationships.   3. Adopted children — Family relationships.
I. Title.
RJ507.A77H84   1997
155.44'5 — dc20   96-30402

Printed in the United States of America. For information and catalog write to Jason Aronson Inc., 230 Livingston Street, Northvale, New Jersey 07647. Or visit our website: http://www.aronson.com

CONTENTS

ACKNOWLEDGMENTS

My therapeutic orientation and interventions have been greatly influenced by the work of Milton Erickson and his followers. While most of his work was developed with adult clients, its value in engaging and leading children with poor attachments is considerable and is limited only by the sensitivity and skills of the therapist. I also frequently employ a psychodynamic perspective in interpreting for a child and his parent how past experiences of abuse and neglect are affecting his current affective, perceptual, and cognitive experiences and his related behaviors.

Contacts with therapists and treatment foster parents at the Attachment Center in Evergreen, Colorado, served as the initial impetus for my exploring ways to touch and hold these children in therapy and to raise them at home. Just as the infant and young child rely greatly on touch to attach to his mother, so, too, does the poorly attached child need to touch and be touched if he is to discover the reality of relatedness. Connell Watkins, Nancy Thomas, and Deborah Hage were especially willing to share their understanding and skills in working with children with attachment problems. While there are various significant differences in our approaches to interventions with these children in therapy, I remain grateful for having been exposed to the Attachment Center and the strong commitment and creative interventions with these very troubled children that these therapists and parents have demonstrated. The parenting principles and techniques employed by the treatment parents in the Attachment Center's therapeutic homes have been very influential in my work.

I have also been affected by the works of Ann Jernberg, Stanley Greenspan, and Allan Schore as well as by various other clinicians, diagnosticians, and theorists who will be quoted.

I am grateful for the opportunity to intervene in the lives of many children and their new families in Maine. I have consulted with many competent and committed caseworkers from the Department of Human Services and with other therapists who treat these sad, angry, and frightened children. My work with various professionals at Community Health and Counseling Services and Casey Family Services has also been beneficial.

I am indebted to the suggestions and criticisms provided by Catherine Monk of Jason Aronson that helped to fashion the final stages of this work.

Finally, I wish to express gratitude to my wife, Barbara, and our children, Megan, Kristin, and Madeline. Without them, I would not have understood the meaning and place of attachment in my life and in the lives of us all.

1

INTRODUCTION

All children, at the core of their beings, need to be attached to someone who considers them to be very special and who is committed to providing for their ongoing care. Children who lose their birth parents, especially those who have experienced the trauma of abuse and neglect, desperately need such a relationship if they are to heal and grow. Providing psychological treatment to such children is a challenge, a responsibility, and an opportunity for great professional satisfaction and personal joy. However, if the child in treatment is not experiencing an attachment to a parent, whether because of lack of ability or opportunity, the therapist is greatly limited in her efforts to assist the child in beginning to heal and in wanting to work to become "special" to self and others.

When these children fail to form an intense attachment to a parent, their developing sense of self is experienced as being bad and incomplete and their autonomy develops in a very limited and fragmented manner. They are very likely to experience deep shame, intense rage, pervasive anxiety, and extreme isolation and despair. They are also likely to manifest a variety of destructive and self-destructive symptoms whose functions are to attempt to make life bearable when it is lived outside the basic reality of interpersonal relatedness. When, as adults, these children do attempt to develop intimate relationships with others, they often experience much conflict, heartbreak, jealousy, violence, and abandonment since they lack the abilities needed to become intimate with another. They relive, alone and in very compulsive ways, the abuse and/or neglect that they lived as children. On those occasions when we have the opportunity and ability to facilitate both a basic attachment between a child and parent as well as the development of a positive and well-integrated autonomous self, we live with the knowledge that the child now has a chance to adequately pursue happiness and success within the human community. These children now have the most fundamental skills necessary to break the generational cycle of abuse.

Stopping the abuse is not enough. The results of the abuse often live on within the child and render him unable to take advantage of the new opportunities presented to him. Many children enter foster care or are placed in an adoptive home and then proceed to prevent their parents from enabling them to develop in healthy directions. These children often make their new parents' love, support, guidance, and directions ineffective and permeated with stress, conflict, and disillusionment. Why do they not take advantage of the opportunities given to them within these good families? Why do they continue to work so compulsively to re-create the circumstances of abuse and neglect that they experienced in the past? Too often we have "saved" these children from abuse, but we have failed to encourage their healing. We have failed to show the child how to respond positively to a relationship with a parent. We have failed to show the parent how to structure the relationship so that the child is more likely to become meaningfully engaged. With these children, our primary respon-sibility is to provide them with the opportunity for an attachment to a caring and capable parent and then to focus all our energies on success-fully facilitating this attachment. Within this context, the child has the means of developing a sense of self that is both positive and competent.

Let me briefly list qualities common to many of these children that make it very difficult for them and their new caregivers to establish a positive, reciprocal relationship:

1) They work very hard to control all situations, especially the feelings and behaviors of their caregivers;
2) They relish power struggles and have a compulsion to win them;
3) They feel empowered by repeatedly saying "No!";
4) They cause emotional and, at times, physical pain to others;
5) They strongly maintain a negative self-concept;
6) They have a very limited ability to regulate their affect;

7) They avoid reciprocal fun, engagement, and laughter;

8) They avoid needing anyone or asking for help and favors;

9) They avoid being praised and recognized as worthwhile;

10) They avoid being loved and feeling special to someone; and

11) They are enveloped by shame at the origin of the self.

Certain factors cause the development of these qualities. These factors, which need to be explored and understood if we are to uncover ways of facilitating the child's readiness to form an attachment to his new parent, include the following:

1) Repeated abuse and neglect leads to an anxious and disorganized attachment that creates a poor working model both for the developing self and for subsequent attachment relationships.

2) This poor working model creates chronic vigilance and lack of trust in future caregivers.

3) This poor working model creates a sense of self as "bad"—a self that becomes limited and fragmented in physical, affective, behavioral, and cognitive development.

4) The loss of birth parents is unresolved; the child is not able to establish new relationships and must compulsively reenact the loss.

5) Early experiences of a reciprocal mother/child dialogue are minimal; the self is both unaware of the realities of attachment and has weak internal skills needed to become engaged in one.

6) Early socialization experiences are characterized by humiliation, terror, and rejection. There is intense opposition to new socialization experiences.

Increasingly we are realizing that a healthy infant and child develop as part of a primary attachment to a caregiver. The existence of this attachment constitutes the womb for the "psychological birth" of the infant. Increasingly, too, we are realizing that an individual's healthy identity requires the presence of relatedness with others as much as the presence of individuation. The "working model" for our manner of relatedness, evolving over the first four years of life, is our first attachments to the primary caregivers in our lives. It reflects the *developmental attachment patterns* (as described by Stanley Greenspan 1988) which define the nature and qualities of our physical, affective, behavioral, and cognitive development. From this model, we define our basic communications, comfort, empathy, identifications, conscience, care giving, and styles of relating to the various individuals in our lives. When the initial working model is insufficient for the full development of these qualities, every effort must be made to provide other models of sufficient emotional depth, behavioral variation, and cognitive meaning for the child to utilize in order to proceed with his development.

This task of facilitating attachment to new caregivers is rendered more difficult by the pervasive working model distortions caused by abuse and neglect. These children perceive caregivers as violent, cruel, rejecting, and unpredictable. Safety is increased through avoidance, silence, denial of one's own feelings and thoughts, lying, manipulation, and developing an attitude of constant vigilant control over one's environment. This working model does not include any reality of mutual enjoyment nor does it include accepting the caregiver's socialization expectations as the best means to remain safe and to develop with a balance between individuality and relatedness. This working model also involves the child seeing himself as bad, lazy, selfish, mean, and probably stupid. He sees himself as incapable of and undeserving of enjoyable experiences and loving relationships.

When the child with a weak attachment interacts with a seemingly caring and giving adult, the child assumes that it is his own successful manipulation that is causing the adult to act in a caring way rather than any nurturing quality of the adult or any intrinsic worth of the child. When the adult disciplines him, he interprets the discipline as abuse, rejection, and humiliation, further proof that caregivers are not to be trusted, and the need to rely on manipulative control of others becomes greater. Thus, the new parent's care giving does not facilitate trust. Adults who "give" the most are seen as those who are easiest to manipulate rather than as those one can trust. Acts of nurturance from parents are often seen as means to control parents rather than opportunities to become attached. If these parents want to "give" to the child, the child is quite willing to take advantage of the situation for his own self-focused reasons that have little to do with relatedness.

These children are often drawn to new adults, who are easier to charm and manipulate, rather than to their foster or adoptive parents, who are beginning to make realistic demands on them. The child's affection is often indiscriminate since it does not represent a developing attachment but rather a means of controlling an adult, any adult.

Within a healthy attachment, discipline is a fact of life. The child may grumble, but he accepts the fact that one parental role is to teach. He has a basic trust that this teaching (though at times annoying) is ultimately given in his best interests. Discipline leads to his socialization and helps him to move from the healthy narcissism of the infant to the engaging mutual relatedness of the preschool child. The healthy child's working model for parent–child relations incorporates the value of such teaching into all aspects of his developing identity. It is a model for behavior, skill development, values, and interests.

The child who is poorly attached to a caregiver views discipline as arbitrary, cruel, and rejecting. When discipline is not perceived as being actually abusive, it is probably seen by the child as neglecting his wishes and needs and being deeply humiliating at the core of the developing self. It represents the child's failure to adequately manipulate and control the adult, leaving the child feeling more vulnerable to future abuses beyond his control. He does not see that discipline is directly associated with his behavior nor that it is in his best interest. Rather, it is proof that this adult, too, is cruel. The adult's other "nice" behaviors were deceitful.

Affection, discipline, and mutually enjoyable communication and activities emerge naturally within a healthy parent–child attachment and, in turn, further intensify and develop this attachment. A great variety of emotions emerge naturally within this relationship. Joy and anger, sadness and excitement, affection and anxiety all come and go within the profound security of a basic attachment. The toddler does feel shame when limited and this serves a healthy purpose in early socialization experiences when it is not associated with disgust and rejection. As he continues to develop, conflicts are resolved, wishes emerge, and separate interests are pursued. Every activity is colored by the attachment. The child discovers that he can develop himself as a worthwhile and competent individual without sacrificing the basic attachment with his parent. He does not have to sacrifice his autonomy in order to try to satisfy his basic attachment needs.

Regretfully, affection, discipline, and mutually enjoyable interactions are much less successful in achieving these ends for children who are poorly attached to their caregiver and who possess a working model that emerges from profound abuse and neglect. The parents who attempt to raise these children quickly discover that their parenting skills are not very effective. Their love is rejected, misinterpreted as weakness, and used against them. The child may well take advantage of their love as a way to hurt or control them. Discipline is misinterpreted, strongly resented, and resisted. Mutually enjoyable activities that the child cannot control are rejected and turned into battles.

Poorly attached children try to control everything in their daily interactions with their caregivers. This compulsive need to control functions to manage their unmet needs for both attachment and autonomy. Since they do not feel attached to their caregivers and thus cannot feel safe through their relationships with them, their only means of trying to establish a sense of safety is through successfully controlling whatever happens. At the same time, this frantic control is manifested as constant oppositional and/or avoidant behaviors that represent their primary maladaptive means of trying to meet their developing autonomy needs.

The majority of children who enter foster care or who are placed for adoption are able to make the transition to their new homes successfully with traditional social and mental health services. They do manifest the ability to attach to their new homes despite various past traumas. This book is focused on the smaller group of foster and adopted children who have disorganized, insecure, and disrupted attachment histories and who lack the ability and readiness to form a secure attachment with their new parents. When such children are placed in foster homes, they immediately prove to be a profound challenge to the skill, caring, and commitment of their new foster parents. These parents often work harder with their poorly attached child than they ever did with their other foster or birth children. They believe, and are often told by professionals, that love and patience will be enough. They seek assistance and find waiting lists, a series of helpers involved in career or job changes, and counseling and recommendations that do not effect meaningful change. Having begun with an idealistic desire and an actual passion to make a difference in the lives of a few traumatized children, they often drift toward discouragement and self-doubt. They blame themselves for not getting through to their child. Often, with considerable guilt, they finally ask that the child be moved to another home. Tragically, this sequence occurs for countless foster children. For many of these children, it happens over and over.

It is in these situations that intensive therapeutic interventions are required. These interventions must make use of the parents' commitment, basic skills, and own capacity for attachment. They must demonstrate very directly and intensely to the child how much the parents have to offer him and how totally he needs these parents for his own basic psychological development and survival. These interventions must engage and enhance the child's physical, emotional, behavioral, and cognitive traits if he is to learn to use this opportunity to form a healthy attachment.

To be effective, the child must be engaged by the therapist at the level of preverbal attunement rather than in a setting of rational discussions.

The therapy must also involve a great deal of physical contact between the child and the therapist and parent. During much of the most intense therapeutic work, the child is being touched or held by the therapist or parent. His intense emotions are received, accepted, and integrated into the self. Within a therapeutic atmosphere based on attunement, he is able to begin to explore aspects of himself and his relationships with his parents that have previously not been accessible. The development of both the child's attachment to his parents and his integrated self is the primary goal of the therapist; all else is secondary.

In traditional child therapy, the child's relationship with the therapist is the critical foundation for change. This relationship develops trust between the child and therapist, and the trust then allows the child the freedom to explore trauma, work through conflict, integrate troubling experiences, and so forth. However, with a child who has a profound lack of experiences of trust, there is a great deal of difficulty on his part in beginning to trust the therapist. The relationship is too circumscribed and brief and it lacks the crucial quality of 24-hour-a-day engagement that a parent has with a child. The child perceives the therapist's acceptance and nondirectiveness as qualities that are easy to control and which result from his successful manipulations. The child's goal is often only to maintain control of the therapy session.

These children, in fact, show their capacity to manipulate the therapist by providing some disclosures in order to insure that the therapist will allow the sessions to proceed according to the child's wishes. They "give" the therapist some of what they know that she wants in order to be able to do what they want. They benefit little from such disclosures. These children also learn in therapy that there are advantages to recalling the abuses of the past because they make great excuses for their present disruptive, aggressive, or defiant behaviors. Once a child lacking a secure attachment learns that adults respond with sympathy to accounts of abuse, his motivation to accept responsibility for his current behavior decreases unless this tendency is directly and forcefully dealt with in the treatment. Even then, it may remain a problem since he is often good at finding other adults who will accept past abuses as legitimate reasons to maintain present distorted perceptions and inappropriate behaviors.

In psychotherapy with children who have attachment problems, parents need to be present and actively involved in the sessions. The parent–child attachment is the central therapeutic goal. The relationship between the child and therapist is certainly important as well, especially in so far as it serves as a "working model" for the child's relationship with the parent.

The parent's presence enables the therapist to model crucial ways of engaging for both the parent and child. There is frequent shifting between the therapist–child relationship to the parent–child relationship in any given session. The parent becomes a co-therapist in important ways.

In psychotherapy, all aspects of the child's relationship with the parent are explored. Love and fun and also conflict and discipline have equal weight. Since love and fun tend to consistently decrease in families with poorly attached children, they must begin to increase in therapy and then both parent and child must learn ways to facilitate and protect that experience in the home. The child's fears of love and fun are explored and his means of sabotaging these experiences are uncovered. Activities to build love and fun are developed and ways of maintaining or reestablishing love and fun during conflict and discipline are also found.

Discipline is explored, discussed, and reenacted in order to frame the child's response to discipline as evidence of his difficulty with trusting the parent and with accepting the self rather than as evidence of the parent being mean or of the child being bad. Above all else, discipline must be structured so that it does not break the developing engagement between the parent and child. The child may misbehave in order to avoid any emerging attachment. He may also misbehave in order to control the parent's emotional reactions. Misbehavior may reflect his intense ambivalence about attachment. The parent must respond in such situations in ways that build, not weaken, the attachment.

The child's difficulty with trusting the parent is explored, discussed, and reenacted. It is related in part to his perception of discipline as being abusive. He generalizes constantly from his experiences with the abusing parents to experiences with his new parents. A differentiation between the old and the new is made in many ways over a variety of family life situations in order to begin to reduce the generalization. Helping the child to differentiate the old from the new parent is critical if he is to begin to trust the new. Framing misbehavior, discipline, conflicts, and parental authority as important aspects of the child's learning to trust is a critical component of therapy and psychological movement within the child. Otherwise these issues simply represent "behavior management," which is not enough to effect lasting development and change. Trust is also difficult to experience for the child who is full of shame and is convinced that he is not worthy of trust. Such children resist any encounter that would facilitate the experience of mutual parent–child trust.

Treatment of children with attachment problems must be intensely engaging if the child is to become receptive to a new and emotionally rich way of relating to his parent. Many instances of delight, anger, fear, and sadness—expressed through yelling, whispering, crying, and laughing—occur during the sessions so that the child remains engaged with the therapist and parent and experiences a deep, positive, reciprocal interaction. The therapist constantly directs the child to the parent for expressions of permission, sorrow, gratitude, fun, surprises, conflict resolutions, and so forth. Parents hold, rock, hug, and tickle the child, not in an artificial prearranged way, but as a natural part of a sequence of interactions.

Another crucial aspect of the psychological intervention is facilitating the parent–child interaction outside of the treatment session. This is too crucial to be left to parent-education classes or support groups. These interactions must be integrated with the treatment interactions. The therapist needs to demonstrate to both parent and child a general framework for raising a child who has significant difficulty with attachment. She must also suggest numerous specific ways to relate with the child in day-to-day situations.

This book presents a framework for therapeutic interventions with children who show significant difficulty forming and maintaining an attachment to their primary caregivers. Much of this work focuses on children who were abused and/or neglected by their birth parents. Most often these children did not return to their birth parents and so were left with the task of developing attachments with their foster and/or adoptive parents. Many of these interventions might also apply to children who are with their birth parents but for various reasons have weak or maladaptive attachments with them. However, the interventions assume that the parents with whom the children are learning to attach do themselves show the ability to engage in appropriate attachments with children and demonstrate a level of psychological health superior to that of their children. These children cannot and should not be expected to work for and take risks toward becoming attached to adults who are not able or willing to interact with the child in a competent and committed manner.

Regretfully, as is true with much of the psychological treatment of children (Kazdin 1993), there is little supporting research for these treatment interventions. Most of the research on the psychological treatment of children does not focus on the treatment of abused and neglected children. Research often focuses on cognitive-behavioral interventions in treatment programs in university settings. I have done what most clinicians do in their practices, namely, study, read, talk with other clinicians, review and develop my own framework and techniques, observe the results, and then begin the process of learning again and again.

When I use the term attachment I am referring to the unique relationship between a child and his parent that facilitates the healthy developmental patterns that require such a relationship. Such a relationship does not occur with the child's therapist, teacher, or other potentially important adults in his life. Just having a relationship with a parent does not insure that the child is "attached" to her. Attachment refers to the unique relationship between child and parent through which the child is able to proceed with the major qualities of his own psychological development.

Stanley Greenspan (1988, 1989) refers to *developmental attachment patterns* that emerge, in sequence, through the child's relationship with his parent and his own psychological state over the first 4 years of his life. The child who has had a weak and disorganized attachment with his parent during part or all of those first years manifests many significant problems in his developmental attachment patterns. To have a chance for a good life, he must be able to form a secure attachment with his new parents and develop healthy attachment patterns that facilitate his affective, behavioral, and cognitive development.

This work is motivated in part by my convictions formed over my first 15 years of psychological practice that traditional interventions of play therapy, parent education, and cognitive-behavioral techniques are not sufficient to effect significant progress with the poorly attached child. Although traditional interventions are often effective with foster and adopted children who have positive and stable working models of relationships and of the self, they are much less so with the poorly attached child. I have seen many children who never benefited sufficiently from these interventions to be able to begin to live well within the human community. I have also seen many foster and adoptive parents give overwhelming blood, sweat, and tears to these children without having a significant effect on their child's ability to benefit from these gifts. This work is written with the hope that others will become more aware of this tragedy and more committed to the search for ways to provide meaningful assistance.

2

ATTACHMENT:
THEORY and RESEARCH

HEALTHY ATTACHMENT

Attachment as Dancing

A nine-month-old girl becomes very excited about a toy and reaches for it.
As she grabs for it, she lets out an exuberant "aaah" and looks at her mother.
Her mother looks back, scrunches up her shoulder, and performs a terrific
shimmy with her upper body, like a go-go dancer. The shimmy lasts only
about as long as her daughter's "aaaaah" but is equally excited, joyful, and
intense. [D. Stern 1985, p. 140]

Daniel Stern has given us this and many other examples of *affective
attunement* in the mother–baby relationship. Any one of these interactions
might last only a few seconds. But there are hundreds, no, thousands of
such experiences in the first two years of the mother–child attachment.
They serve as the building blocks for the strength of the relationship. The
relationship, in turn, is the basis for the full development of the child. All
aspects of the child's development—neurological, physical, emotional,
behavioral, cognitive, and social—are fundamentally effected by the qual-

ity of this unique relationship. The individual characteristics of this mother and this child are brought into harmony within this most crucial bond.

Stern (1985, p. 141) regards attunement as the "intersubjective sharing of affect." In his detailed work on attachment, Robert Karen (1994, p. 348) indicates that important early development and attachment theorists— Stern, Bowlby, Ainsworth, and Winnicott—consider attunement to be "central to every aspect of the infant's psychological development."

According to Stern (1985), in affective attunement the mother's activities match the feeling state of her infant and do not simply imitate his behavior. When attuned to her infant's affective state, her response closely matches the intensity, duration, and shape of her infant's behavioral expressions. During the first 9 months, her response is most often in the same modality of her infant's. If he vocalizes, so does she. When he makes a face or waves his hands, she immediately follows with a very similar expression. As he continues to mature, her responses increasingly use other modalities to express the same affective state. She may make a face in response to his vocalization or make a particular vocalization in response to a given movement. In this way she is leading her infant into more complex experiences of interpersonal enjoyment and union. Through these experiences he also is becoming more able to integrate his various affective states and activities.

Attunement experiences are recurring moments of interpersonal communion that rest upon affect. Research (Stern 1985, p. 147) suggests that when the mother and infant are playing, these experiences are observed every 65 seconds. These countless experiences are the foundation for later affective communication between the child and others. We describe this communication as empathy.

According to Stern (1985, p. 156), most attunement experiences relate to vitality affects rather than categorical affects. By vitality affects he is referring to the underlying feeling states that are always present within any living individual. These states are characterized by intensity and pleasure/displeasure. With infants, these continuous feeling states are distinguished by sudden, abrupt shifts and extreme levels of intensity. We all have experienced how a baby is "putting everything into it" when he is crying and then a moment later he is laughing just as intensely. By attuning to these underlying vitality affects, the mother is constantly connected with her infant at a preverbal level of experience and he feels continuously connected to her. Attunement experiences also help her infant to learn to regulate and integrate these feeling states so that they come to form the early experience of "self." As will be shown later, such attunement experiences are crucial in therapy in helping the poorly attached child to feel connected to his therapist and parent at the preverbal level and to begin to regulate his affects and integrate divided and rejected aspects of the self.

John Bowlby's work over the past several decades is considered by many to be the foundation of our understanding of the nature and importance of attachment in the lives of human beings. In describing how an infant's attachment to his mother develops, Bowlby focuses on the moment-to-moment, day-to-day interactions between mother and infant. It is these small, ordinary moments—not dramatic, out of the ordinary experiences—that build a strong attachment. In *A Secure Base*, Bowlby (1988, p. 7) describes this process well:

> When a mother and her infant of two or three weeks are facing one another, phases of lively social interaction occur, alternating with phases of disengagement. Each phase of interaction begins with initiation and mutual greeting, builds up to an animated interchange comprising facial expressions and vocalizations, during which the infant orients toward his mother with excited movements of arms and legs; then his activities gradually subside and end with the baby looking away for a spell before the next phase of interaction begins. Throughout these cycles, the baby is likely to be as spontaneously active as his mother. Where their roles differ is in the timing of their responses. Whereas an infant's initiation and withdrawal from interaction tend to follow his own autonomous rhythm, a sensitive mother regulates her behavior so that it meshes with his. In addition, she modifies the form her behavior takes to suit him: her voice is gentle but higher pitched than usual, her movements slowed, and each next action adjusted in form and timing according to how her baby is performing. Thus she lets him call the tune and by skillful interweaving of her own responses with his, creates a dialogue.

Countless such interactions between mother and child occur during each and every day. It is in these moments that a *living attachment* exists, develops, and becomes a unique reality to this specific mother–child pair. Play between mother and baby both reflects and facilitates this vital reality that exists within their relationship. These interactions contain eye contact, physical contact, movement, rhythm, excitement, anticipation, and, at times, mild anxiety. Most of all, they contain a wonderful emotional tone that carries the parent and child with joy, merriment, and full engagement.

While singing, laughing or smiling, caressing or clapping, moving with alacrity or slow waltzes, nothing else exists for this parent–child. As I will indicate later, because such universal interactions are so vital in the living attachment of the normal parent-infant bond, they also most certainly have a role in facilitating attachment for much older children who are entering a relationship with a new parent. Their effectiveness is evident immediately. I have even seen teenagers become lost in such mutually enjoyable interaction with no trace of self-consciousness and with considerable merriment.

Stern (1985, p. 72) describes well how the infant, beginning at two months of age and lasting for several months, is overwhelmingly focused on his mother. His psychological development rests primarily on maintaining an intense relationship with her for most of his waking moments.

> The period roughly from two to six months is perhaps the most exclusively social period of life. By two or three months the social smile is in place, vocalizations directed at others have come in, mutual gaze is sought more avidly, predesigned preferences for the human face and voice are operating fully, and the infant undergoes that biobehavioral transformation resulting in a highly social partner.

Stern (1985, p. 70) states that the infant's "first order of business," accomplished to a large extent during these early 4 or 5 months, is to form "the sense of a core self and core others." During the first year the infant is not fully differentiated from the mother, but the origins of the sense of self are evident as the child is becoming more autonomous. He is becoming defined within this intimate relationship with his mother. The self and mother are the two sides of the same coin. Stern speaks of the mother–infant interactions as clearly not cognitive events but as those that "mainly involve the regulation of affect and excitation" (p. 75). Allan Schore (1994) also stresses that affect regulation, forming within the mother–infant attachment, is at the core of the origin of the self.

In her recent work, *No Voice Is Ever Wholly Lost*, Louise Kaplan (1995) stresses the crucial role of empathy in the reciprocal communication that occurs between the infant and mother. She indicates that this dialogue between the infant and mother breaks down "whenever there is a consistent and prolonged failure of empathy" (p. 25). She also beautifully describes the mother–infant dance as a reciprocal dialogue which is "the heartbeat of a human existence" (p. 20). She describes it as the means by which the mother "nurtures an infant and conveys the meaning of love" (p.

25). She further states that this dialogue "is crucial to the learning of love, of hate, of joy, of mastery, of play, and in the human being, the acquisition of verbal language and the symbolic communications of human culture (p. 25)." I am convinced that Dr. Kaplan is not overstating the value of the mother–child dance in human development. She convincingly demonstrates that when a child is abandoned by a parent through death, the dialogue continues within the child. The child remains attached to the dead parent in profound ways and this attachment has a great deal of influence on the child's thoughts, feelings, plans, and behaviors throughout his life. The same can be said for the child who is abandoned by the parent who is still living. This continuing dialogue cannot be ignored; it must be integrated into all efforts to help the child to form a dialogue with his new parent or caregiver.

Developmental Attachment Patterns

Various theories and bodies of research on child development conceptualize the emerging characteristics within the young child that occur within the context of a secure attachment with his primary caregiver. The quality of the mother's emotional attunement with her child is crucial in determining the nature of his biological, affective, behavioral, and cognitive development. Because the infant or toddler is engaged in his dance with his mother, his development proceeds normally; without the dance, profound distortions and deficiencies in development will result.

Margaret Mahler and colleagues (1975) describes attachment from a developmental perspective. Stanley Greenspan (1988, 1989) also considers attachment to be a developmental process. He presents *developmental attachment patterns* that emerge over the child's first 4 years of life. He describes one pattern that he considers to be a normal attachment as well as two variations of dysfunctional patterns.

Normal developmental attachment patterns consist of the following:

1. **Homeostasis**: (0 to 3 months) Concrete attachments, interest in the world and self-regulation; relaxed and alert; increasingly responsive to interesting stimuli.
2. **Attachment**: (0 to 7 months) Personal (emotional, joyful, synchronous) attachment, very interested in caregiver; especially responsive to smiles and touch with pleasure and interest.
3. **Somatopsychological Differentiation**: (3 to 10 months) Inten-

tional attachments, purposeful communications; reciprocal, cause and effect interactions with caregiver. Initiates and responds purposefully, with all sense modalities and motor system and with range of emotions.

4. **Behavioral Organization**: (9 to 18 months) Conceptual and integrated attachments; initiative and internalization; shows wide range of socially meaningful behaviors and feelings in an organized manner; able to go from interaction to separation; accepts limits while initiating much; surprising and delightful behaviors.

5. **Representational Capacity**: (18 to 30 months) Internalized, symbolic attachments; words are being used to indicate wishes, intentions, and emotions with caretaker.

6. **Representational Differentiation**: (24 to 48 months) Differentiated attachments; symbols are used to separate self from nonself and relate to others across a wide range of emotions in a balanced manner.

As one can see from this brief summary of the initial six stages of human development, the crucial characteristics of homestatic state, *emotional* responsiveness (regulation and integration), *behavioral* purposefulness (initiation, inhibition, and organization) and *cognitive* understanding (differentiation, planning, and integration) all occur within the meaning of the attachment with the caregiver. *Language*, too, emerges naturally as a means of communicating one's wishes, desires, and emotions to the caregiver. Language becomes a tool for further differentiation of self from nonself and for the development of the child's inner world of thought and emotion. Attachment with one's parents is the setting in which these developmental patterns occur.

In his work, Greenspan stresses the central qualities of differentiation and integration in the child's early development. With each step, the child is increasingly able to differentiate among his emotional, behavioral, and cognitive states and then to integrate these various states in a way that best meets the "best interests" of the whole child. Without such differentiation and integration, the child's development proceeds with significant gaps, abrupt shifts, fragmentations, and lack of maturation across all areas of functioning. The parent's consistent, congruent, and deeply engaged presence enables the healthy child's development to proceed in a fluent, integrated, and spontaneous manner.

Cicchetti (1989) also stresses the presence of "differentiation and hierarchical integration" in normal childhood development. He contrasts such development with what is present in developmental psychopathology:

Pathological development is perceived as a lack of integration of the social, emotional, cognitive, and social-cognitive competencies that underlie adaptation at a particular developmental level. Because early structures are incorporated into later structures, an early disturbance in functioning may ultimately cause much larger disturbances to appear later on. [1989, p. 379]

In an excellent, detailed, and integrative work, *Affect Regulation and the Origin of the Self: The Neurobiology of Emotional Development*, Allan Schore (1994) describes the first 18 months of life from the perspective of both psychoanalysis and neurobiology. Schore details the crucial role of the mother–child relationship in both affective and psychological development and in the physical development of the brain. He demonstrates how this primary attachment relationship truly becomes the "working model" for future intrapersonal and interpersonal development:

By providing well-modulated socioaffective stimulation, the mother facilitates the growth of connections between cortical limbic and subcortical limbic structures that neurobiologically mediate self-regulatory functions. The dyad's response to stressful transactions, such as occur in socialization experiences in the second year, is particularly instrumental to the final structural maturation of an adaptive cortical system that can self-regulate emotional states. The core of the self lies in patterns of affect regulation that integrate a sense of self across state transitions, thereby allowing for a continuity of inner experience. [1994, p. 33]

Schore describes how attunement, which characterizes the mother–infant dance, facilitates the development of the limbic system that is responsible for the gradual increase in the frequency and intensity of positive affect within the infant over the first year. This positive affect culminates in the early stages of the Practicing Stage of Attachment at 10 to 12 months. During this time, the affects of Interest-Excitement and Enjoyment-Joy are at their peaks. These months of exuberance and pleasure, based on many months of prior attunement experiences, are crucial in the entire life cycle:

The practicing phase in which the infant truly becomes a behaviorally and socially dynamic organism represents a critical period for the formation of enduring attachment bonds to the primary caregiver. The nature of the attachment to the mother influences all later socioemotional transactions. [1994, p. 98]

Schore goes on to document the equally important aspects of the later phase of the Practicing State (15 to 18 months), during which the mother begins to place limits and directives on the infant's expansive behaviors. The mother is now "misattuned" with the infant. She is experienced as "stranger" not as "mirror" and the child experiences shame, the affective component of the early socialization processes. Shame causes a break in the affective bond with the mother. It falls on the mother then to initiate "interactive repair," which serves to cause an affective reunion between mother and infant. This reassures the infant and enables him to continue with his autonomous development while maintaining an attachment with his mother. It also enables him to integrate both pleasure and frustration and affection and anger within the self and in relationship to the mother.

Schore also documents how the early Practicing Period facilitates and is furthered by the development of the sympathetic system in the right hemisphere orbitofrontal cortex. In the later Practicing Period, a similar development occurs in the parasympathetic system in the dorsolateral prefrontal cortex. However, this development only occurs optimally when the socialization experiences are followed by "interactive repair," in which the infant is reassured by the mother. Without such reassurance, the sympathetic system is again stimulated and impedes the development of the parasympathetic system. The development of both neurological structures is crucial for the establishment of affect regulation, integration, and balance. Let Schore summarize his important work:

> A central thesis of the volume is that over the first 1½ years of life the infant's transactions with the early socioemotional environment indelibly influence the evolution of brain structures responsible for the individual's socioemotional functioning for the rest of the life span. Such events occur in the context of a one-to-one relationship between the infant and the primary caregiver. . . . To be attuned to the child's internal states and the changes in these states takes a significant amount of empathic attention and emotional involvement on the part of the primary caregiver. Her participation in face-to-face merger experiences generates and sustains sufficient levels of positive affect that trophically induce the growth of new connections between neurons. [1994, p. 540]

Schore, Mahler, Greenspan, and others rightfully stress that attachment does not only consist of the magical moments of attunement during the first 10 months and the joy and vitality of the early practicing phase. They also stress the importance of the toddler's experience of separation and shame. Such experiences must lead to a reunion with the mother, one that is not a return to the earlier merging moments but a more mature attachment that is able to integrate the autonomous self with the continuing bond. This attachment also must integrate the "good" and "bad" in both the self and mother. Finally, it must move from the preverbal communion of the attunement experiences to the level of verbal communication, which greatly facilitates the child's ability to differentiate and integrate his affective experiences. The successful journey through this entire sequence is crucial for the child's development to continue in a healthy manner. I will describe the consequences of not completing this journey later in this chapter.

Attachment into Adulthood

Before presenting the consequences of a weak attachment on children, I wish to briefly mention that professionals are studying the importance of attachment with one's parent throughout the life cycle. The permanence of the relationship between the parent and child is the context in which the individual proceeds from one developmental task to the next. Adults who have such a continuing, living, evolving attachment with their parents are able to explore their world and master it, develop new attachments and relish them, and present the gift of relatedness to new generations. The "emotional refueling" that Margaret Mahler describes, where the toddler explores the new person or object and then runs back to mom for security and confidence in self and the situation, occurs again and again, year after year, when the parent and child maintain a meaningful relationship.

When an adult is able to assume that his parent would have interest, concern, and empathy for him, the present moment can be met with greater confidence and intensity. Certainly adults can experience deep and meaningful "refueling" experiences through relationships with a spouse, partner, friend, or mentor. However, such relationships are harder to develop when the "working model" of the parent–child attachment is limited and distorted. The adult who has meaningful attachments to one or both of his parents, as well as to other adults, is truly blessed.

It is much harder for the developing adolescent or young adult to function well without having a meaningful attachment with a parent with which to "refuel" the self as one enters the world of peers and life away from home. Having such an attachment at that stage of the life cycle is often crucial if the adolescent is to make the transition well. In my psychological treatment of college students, I have repeatedly encountered the profound depths of anxiety and despair that many experienced when they did not feel a part of their new world at college, did not feel confident that satisfying relationships or interests were likely to develop, and at the same time, experienced little emotional connection with their parents. Their experience of intense loneliness was all-pervasive. One young woman, when asked if she could contact her parents for support about a very difficult time that she was having at college, replied, with cold certainty: "I am nothing but an investment to them. They'll now see me as an investment gone bad."

For years professionals have emphasized that in order for an individual to develop and experience his own autonomy, he first had to separate from his parents. Without such a separation, it has been assumed that one remained dependent upon one's parents and never truly became "one's own person." That assumption is being reconsidered by many individuals who are studying adolescent development, women's psychological development, adult development, and attachment throughout the life cycle. A model of *individuation and connectedness*, rather than *individuation and separateness*, is being created.

Many professionals are now asserting that the assumption that one needs to separate from one's parents to become autonomous is not a valid model of psychological development for women nor, possibly, for men. This point is made repeatedly by Janet Surrey (1991) in *Women's Growth in Connection*. Surrey (1991, p. 57) describes a girl's relationship with her mother as containing three features. First, the girl has "an ongoing interest and emotional desire to be connected to her mother." Second, the girl greatly increases her capacity for "mutual empathy" within the matrix of the relationship. Finally, she views this reciprocal relationship as the source of "mutual self-esteem." The girl, as she becomes an autonomous woman, knows "the capacity to 'become one's own mother'—that is, the internalizing of the attentive, listening, caring relationship to oneself—does not occur in isolation but within relationship" (p. 62).

Surrey contrasts this description of the developing attachment between the mother and girl with the disruption of the boy's relationship with his mother. Surrey refers to a male colleague who "described his childhood experience as 'learning not to listen, to shut out my mother's voice so that I would not be distracted from pursuing my own interests,'" (1991, p. 55). I do not believe that his experience is unique. Surrey (1991, p. 55) concludes: "For boys then, 'separation' means not only a simple physical but an emotional disconnection, often with the goal of not being bound or 'controlled' by mother's feeling states or needs" (p. 55).

The problems inherent in the boy's disrupted attachment with his mother are described by Olga Silverstein (1994) in *The Courage to Raise Good Men*. Silverstein presents many reasons to believe that society's emphasis on a boy "cutting the apron strings" if he is to ever discover himself as a man is, in truth, interfering with the man's ability to experience himself as a competent and caring individual who is able to establish and maintain meaningful connections with others. The adolescent male's continuing attachment to his mother if he is to transition well into adulthood is as necessary for him as it is for his sister. The model of autonomy and relatedness being developed for women might be considered as the preferable model for all human beings. Intense, intimate relationships, beginning with and modeled on a healthy parent–child attachment, are central components of one's self, not simply an "add on" to be "well-rounded."

WEAK ATTACHMENT

Trauma & Neglect and Weak Attachment

There are profound obstacles in our attempts to make significant therapeutic interventions with children who have problems in forming an attachment to their primary caregivers. The problems of these children in relating to adults are pervasive and intense, and traditional mental health interventions are often insufficient. These children have limited skills for engaging others in mutually enjoyable, reciprocal interactions. Their developmental attachment patterns are immature and contain many interrelated deficiencies in affective, behavioral, and cognitive development. They are often hypervigilant in relationships and not receptive to the positive influences, messages, and experiences being provided by competent and caring adults. They do not "dance" well and they are reluctant to learn how. Even if they have some motivation to learn, they often cannot hear or understand the music. They are masters at driving away, or at least maintaining a barrier against, those who attempt to engage them.

Children who have been abused and neglected are at high risk of having established an insecure, dysfunctional attachment to their primary caregiver. Cicchetti (1989) indicates that many studies document that maltreated infants and toddlers are likely to form such insecure attachment relationships. Estimates of the number of such children who develop varying degrees of insecure attachment patterns range from 70 percent to 100 percent. He notes that in forming an insecure attachment to his primary caregiver, the child has developed a working model for all subsequent relationships as well as for his own view of himself. Because of the central importance of such a working model in one's psychological development, Cicchetti (1989, p. 389) concludes that "attachment dysfunction may be a prime etiological factor for the occurrence of maltreatment as well as for its continuation across generations." In a related article, Aber and others (1989, p. 614) clearly state their similar conclusion originating from research based on attachment theory:

> Many of the other problems maltreated children exhibit (poor self-esteem and self-regulation, aggressive/rejecting and/or withdrawn/isolated relations with peers; lags in cognitive and academic competence; elevated levels of behavioral symptomatology) appear to us to be derivative of the central problem—an overconcern with security issues reflecting an expectation of unresponsive, unavailable, rejecting adults.

Research using The Strange Situation Paradigm has shown that children who have experienced abuse and neglect are at high risk for manifesting all three forms (ambivalent, avoidant, disorganized) of anxious attachment with their primary caregiver (Cicchetti 1989). For example, Patricia Crittenden (1988) found that among children who experienced abuse, neglect, or both, only 5 percent to 13 percent manifested a secure attachment. Of the children who had experienced marginal maltreatment, 36 percent manifested a secure attachment. Of those children who were in "adequate" homes, 59 percent manifested a secure attachment. Differences in anxious attachments were also noted between those children who primarily experienced abuse and those who experienced neglect or marginal maltreatment. Among the abused groups, over 50 percent manifested very disorganized attachment behavior with features of both avoidance and ambivalence. In contrast, children who experienced only neglect were much more likely to manifest the anxious-avoidant pattern of attachment. These and similar findings lead Crittenden (1988, p. 163) to raise a very important issue, namely, whether "maltreated children can remain sufficiently flexible to modify their behavior further if conditions improve." Crittenden goes on to indicate that the maltreated child must inhibit his displeasure at his experiences. She believes that this occurs at a price, namely, "The child's internal feelings are consistently denied by her/his behavior. This may be maladaptive for the individual's long-term development and relationship with others" (p. 163). In another article Crittenden and Ainsworth (1989, p. 439) refer to research which suggests that "it is the withholding of close bodily contact—with or without rejecting attitudes—that accounts for the anxious/avoidant pattern." Children who are subject to profound neglect have few of the experiences of physical comforting and affection that are central to attunement and which are necessary for secure attachment.

The latest manual for psychiatric diagnosis (*DSM-IV*) describes Reactive Attachment Disorder of infancy and early childhood and then indicates that this disorder is due to "pathogenic care." Such care is characterized by:

1. Persistent disregard for the child's emotional needs for comfort, stimulation, and affection;
2. Persistent disregard for the child's physical needs; and
3. Repeated changes of primary caregivers.

These three traits of pathogenic care are elements of emotional and physical neglect, and they are frequently present as well in families where children are at risk for abuse.

Years ago there was a study of infants who lived in an institution from shortly after birth until they were from 9 to 29 months of age. The authors, Sally Provence and Rose Lipton (1962), found that whereas these infants' physical needs were well met, they were not provided with the opportunity to form an attachment with a primary caregiver. When the children were 5 years of age and in permanent homes (2 to 4 years after leaving the institution), they still demonstrated features in their functioning that reflected abnormal developmental attachment patterns emerging from the first year or two of their lives. These features included being slow to ask for help, being indiscriminately friendly, poor impulse control, and difficulty delaying gratification and making transitions. They also demonstrated poor problem-solving ability.

It is evident that for these very young children there were significant, ongoing effects from the failure to be provided with a responsive, sensitive caregiver who comes to know their unique needs and responds to them with the attunement so necessary for their development. The effects are evident in the child's later relationships with caregivers as well as in their developing affective, behavioral, and cognitive abilities.

Doris Brothers (1995) describes, from a psychoanalytic perspective, the development and central importance of trust in psychological well-being. She proposes that at the core of the effects of trauma on the self is the betrayal of trust that such trauma represents. She describes how one's abilities to trust others develop throughout the life cycle, becoming increasingly realistic, abstract, complex, and differentiated over the course of development. Trauma impedes the development of these qualities of trust and so hampers the overall development of self and the ability to relate successfully with others. When the child experiences trauma at the hands of his primary caregiver, he is most vulnerable to forming a maladaptive developmental attachment pattern that greatly impairs his overall development.

Children who have experienced abuse and neglect are very likely to manifest significant difficulty forming and maintaining a secure attachment to their caregivers and this has profound implications for efforts to treat their traumas and facilitate their psychological health. Richard Small and colleagues (1991), at the Walker Home and School in Massachusetts, state emphatically that "a large proportion of children in residential treatment . . . suffer from severe attachment disorders and abuse reactivity" (p. 327). They go on to say, "most of our clients have severe difficulty making and maintaining basic human connections" (p. 331). They conclude that "the severity of the attachment disorders and accompanying problems in social relationships . . . pose particular problems for models of treatment which purport to provide an experience that corrects the continuities of early development" (p. 331–332).

Small and colleagues (1991) note that the traditional treatment modalities for children in residential treatment, namely long-term psychotherapy, milieu therapy including designs with a cognitive-behavioral approach, and family therapy are not sufficient to effect significant change in the child's functioning. They state that the treatment models are not "comprehensive enough to give us clear guidelines for moving from effective therapeutic behavior management to the restoration of developmental momentum for each child" (p. 335). These authors very clearly describe the reality of disturbance and the insufficiency of our interventions that many parents and clinicians see daily but which are not sufficiently discussed. Too often, elaborate diagnostic workups do not contain equally elaborate treatment recommendations. The question of how to move from describing the problems to successfully intervening in treating the problems needs much more consideration. If we know diagnostically that the roots of the child's psychological problems lie in disrupted and/or distorted early attachments, then we need techniques that will facilitate the child's ability to form new attachments to caring and competent adults.

Abnormal attachment patterns may be the most devastating effect of abuse and neglect on the child's development. The work of Cicchetti and others strongly indicates that for the child to heal and become whole, the child needs to go far beyond resolving the immediate effects of trauma. He needs to develop working models of self and others that allow for a positive experience of self and a sense of trust in his primary caregivers' nurturance and commitment.

Specific Symptoms of a Weak Attachment

When we speak of the importance of the child having a secure attachment to his caregiver, we are not just referring to the emotional meaning and sense of security generated by his first relationship. We are referring especially to the central role of attachment in all areas of the young child's psychological development. We cannot understand his physical, affective, behavioral, or cognitive development without understanding the nature of his attachment. If the attachment pattern is insecure, anxious, and fragmented, the child's development will unfold in numerous abnormal ways.

As was noted in the last chapter, Stanley Greenspan (1988) not only described the normal developmental attachment patterns, but he also presented two abnormal developmental attachment patterns that result from significant deficiencies in the infant-caregiver relationship.

In the first abnormal pattern, the infant quickly becomes disinterested in his immediate world since it provides him with few experiences of attunement that would bring the interpersonal world to life. His cries and movements elicit little response, so he does not develop the sensory and motor skills needed to actively engage in an intentional manner. He withdraws from touch. Motions are repetitive since there is little reciprocal activity. Concepts and language are also slow to develop since there is little value in communication needed to facilitate the recognition and expression of thoughts and ideas. The inner life of this young child is poorly differentiated, experienced, and understood. What little satisfaction there is reflects his lack of affective engagement. Manipulating objects with little interpersonal meaning or withdrawing into solitary fantasy is the most safe and desirable activity.

In the second abnormal pattern, the infant becomes very interested in his immediate world and tries to make sense of it. This young child does get a response from his caregiver, but it is inconsistent and unpredictable. The child tries to find out what he must do to elicit the interpersonal response that he craves. He discovers that he is most likely to get a response through intense affective expression. His frantic mission becomes one of trying to establish an empathic attunement with a caregiver, any caregiver. All of his efforts end in failure and he is never able to establish the inner sense of security, self-regulation, and integration that emerges only when empathic attunement is present—moment-to-moment and day-to-day—without the need for desperate efforts on his part. His behavior and affect remain random, with abrupt shifts and fragmented meanings. Symbols become used to express intense, disjointed inner states rather than being used for reciprocal communication about the self, other, and the world.

These two abnormal patterns are similar to the two accepted patterns of insecure attachment: avoidant and ambivalent. Crittenden (1995) considers the first pattern to be the "defended" children who use "false affect" and "coy behavior" to try to get by in the world. They experience neither genuine affect nor enjoyment of reciprocal relationships. They deny their feelings. They rely on cognition to analyze the external world for survival since they cannot rely on their caregiver to be aware of and responsive to their thoughts and feelings. The second pattern she describes as "coercive" children who employ exaggerated affect in an effort to make their caregivers more predictable. They employ threats and bribes to get what they want. Affect—intense and impulsive—not cognition, directs their behavior.

Bruce Perry (1995) also describes two persistent patterns of traumatized children that are quite similar to those described by Greenspan and Crittenden. In the first pattern, the children are characterized by a high degree of dissociation and withdrawal. The children in the second group are noted for their persistent highly aroused, vigilant state. Similarly, Beverly James (1994) speaks of dysfunctional children as manifesting dissociation and/or constant vigilance.

The abnormal patterns described by Greenspan show a severe deficiency in the development of biological regulation, affect integration, behavioral purpose and direction, and general cognition. Deficiencies in every area lead to various forms of psychopathology. Both patterns show an extreme lack of the development of words to convey intentions and emotions as well as to differentiate self from nonself. Whereas the securely attached preschool child has begun to use symbols to communicate with his primary caregiver and others about a wide range of "socioemotional" themes, the poorly attached child often uses symbols to describe things in the present. Efforts to communicate tend to be chaotic with fragmented meaning. In any attempt to facilitate the development of a child who manifests one of these two dysfunctional attachment patterns, one must initially engage him in the early stages of the development of these patterns. This necessitates a preverbal engagement based on the affective attunement of the mother with her young child.

Cicchetti (1989) and colleagues (1990) have found that maltreated children show disturbances in "internal-state (or emotional) language usage." These researchers indicate that the ability to "master internal state labels" is critical if young children are to "communicate about past or anticipated feelings, goals, intentions, and cognitions." Moreover, Cicchetti, in Cicchetti and colleagues (1990) demonstrated that the ability to use internal state language allows them to clarify misunderstandings and misinterpretations with their companions during ongoing interactions. They also found that maltreated children talked less about their own activities and made fewer requests for information. They used words primarily to speak of the "here and now." Cicchetti and colleagues (1990) found that children who are securely attached at 24 months demonstrate more internal state language at 30 months than do insecurely attached children.

Allan Schore (1994) demonstrates how early language learning evolves from the infant–mother affectively based utterances during the first 18 months of life. Whereas more mature language development involves the left hemisphere of the brain, these initial transactions involve the right hemisphere. It is the dynamic infant–mother dyad that is crucial for the neurobiological development of the significant structures within the right hemisphere.

R. Rogers Kobak (1993) summarizes research that demonstrates how there is a strong positive relationship between early language development and secure attachment. The ability to communicate coherently on personal themes is seen as reflecting secure attachment relationships throughout the life span.

Taken as a whole, the above findings and theory suggest that one's ability to use language to communicate about one's "socioemotional" life to another reflects the health of one's attachment history and, moreover, is crucial to foster and maintain one's primary attachments throughout life. Such use of language is based on successfully developing earlier developmental attachment patterns which established biological, affective, and behavioral regulation and integration. Without this foundation, language will remain detached from the "socioemotional" meaning of one's life. There should be some value in psychotherapy that facilitates one's ability to identify and communicate coherently about one's "inner state" with someone with whom one is trying to develop an attachment. Cicchetti (1989) and Kobak (1993) come to a similar conclusion.

The work of Bruce Perry (1995) at the Baylor College of Medicine also has implications regarding the negative effects of a poor early attachment. Dr. Perry describes how the infant and young child's brain develops, the brain stem developing first, to be followed by the midbrain, limbic system, and cortex. He shows how emotional reactivity, affiliation, and attachment occur within the interaction between the caregiver and the young child's midbrain and limbic system. These parts of the brain need to be activated if attachment is to occur. Dr. Perry suggests that a critical period, or at least a sensitive period, for such interaction to occur is early in the child's life. At a later age, he may be much less receptive to attachment. Moreover, trying to teach the child attachment through "cognitive" means is unlikely to succeed since the cortex is not crucial in the early development of attachment. Since these traits involve the more primitive structures and functions of the brain, they are likely to be much more resistant to change than are experiences involving the cortex of the brain.

Allan Schore (1994) documents extensive neurobiological research that is supportive of Perry's conclusions. Schore indicates that the quality of the initial attachment relationship has direct effects on the neurological development of significant areas of the brain. This neurobiological development has major implications for the development and regulation of affect, which he considers to be at the "origin of the self." He shows convincingly how the origins of significant psychopathology throughout the life span have their roots in the mother–infant relationship during the first 18 months of life. The infant who experiences a lack of attunement perceives the preverbal self as being basically flawed, and thus he feels empty, helpless, and hopeless. Without having the mirroring mother to regulate and integrate his emerging affective self, he is left the victim of his own poorly regulated impulses, affects, and psychological-behavioral-biological states. The infant in the practicing phase who experiences the stress of misattunement without sufficient maternal availability to reduce the inner turmoil through a reunion with the mother is left without little internal resources to cope with stress.

Schore also describes how the experience of healthy shame, so important in socialization, becomes unregulated and overwhelming when it is associated with maternal humiliation and rejection rather than "interactive repair" and reunion. Such humiliation and rejection lead to "narcissistic rage" with extreme unregulated affect. The lack of reunion impedes the ability of the child to regulate the effects of stress and develop a moderating, integrative, affective state. Schore (1994, p. 341) perceives the increase in violent acts by children as representing "the major threat to the further development of our species" and he traces these acts to "unregulated unconscious primary narcissism and humiliation-induced rage." To Schore (1994, p. 207), extreme pathogenic shame-inducing experiences are seen as being central in later pathology:

> Early unregulated contempt-humiliation exchanges may be a common form of practicing dyadic pathology and an important source of transmission of severe emotional disorders associated with the under regulation of aggression. For example, there is now strong evidence that shame-humiliation dynamics always accompany child abuse.

Schore traces the development of the borderline personality disorder to disorders of attachment in the first year of life. He traces narcissistic personality disorder to disorders of attachment in the Practicing Stage.

Lieberman and Pawl (1988), in summarizing the clinical work of Fraiberg, describe the symptoms of "Nonattachment" as showing impairment in three major areas: interpersonal relationships, cognitive functioning, impulse control and the regulation of aggression. Let me quote them as they describe the tragic consequences of children who have not been given the basic human right to form an attachment to an adult:

> These children are considered to suffer from a structural ego deficiency that seriously handicaps their long-term capacity to establish emotionally meaningful human relationships. Their connections to people are based on need and satisfaction of need, regardless of the specific personal qualities of the partner. There is no apparent emotional claim for one partner over another, and no signs of longing or distress when one caregiver leaves and another arrives. Thus, one person can easily replace another provided the child finds her/his needs and wishes satisfied. Cognitively, nonattached children tend to show impairments of intellectual functioning, particularly of language. Finally, there is a marked deficiency in the child's ability to regulate aggressive impulses and to modulate responses to frustration and displeasure. [p. 331]

In a recent study, the best predictor of oppositional defiant disorder was a lack of attachment security in preschool boys (Speltz and colleagues 1995). The central role of insecure attachments in conduct disorders has also been found (M.T. Greenberg and colleagues 1993).

DSM-IV (1994) presents the criteria for the diagnosis of Reactive Attachment Disorder of infancy/early childhood. This disorder has two forms: inhibited or disinhibited. It is said to be present when the child manifests "markedly disturbed and developmentally inappropriate social relatedness beginning before age five." In the "inhibited" form, the child shows "persistent failure to initiate or respond to most social interactions." The child's social responses are inhibited, hypervigilant, highly ambivalent, and contradictory. In the "disinhibited" form, the child shows "diffuse attachments and indiscriminate sociability." There is a lack of "selective attachments." The incidence of this disorder is said to be unknown at present.

The developmental phases described by Greenspan and Mahler, as well as the research of Cicchetti, Schore, Perry, and many others, all illustrate how intimately the child's early attachment is connected to all areas of his development. Clearly, children who manifest a dysfunctional attachment pattern will demonstrate psychopathology in many, if not all, areas of their development. Problems in *relationships* (aggression, lack of discrimination, ambivalence, clinging, lack of empathy, withdrawal, manipulation, demanding, poor cooperation), *emotional development* (limited range of recognition and expression, lability, poor frustration tolerance, habitual depression, anxiety), *behavioral control* (impulsive, unpredictable, chaotic, or passive and repetitive), and *cognitive development* (inner-state language, anticipation of rejection/aggression, inability to learn from new experiences, failure to understand cause and effect in daily living) are all likely to be evident in the more severe forms of attachment disorder.

My own clinical experiences suggest that the following symptoms are very noticeable in children who exhibit significant attachment difficulties. These have been mentioned above or, I believe, can be inferred from the above developmental descriptions and research:

1) Compulsive need to control others, including caregivers, teachers, and other children;
2) Intense lying, even when "caught in the act";
3) Poor response to discipline: aggressive or oppositional-defiant;
4) Lack of comfort with eye contact (except when lying);
5) Physical contact: wanting too much or too little;

6) Interactions lack mutual enjoyment and spontaneity;
7) Body functioning disturbances (eating, sleeping, urinating, defecating);
8) Increased attachment produces discomfort and resistance;
9) Indiscriminately friendly, charming; easily replaced relationships;
10) Poor communication: many nonsense questions and chatter;
11) Difficulty learning cause/effect, poor planning and/or problem solving;
12) Lack of empathy; little evidence of guilt and remorse for others;
13) Ability to see only the extremes: all good or all bad;
14) Habitual dissociation or habitual hypervigilance; and
15) Pervasive shame, with extreme difficulty reestablishing a bond following conflict.

While many of these symptoms can be related to the immediate effects of trauma, their persistent expression, despite quality caregiving and psychological treatment, is related to poor developmental attachment patterns. These symptoms will certainly interfere with the development of a secure attachment with a foster or adoptive parent. Issues of a "poor working model," abnormal developmental attachment patterns, and maltreatment, all need to be addressed if the new attachment is to "take."

A secure attachment contains a sequence of mother–child experiences over the first 24 months that are crucial for all later development. During the first 10 months, there are countless attuned interactions in which the mother and infant merge, leading to a number of months in which the child moves with pleasure and interest into the world. This is followed by an increase in socialization experiences in which the infant experiences shame, signaling a break in the attachment and enabling the child to evaluate his behavior in light of the mother's "gaze." The shame experiences are crucial for the child's subsequent development. However, to be a positive experience, it must be brief and lead to a reunion with the mother fairly quickly. The child then has learned to reflect on his behavior without losing his attachment. He is learning to deal with ambivalance and to integrate autonomy with intimacy.

In children with poor attachments, there are often recurrent failures of the mother–child bond. First, the attuned experiences over the first 10 months tend to be too few and weak. Experiences of neglect and abuse are likely to greatly undermine any "secure base" that is so crucial for later development.

Second, the child's developing self in the early practice stage is restricted by the fears and doubts inherent in not feeling fully attached to the mother. The "self" remains quite limited and is not expanding with new interests and pleasures as it must.

Third, when the child does encounter shame experiences, he is poorly equipped to deal with the stress of this break in the sense of attachment. The attachment was insecure already and is further strained now.

Fourth, the shame experience is generally associated with contempt and rejection. Even if the initial 10 months had fostered a secure attachment, such later experiences certainly restrict all future expansion and impair the integration of autonomy and intimacy. The child quickly withdraws to the psychological state of the original 10 months, hoping to again feel secure. Commonly, the parent would either reject such "baby" behaviors or infantilize the toddler, communicating that remaining merged with the mother was the only safe choice.

Fifth, there is also likely to be a lack of opportunity to reunite with the mother after contempt and rejection. The child is abandoned, terrified, and enraged at this negation of both the developing self and whatever prior attachment had been achieved. Thus, the healthy sequence of union, exploration, shame, and reunion has been replaced by neglect, self-minimizing, contempt/rejection, and isolation/splitting.

As with most psychological realities, there is a continuum of attachment problems ranging from mild to severe. The *severity* of the child's difficulty in forming a secure attachment to a capable and receptive caregiver is based on many factors. First, the severity, pervasiveness, and duration of abuse and neglect by the initial primary caregiver are certainly crucial.

Second, if an alternative caregiver (grandparent, older sibling) provided good secondary care consistently over time, the severity of the attachment difficulties should be less.

Third, if severe maltreatment occurred during the first 2 years of life, attachment abilities are likely to be more severely impaired than if the maltreatment began when the child was older.

Fourth, if the primary traumas occurred during the practicing period of attachment rather than the initial merging phase, the severity of the disorder should be less.

Fifth, children with a larger number of alternative placements are likely to have a harder time forming an attachment to a new caregiver.

The severity of the symptoms as well as their pervasiveness are important factors to know in assessing difficulties and the child's possible response to therapeutic interventions. The age of the child is very relevant. Younger children show greater responsiveness to interventions for various reasons, most importantly the fact that they openly desire an attachment more readily than do adolescents. Their dysfunctional developmental attachment patterns are also less ingrained. Many clinicians believe that interventions with children older than 10 or 11 who manifest severe attachment problems are much less likely to be successful, as well as being much more difficult. Regardless of these factors, I believe that one cannot predict with certainty how a child will respond to intensive therapy directed toward facilitating attachment. If the child can be initially engaged in therapy, with some degree of commitment to the process, he may well surprise the therapist and caregiver with therapeutic change. Since there is little enough clinical experience and research, each child warrants a chance if he can be engaged with both the caregiver and the therapist in the necessary hard work.

The treatment proposed in this book for the poorly attached child may not be necessary for abused and neglected children with only mild attachment problems. Those children may respond readily to more traditional therapeutic and child-rearing practices. This book is written for those with the more severe forms of attachment problems that correspond to Reactive Attachment Disorder.

It is a tragedy for children not to have a meaningful attachment to their parent. When their relationships to their birth parents are permanently disrupted, it is crucial for them to begin to form an attachment to their new parent. This is a necessity if they are to be able to proceed with the developmental tasks of childhood within a matrix of love and commitment that enables them to flourish and that can serve as a model for other attachments in later years. It is also necessary to provide these children with permanent attachments so that as adults they will always have a place to go home to and to parents who cherish them. Adults who have achieved no such relationships through a successful adoption or a long-term foster-care relationship will return to the abusive parent, searching for a connection with a parent, generally with no chance of either healing or developing a new attachment. They then wander the world, experiencing and causing pain and despair.

The model for interaction with the poorly attached child must be the infant–mother dance. Through repeated experiences of attunement between him and his therapist and parent, the child will gradually begin to proceed in a healthy manner through the developmental attachment patterns with his new parent. The poorly attached child will intensely resist that process.

3

CHILDREN, THERAPISTS, AND PARENTS

Before presenting the treatment described in this work, it is first neces-sary to summarize the individuals who are involved: the children, thera-pists, and parents. Many of the treatment interventions suggested are very difficult for all three individuals to experience. By their very nature, interventions designed to facilitate a child's ability to attach must engage him in a deeply emotional and intensive manner. The child's memories and affective responses associated with his original poor attachments to his birth parents are elicited and directly related to his current relationships with his caregivers and therapist. Thus, he is encouraged to *transfer* deeply meaningful relationship features from his past to both therapy and his life at home. Anticipated thoughts of rejection, abuse, and humiliation will emerge along with associated emotions of shame, rage, fear, and sadness. Many of the following interventions are indicated only for children who have the characteristics of the poorly attached child presented in the previous chapter.

CHILDREN

The children described in this work have been or still are foster children who have experienced considerable abuse and/or neglect. They also are children who have a high degree of difficulty forming attachments to their primary caregivers. They have entered a foster home or an adoptive home and are unable to take advantage of the good care which they are receiving because they have been deprived of sufficient attunement experiences to enable them to form an affective union with their new parents. I am not describing the majority of children in foster care but, rather, the child with the greater psychological problems who is at risk for many disrupted placements and a lifetime of rejection and loneliness.

Foster care serves to provide a temporary home for children who have been abused and/or neglected by their parents or guardians and who are at risk for further maltreatment if they are allowed to remain in their home. At any one time there are 500,000 children in foster care throughout the United States. In theory, the child remains in foster care for months, not years. He lives in one foster home while his parents resolve the problems that placed him in jeopardy for abuse or neglect. Once his parents are able to safely assume his care, he returns home. If they are unwilling or unable to remove the circumstances of jeopardy within a time that will meet his needs (for example, 6 to 12 months), then the child is legally freed to be adopted. Once free for adoption, he is placed in an appropriate adoptive home within 3 to 6 months.

The reality often does not resemble the theory. Many children are abused and neglected for months or even years before their circumstances are made known to legal authorities or before these authorities take action to place the child in foster care. Once the children enter foster care, they often wait for extremely long periods of time due to court delays, long delays in providing services to their parents, an overworked social services system, and, finally, because of a frequent tendency to give their parents numerous chances to reduce their problems, even when the parents are poorly motivated and show no signs of progress. As a result, months in foster care become years. During this time, the child often moves from one foster home to another either because of his own problems that make him difficult to raise or because the circumstances in the foster home change over time and the foster parents are no longer caring for foster children. As a consequence of these delays and multiple placements, the children who are traumatized by the original abuse are retraumatized by the foster care system. Their attachment difficulties upon entering foster care often become even more severe a few years later.

If America is to meet the needs of its foster children, it is crucial that the reality more closely approximates the theory. Services and decisions must be made in a fashion that will meet the needs of the children who are waiting in their temporary homes. The children need to be provided with a permanent home, and if their parents are not able or willing to assume their permanent care within 6 to 12 months, they should be placed as soon as possible in an adoptive home. If they have the ability to form a secure attachment with adoptive parents, they need to leave foster care as soon as possible so that their attachment with their permanent caregivers can begin. They need to receive traditional psychological and social services to assist them to resolve their traumas, grieve their losses, and make the transition into a capable and loving family. The present work is not meant for these foster children. If the system worked as it were designed, their needs could be met in an ethical and professional manner. The failures of this system are not the focus of this work.

The children described in this book are the more severely traumatized children who are restricted in their ability to form an attachment to their foster parents. These children had very poor attachments to their birth parents, and these deficiencies may also have been exacerbated by long delays and many foster placements. These children still need to have their legal uncertainties resolved. If their parents are unable or unwilling to resolve the circumstances that created the abuse and neglect in a timely fashion (say, in 6 to 12 months), efforts to reunify with their parents should cease so that the children can refocus their psychological energy and receive specialized services that will facilitate their ability to form a secure attachment with their new parents. It is for these children that this book has been written.

"Therapeutic" foster care is offered to many children who manifest a moderate degree of psychological problems. The assumption is made that these children require a different level of care than is furnished in regular foster homes. The foster parents are provided with additional training and various supports to raise this very difficult child. Many private nonprofit agencies contract with their state foster care system to provide these special services to enable the child to remain in a home rather than be referred to a residential facility. The state of Maine has several such programs. There are nationally known programs such as Pressley Ridge in Pittsburgh, Pennsylvania, and the Oregon Social Learning Center in Eugene, Oregon. Casey Family Services has programs throughout the country to provide similar services for children who require long-term foster care. The Attachment Center in Evergreen, Colorado, is a therapeutic foster care program that has been specifically developed for children who manifest Attachment Disorders.

Some therapeutic foster care programs too often "micromanage" their foster parents, instructing them to raise the foster child in very specific ways and second-guessing their day-to-day decisions. Foster parents are helped more by assuming that their knowledge and commitment to this unique child is probably greater than the other members of the treatment team. They should not be expected to change basic family routines and interactions to match some child-rearing "cookbook." Rather, they need to understand basic principles of raising a poorly attached child and need to be presented with ideas that will translate these principles into their unique family structure. If these parents habitually can maintain an empathic and comfortable atmosphere in their home while presenting reasonable choices and consequences for the child, their daily decision-making should be supported, not constantly scrutinized.

Many of the children with whom I have worked have been in therapeutic foster care programs. These children have moderate to severe difficulties forming an attachment to their foster parents. With most of them there is no longer any active effort to reunify them with their birth parents. Many have been freed for adoption and some have already been adopted or are in a foster home in which their parents intend to adopt them. With these children it is often not in their best interest to move them out of foster care and into a new adoptive home quickly. They first need to learn to attach to their foster parent before they can be placed in an adoptive home without a high risk of disruption.

One might think that poorly attached children should be quickly placed in an adoptive home so that they would not have to leave the parents with whom they have finally learned to form an attachment. Why not teach them how to form an attachment with their adoptive parents? There are various reasons. First, these children require a type of child rearing that is difficult and often different from the way many parents naturally raise their children. Foster parents who take these children must be committed to learn how to provide them with the family life that they require. These parents are able to do this difficult work in part because it is not a lifetime commitment. Moreover, they are not looking for the same parental satisfactions that motivate individuals to apply to adopt children. Therapeutic foster parents who are effective are able to allow their children to "use" them to meet their profound affective, interpersonal needs. They expect little in return during their day-to-day work. Adoptive parents instinctively want something in return although it is little compared to what they are giving their child. They want to be special to their child and they anticipate a lifetime of mutual enjoyment and respect. When I do work with adoptive parents, I frequently must work hard to convince them that if they want to elicit progress, they must first "detach" and raise their child as if he were a foster child. Their poorly attached child often sees how important it is to his adoptive parents to establish a bond with him. He uses this desire against them by hurting them through rejecting their love. Trained foster parents expect less "love" from their child and are more able not to react personally when their child repeatedly betrays their trust in numerous ways.

Many of the foster parents with whom I have worked have adopted their foster child. They were in a position to be able to adopt or the adoption was subsidized because of the child's difficulties and because of their financial situation. However, other foster parents, for various good reasons, did not adopt the child after he had formed an attachment to them. They were quite direct with their child during the entire placement that their role in his life was to teach him how to get close to and trust them so that he would be able to go on to have a similar relationship with his adoptive parents. Their child's grief and anger are accepted as natural and are worked through. While the loss of his foster parents with whom he has formed an attachment is painful, he has developed the inner resources necessary to work through the loss and to develop an attachment with his adoptive parents. I have seen this happen a number of times without causing trauma to the child or without interfering with his ability to become attached to his new parents. These children have retained an important bond with their foster parents long into their adoptive placement. Their foster parents often become "extended family," similar to grandparents or aunts and uncles.

When a child is not going to be reunified with his birth parents, it is important to determine early in his foster placement whether he is able to attach to adoptive parents or if he first needs to learn how to attach through a therapeutic foster placement. If he has the ability to attach, his foster parents do not have to teach this. Instead, they provide appropriate care for as short a time as is possible until he can be adopted.

However, if freed for adoption, a foster child should not be rushed into it before he is able to respond well to a good home. At the same time, he certainly should not wait indefinitely in foster care. He should be receiving a specialized program that actively works with him to learn how to become attached to his parents. Committed and competent foster parents in close collaboration with a knowledgeable therapist must provide the interventions needed for him to learn to attach in as timely a fashion as is possible. The therapist and foster parent(s) are a team who teaches him what he needs to learn in order to live well within a family. If this service is not provided for the poorly attached child, all the other services that he has received to reduce his jeopardy will be only partially successful. He may be safe and the abuse may have stopped, but he remains at high risk for serious psychological and interpersonal problems. His adopted parents will often fail to reach him and they and he will experience years of disillusionment and pain.

Foster children who manifest the features of the poorly attached child are the subject of this book. As noted earlier, they exhibit an intense need to control others and they show this need through manipulative and/or aggressive and defiant means. They are indiscriminate in their affection, using their charm to get what they want rather than for developing an attachment with selective adults. Because of their history of a lack of attunement experiences, they lack empathy for others. Because of their humiliation and rejection during acts of autonomy, they experience pervasive shame that frequently leads to outbursts of rage. They become anxious during experiences of mutual enjoyment and affection. Because of the severity of their symptoms and the rigidity of their interpersonal patterns, they are extremely resistant to forming an attachment with their new parent. They require extensive interventions both at home and with their therapist before they are able to be successfully adopted.

THERAPISTS

If a therapist is to provide effective intervention to a child who is unable to establish a secure attachment to his foster or adoptive parent, she must be ready to bring his parent into the office and bring the therapy into the home. This therapist needs to consider the parent as a co-therapist who provides a vital component of the overall treatment. The therapist provides her knowledge of attachment and attachment disorder. She also provides her expertise in facilitating developmental momentum for the child and she communicates her understanding of how the parent needs to relate to her child in the home. During the sessions she is deeply engaged with the poorly attached child, modeling attunement and continually reestablishing it following the child's experience of shame and by providing empathy for the difficult work. The parent, in turn, provides 24-hours-per-day love and commitment to her child. For her child to learn attachment, he needs her for experiences of attunement, mutual enjoyment, and healthy shame that do not harm the relationship. If he is to proceed through his developmental attachment patterns, his attachment with her must be developing.

The therapist who provides treatment to a poorly attached child needs to have a high degree of professional and personal maturity if she is to successfully provide the intensive interventions necessary to effect therapeutic change. There are a variety of factors on all levels that will challenge her abilities.

In facilitating the child's readiness to attach, the therapist needs to be ready and able to offer ongoing experiences of *affective attunement* to him. This is a primitive, preverbal manner of engaging the child and it is a skill that would be difficult to learn in a formal, conscious manner. To be able to provide attunement well, the therapist will have experienced a great deal of attunement with her own parents when she was very young. She also would benefit from being a parent herself where she would participate in countless attunement experiences with her own child. If she is not a parent, then it would be desirable that she have experience observing parent–child attunement experiences and/or participating in such experiences with a healthy infant or toddler. Finally, she needs to be receptive to her attunement "instincts" so that she allows them to be expressed rather than suppressed, as would often be the case in more traditional therapy.

The child's *transference* will be characterized by very strong affect due to his relationship history. When the therapist directs him to recall and reexperience significant memories from his abusive and neglectful past, he is likely to feel intense rage, terror, and despair that will often be focused on the therapist. She will have to be prepared to recognize and absorb such affect if she is to be able to work with it therapeutically. If she personalizes the experience, her response will disrupt the child's work and even subject him to possible trauma. If she reacts to his affect with anger, fear, and discouragement of her own, the child will be unable to process the experience in a positive fashion. It is crucial that the therapist be able to respond to the child's transference with empathy and acceptance. She needs to be able to remain detached while responding to the unique needs of the child.

In adopting a directive stance while focusing on the most difficult areas of his past history and development, the therapist is assuming a position of significant *power* over the child in the session. While it is my thesis that assuming such a position is crucial for success given the child's very defended, controlling stance and his inability to trust, it must be recognized that this position could easily become abusive. If the therapist seeks power for its own sake, consciously or unconsciously wanting to control the child for her own personal needs, then he will again experience himself as being used by an adult and his damaged ability to trust will be further shattered. Power struggles are an easy trap to fall into, one that these children are very adept at setting for the unwary adult. If the therapist is not aware of the traps or uses these interventions simply to become good at winning power struggles, then I fear that therapeutic gains will be minimal, or worse.

It is my belief that the most therapeutic position for those children who are healthy enough to benefit from it is one of *nondirection.* In working with poorly attached children, the therapist assumes a directive stance only because it is necessary to do so. As soon as it is no longer necessary, the therapist is ready, and even eager, to give the control and direction to the child, who is now able to use it therapeutically rather than continuing to avoid or compulsively repeat the past while manipulating and controlling others.

Because of the frequency of *physical contact* with the child, the therapist needs to be very sensitive to the effect of such contact on herself and on the child. While a degree of safety is insured for both the child and the therapist because of the presence of the parent in each session, nevertheless, care and constant awareness of the moment-to-moment physical interactions remain crucial if the experience is to be therapeutic. The therapist must be aware of the child's potential fears and sexual feelings as well as any sense of helplessness and victimization that he might be experiencing. The physical contact itself is likely to cause her to have a more intense and immediate reaction to the child's activity than would otherwise be the case. If the child feels sudden rage and attempts to hit or bite the therapist, it is absolutely necessary that she be sufficiently alert, prepared, and detached enough so as not to respond in kind. If the therapist feels any rage or sexualized feeling toward the child when she is holding him, there is a strong likelihood that he will unconsciously sense her feelings and feel misused, if not traumatized.

Psychodrama, when used to reenact past traumas and destructive relationships involving the child's primary caregivers, is an intervention that requires considerable sensitivity to his current psychological functioning. If his response is becoming regressed, rigid, or frantic, the therapist must immediately reduce the intensity or change the focus. She needs to make more obvious the "make believe" quality of the intervention and help the child regain a sense of mastery of the activity. As with all interventions, it is the child's responses, not the therapist's plans, that should dictate the direction of the session.

Humor and teasing are valuable ways of engaging a child by setting a relaxed and playful tone, increasing attention, and exploring shameful experiences and conflicts. However, humor and teasing also may be used in an aggressive and hurtful manner with little sensitivity to how the child is reacting to the comments. The therapist needs to continuously assess her motives in using humor as well as to assess the immediate effects of the humor on the child.

The therapist's *recommendations to the parent* regarding consequences to give the child for certain choices as well as homework assignments for the parent also contain the potential for misuse. This is especially true with the very defiant and oppositional child, whose repetitive behaviors require strong and lasting consequences to produce any lasting change. The therapist needs to constantly stress that all such consequences must be given with considerable acceptance, nurturance, and empathy—never with anger—or they are likely to be experienced as punitive and cruel and are likely to directly hinder the therapeutic progress and the child's ability to attach.

To be therapeutic, these interventions need to be employed by a therapist who has a strong understanding, empathy, and compassion for the overwhelming loneliness and pain that are chronically experienced by children who are unable to adequately establish and maintain a secure attachment to their primary caregivers. The therapist must never lose sight of this underlying reality in the lives of these children if she wants to be able to adopt a directive, powerful position, engaging the child intensely through providing physical contact, maintaining affective attunement, giving cognitive interpretations and challenges, and applying behavioral consequences without further violating the child's developmental path. If the therapist loses sight of this reality, she is at risk for misusing her therapeutic position.

To use these interventions in a beneficial way, the therapist needs to be secure in her own personal life. She needs to have formed attachments and to have a history of successful attachments in the past and present. If the therapist is to give the poorly attached child an ongoing experience of emotional attunement, it is crucial that she have had the experience in her own life. She needs sufficient abilities for introspection and an understanding of her own thoughts and emotions to be aware of the child's inner life. She needs to have attained a strong integration and regulation of her affective life so that she can use it in the service of the child. She then can form a union with the child's affective life and go on to communicate empathy and acceptance of him.

For the interventions recommended in this work to be beneficial and not detrimental to the child's developing attachment abilities, it is necessary for the therapist to manifest a high level of personal and professional maturity and integrity. These interactions are charged with immediacy and affect and they elicit preverbal, spontaneous responses from the therapist. Her personal qualities and her own responses to intimate family situations often take center stage and influence her engagement with the child at least as much as does her training and theoretical orientation. If she has had and still has difficulties in her own close relationships with parents, partners, siblings, and children, there is risk that similar difficulties will emerge while she is treating these children. The therapist needs to be vigilant that she "does no harm." Her own self-insight, combined with peer consultation and/or supervision, satisfying attachments, and at some point having been a client in therapy herself, may be necessary to both prevent her from doing harm and to also provide a lasting contribution to a child's life.

PARENTS

The personal qualities of the parent who raises a poorly attached child are at least as important as are those of the therapist. The recommended interventions may have to be provided 24 hours each day, 7 days each week. They are provided in the home where the parent's own personal history is likely to have a major influence on how she feels about herself and how she relates to children. Most of her interactions with the child will occur without a therapist or anyone else present. The child's rage toward her is likely to be very intense at times. Her task is extremely difficult and she will need considerable inner strength and maturity and a great capacity to meet her child's very strong needs if she is to do it well.

Although the parent's personal qualities are important, it is not necessary that she have no personal or relationship difficulties. She may well struggle in her personal life, as do most of us. Her maturity must involve her ability to engage him repeatedly with attunement, to communicate empathy, and to demonstrate consistent, patient caregiving.

I have repeatedly found that those foster parents who are most able to provide the poorly attached child with a therapeutic home are those who have a deep and lasting desire to make a significant difference in the life of each child in their care. Many of these parents manifest a deep religious conviction that they are called to make such a difference. They show a passion for the well being of their poorly attached foster child which must communicate to him at some level that he may actually be special and worthwhile. This quality appears to be as important as any other single quality.

Parents who raise a poorly attached child are asked to provide him with a high degree of *affective attunement*. This experience of attunement is the foundation of all change. Her child has such difficulty forming a secure attachment because he experienced so little attunement in his first few years of life. He cannot be expected to relate to his new parent in ways that presume a level of developmental attachment beyond his current functioning. He will not be able to make progress toward a higher level of developmental attachment without the nurturing context of attunement. In order to provide frequent experiences of attunement, the parent should have experienced attunement herself during her early years of childhood. It is hoped that she also would have experience as a parent providing attunement to her own securely attached child. If she has not been a parent, she should have experience interacting with healthy babies and toddlers and observing other parents providing attunement to their children.

The poorly attached child has a history of numerous experiences of abuse and neglect, which greatly impedes his ability to relate to his new parents in healthy ways. Instead, he will generalize from his previous relationships with his caregivers and engage his new parents in destructive and manipulative ways. His *transference* to his new parents will be even more intense than it is toward his therapist. His parents will have to refrain from personalizing such interactions or they will begin to engage their child in ways frighteningly similar to the manner that the original parents treated him. The new parents must understand this process and display a sufficiently high degree of affect regulation and self-insight so as not to react to their child in harmful ways.

The *emotional demands* placed on the parent of a poorly attached child are extremely high. This level of demands is likely to continue for months, if not years. To be able to consistently meet her child's needs, it is crucial for the parent to be able to identify and meet her own psychological needs apart from her relationship with her child. She needs a level of maturity that allows her to engage in self-soothing and self-affirming activity. She needs to have meaningful attachments with significant others who are engaged with her in deeply satisfying ways. Her satisfaction in raising her poorly attached child must come from her realization of the long-term benefits to her child from having become attached to her. Her child must not be in the role of having to provide her with satisfactions or else both child and parent will become resentful and the attachment will be lost.

In parenting a poorly attached child, the parent needs to be willing and able to assume a high level of control over her child's choices and consequences. She is constantly teaching him right and wrong as well as the need to accept the consequences of his choices. Such a position of *power* is subject to misuse. She must not be motivated to find excuses to have power struggles where she will then "do whatever it takes" to win. In fact, she must find ways to avoid power struggles, using natural consequences as the central way to teach her child. While she must limit his choices to a great extent, her goal always remains one of helping her child to have the ability to make his own choices wisely in a variety of settings and relationships.

Conflict is certain to be a central reality at some point in any effort to raise a poorly attached child. The parent will have to be comfortable with conflict. She must neither avoid it nor engage in it in an angry and rejecting fashion. Her child's early history probably contained considerable conflict that led him to feel overwhelming rejection and humiliation. This parent must not re-create those experiences. She must be able to detach and provide empathy during conflicts so that her child will be able to learn from the conflict, continue to experience the strength of a supportive relationship, and develop his ability to regulate his affect and maintain his self-worth.

Raising a poorly attached child requires the capacity to provide a high degree of empathy and nurturance along with a high degree of firm and consistent discipline. Sometimes, these two qualities are not present in the same parent. Such a parent will emphasize one of these traits while ignoring the other and then justify this tendency by stressing the importance of the trait that she employs. When this occurs, I believe that the parent may well be acting primarily from problems in her own attachment history that restrict her ability to provide the full range of experiences that her child needs. In this situation, any attachment that develops will be weak and her child's development will be compromised. A clear communication of both empathy and discipline are necessary for a successful attachment.

It is crucial that the parent of a poorly attached child maintain an open, trusting relationship with the therapist if she is to be able to provide the consistently high level of care that her child needs. The parent needs to feel support and encouragement from the therapist. When she is uncertain about her child's needs or when she has responded poorly to them, she must have confidence that the therapist will not condemn her or second-guess her moment-to-moment decisions. She needs to be certain that the therapist understands how extremely hard it is to raise her child. It is essential that she and the therapist be focused on the long-term progress that her child must make if he is to have a satisfying and productive life. Day-to-day decisions and interventions may sometimes be mistakes but they will not be detrimental to this central goal if both parent and therapist have the personal maturity, commitment, and understanding needed to achieve it.

If parents do present with personal problems or parenting skills that are detrimental to the child and her attachment to them, those issues must certainly be addressed. The child cannot be expected to work hard to learn to attach to parents who place many obstacles in the way. Since the therapist is working very closely with the parents and asking them to relate intensely in therapy themselves, if there are obstacles to the child's treatment, they are likely to emerge fairly soon. It is crucial, however, that the therapist not approach the foster or adoptive parents with the assumption that they are responsible for the child's difficulties. These parents often have blamed themselves strongly for the child's lack of progress in their home. Let us not begin our interventions by further undermining their self-confidence as parents.

4

INTEGRATIVE PSYCHOTHERAPY FOR DEVELOPMENTAL ATTACHMENT IN CHILDREN

Given the pervasiveness and severity of the poorly attached child's psychological problems and deficiencies, any intervention must arouse his emotional responsiveness, engage him in all aspects of his development, and make him aware of new possibilities for the "self" and for his relationship with his parent. To accomplish this, the therapist must be able to deeply engage the child at the affective, preverbal level, and maintain this engagement in spite of the fear, sadness, and anger that the therapy elicits within him. The therapist must also directly and persistently focus with him on those areas of distress from his past experiences and relationships as well as his current thoughts, feelings, behaviors, and relationships.

Traditional child psychotherapeutic approaches for the poorly attached child are often insufficient. They have neither the intensity nor the comprehensiveness needed to elicit therapeutic change within the child who:

1) is rigidly focused on controlling all adults and new situations;
2) consistently manipulates rather than trusts;
3) has had little experience with empathy from an adult who is responsive to his best interests;
4) has numerous deficiencies in his affective, behavioral, and cognitive development;

5) anticipates new trauma, constantly generalizing from old trauma;
6) constantly experiences shame and associated rage;
7) denies the "bad self," while not experiencing himself as "good"; and
8) works to convince the therapist that his new parents are "bad" too.

Maintaining an emotional engagement with the child, regardless of the behaviors manifested by him during the session, is the foundation of all therapeutic interventions with the poorly attached child. His every behavior is utilized to foster the engagement with him. His initiatives or responses to the therapist's initiatives are accepted and then worked with in an emotionally intense and meaningful way. The child is not, however, controlling the session with his behavior. Instead, the therapist maintains very comprehensive, empathic control by using anything that the child does or says for the purpose of maintaining the engagement. This engagement, from which the child cannot disengage through avoidance regardless of his behavior, becomes the moment-to-moment building block for the development of his ability to form an attachment with his caregiver. This principle represents the *utilization theory*, so central to the therapy developed by Milton Erickson (1979, 1980), by which every behavior that the child manifests is used for therapeutic purposes. It also represents the means whereby, through affective attunement, a mother fashions a bond with her baby and facilitates his developmental attachment patterns.

Erickson (1979, 1980), is associated most closely with nontraditional interventions with adults. Though he was originally seen as a hypnotherapist, he has since been embraced by therapists of a variety of orientations, most of whom focus on the client's current functioning, including symptoms which their therapists hope to decrease and living skills they wish to increase. Therapy tends to be brief, with the emphasis on practical interventions to impact on the client's cognitive, affective, and behavioral patterns. I believe this type of the therapy to be relevant in work with poorly attached children who are often resistant and poorly motivated to engage in and respond to traditional interventions. However, given the severity of their problems, which impact on all areas of their development and relationships, therapy with the poorly attached child is unlikely to be brief.

Central to Erickson's therapeutic genius was his willingness and even preference for working with whatever affective, cognitive, motivational, and behavioral functioning the client brought to the session. In this approach to treatment, the therapist *utilizes* anything presented in therapy in the service of therapeutic change. Erickson would perceive the interpersonal meaning of an aspect of the client's presenting behavior and then respond to the behavior in a way that changed its meaning. This would elicit a new response on the client's part, often without any conscious awareness of the purpose of the response or even of the new response itself. The therapist would consequently have some control of the emotional and cognitive impact of the interaction, bypassing the client's habitual manner of maintaining control of his functioning and of the response of others to his functioning. Thus, when a client speaks repetitively about problems in a way to elicit a sympathetic (and eventually bored), pessimistic and negative tone to therapy, the therapist might respond in any number of ways to present a new, and healthier tone, without directly confronting the client about the behavior. Clients who are most invested in maintaining a certain tone may well dismiss the therapist who confronts them directly through a defensive response, a superficial agreement that does not change anything, or by leaving therapy. Erickson instead might ask for even greater details about the problem until the client begins to want to change the topic. He might also suggest that the problem is hopeless, leading the client to convince the therapist that it is not that bad. He might ramble on about similar problems in someone else's life or he might take another tack by speaking with enthusiasm and optimism about how well the client is initiating a resolution of the problem through such a detailed description of it. In essence, once the therapist understands the interpersonal meaning and intent of whatever aspect of functioning the client chooses to manifest in therapy, the therapist then utilizes that behavior to change its meaning at that very moment. The therapist fosters change outside of therapy as well through further discussion, tasks, or stories. The therapist does not interpret the resistance, but utilizes it. The therapist does not contest the behavior, but accepts it, reframes it, enhances it, and/ or associates a unique response to it in order to engage the client and facilitate change.

Erickson's techniques are not frequently used with children, although therapeutic stories and more direct forms of hypnotism have been used. Paradoxical interventions certainly fall within Erickson's utilization framework and are given to parents with positive effects on their child's behavior. When a child is poorly motivated, fairly nonverbal, skeptical, defensive, and somewhat bored, the therapist might well consider ways to utilize the child's immediate functioning in order to engage him in the immediate interaction as well as in the treatment goals. If he shows boredom, the therapist might engage in a yawning game or lean against the child and start snoring on his shoulder. Conversely, the therapist might scream, jump up, and ask the heavens how anyone could possibly not be interested in such matters. If the child laughs and insists that therapy is boring, the therapist might express instant understanding and encourage the child to lie on the couch with his eyes closed while waiting for sleep *or* something else to occur that might be interesting.

One oppositional, poorly attached 8-year-old girl, began her first meeting with me by sticking her tongue out and smiling slightly at her foster mother. I immediately made a fuss about that secret signal she had made since no one both smiles and sticks their tongue out at the same person at the same time. I pressed the girl hard to tell me what this signal meant. I suggested that she must think her foster mother is special or she would never communicate with her in that private, special way. I suggested that she stick her tongue out again so that I could study her foster mother's response. This went on for ten minutes and led to a very engaged, responsive, and motivated meeting with a girl with a history of nonverbal, noncompliant interactions. I could have responded in other ways with equal effects. However, if I had ignored her initial behavior, it probably would have been much more difficult to engage her in a conversation about herself.

Erickson's work is quite relevant to working with poorly attached children. His manner of accepting and utilizing the client's presence in whatever form it takes shows a remarkable *attunement* with the immediate affective state of the client. The therapist maintains an empathic tone regardless of how direct his interventions are. Following each intervention, he observes the client's response to the first intervention and modifies the second one in congruence with that response.

The child's behavior may represent his fear of close personal engagements. That is quite understandable; he is given empathy for the fear, and the engagement continues. The child's behavior may represent his ignorance about how to participate in age-appropriate ways within a close engagement. That also is understandable; he is given empathy for his uncertainties, and then he is shown how to engage in age-appropriate ways. The child's behavior may represent his anger at the therapist for maintaining control of the engagement. That, too, is understandable and his anger is respected. The engagement becomes defined in part as one in which the child's anger is being respected. The child certainly may resist the engagement because of a lack of trust in the therapist and parent. The mistrust, too, receives empathy while the engagement continues.

What permeates each treatment session is the basic therapeutic principle in which anything the child says or does is utilized for the purpose of teaching attachment through multiple emotional engagements with the therapist and his parent. This principle also becomes the primary emotional tone of the child's life at home. The therapist works very closely with the child's parent to demonstrate how this principle is manifested in daily interactions. Each session models ways to maintain a connection with the child in spite of various misbehaviors within the home. Over time, the child comes to realize that he cannot distort, avoid, control, or manipulate the quality of his engagements with his parent because no matter what the child does, an engagement, light or intense, playful or serious, quiet or boisterous, is maintained and the child is becoming more attached.

The children with whom I work actually choose, though the choice may well be unconscious, to resist the influence of their parents. They choose to refuse to follow directions. They do not accept authority. They do not accept the parent's right and duty to exert control over important aspects of their lives. What tends to happen? Too often such choices lead to predictable consequences from both therapist and parent that do not facilitate change. The therapist may focus exclusively on the traumas that underlie these choices in the hope that as the traumas are resolved, the choices will change spontaneously. In that setting, the child's poor choices are often minimized and result in the child thinking that the trauma must therefore be an excuse for that poor choice. The parents think that the therapist is not supporting or validating their concerns. The therapist may ask the parents to be patient with the child's behavior because of the emotional turmoil that the child is experiencing. When specific advice is given, it tends to be "behavioral management," usually involving positive reinforcement. Unfortunately, what is positively reinforcing to most children has little meaning to the poorly attached child. It may actually be aversive given his negative self-concept and wish to avoid affection and enjoyment.

Parents often patiently attempt to wait out the expected "testing" period and try to be as consistent and even-tempered as possible. Over time, however, they become discouraged and experience frustration and anger over the countless, repetitive, defiant, and distancing acts manifested by their child. Eventually, the consequence of their child's behavior is the parents' disengagement from any emotionally meaningful relationship. Parents, then, in grief and confusion, engage in repetitive behaviors themselves that match those of their child. The parents are chronically withdrawn, resentful, or irate. Their response comes under the child's control. The poorly attached child has fashioned for himself parents who will not encourage, expect, or facilitate attachment. The child has won; the parents and child have lost.

When the child's choices function to resist attachment, parents and therapists must develop alternative consequences. These consequences, which become the natural result of the child's choices, are to accept the child where he is and at the same time to expect more. These are consequences that teach a child who does not want to be taught. We do not give up teaching this child even though he wants us to nor do we resent the child for not wanting our "help." He needs it, so he gets it.

I remember a 6-year-old boy who often screamed that he did not want parents and he did not need parents. I responded with confusion over his judgment since at his age, life would be most difficult without parents. I also expressed empathy for his resentment at our efforts to teach him to relate closely with his parents since he was telling us that he did not want them. I mentioned various experiences that children who were close to their parents routinely had. I mentioned laughing together, reading stories, going for walks, playing games, hugging, and baking cookies. I said that he might someday decide that he wanted such activities with his parents. It was my job to show him how to enjoy such activities with his parents if he ever changed his mind. A few months later, as he was beginning to reconsider his earlier choice to live alone, his mother offered to give him a bottle before bed each night. The boy agreed to that experience and he even began to take pride in his participating in being nursed with a bottle. At first I was surprised by his obvious pride, but I then realized that the boy understood what an important step in his life he had taken by his choice.

The following principles of the therapy with the poorly attached child can be understood best within this utilization theory of continuous engagement. They are principles that must come to life in unique ways that are to be determined by the individual qualities of the child, parents, and therapist. They are a means of conceptualizing and loosely structuring the interaction. Within this framework, specific interventions described in Chapter 6 have their meaning. Also, within this framework, the parenting principles and interventions described in chapters Eleven and Twelve can best be understood.

PRINCIPLES

Directive and Empathic

In engaging the child who has extreme difficulty forming an attachment to others, the therapist must take a directive stance. Nondirective approaches are not helpful because the therapist's empathy and unconditional acceptance are coming from a way of life that the child barely knows exists. The child misinterprets the nondirective stance as permissiveness that enables the child to easily manipulate the therapist into allowing him to assume full control of the process, even when that control negates the possibility of therapeutic change.

When the traumatized child who *is* able to attach well to a caring adult is given the opportunity to control the interaction, the child is able to gradually build a trusting relationship with the adult. From there, he is able to gradually rebuild his overall sense of self-worth and work through the trauma so that its impact on his ongoing psychological development is minimized. However, when the child who cannot comprehend the reality of a trusting relationship is given such a nondirective setting, he will simply be motivated to maintain continuous control of the adult and use the therapeutic hour to pursue moment-to-moment gratifications, interests, and impulses. He might also use the therapist to better meet these gratifications, to reduce outside frustrations, and to improve the child's manipulative skills. Unfortunately, the child will not notice the available empathy nor the opportunity for a mutually satisfying human bond. To the poorly attached child, satisfaction is a solitary, internal process of gratifying desires, not an interpersonal, affective experience.

The need to adopt a directive approach with children who manifest significant psychological difficulties is emphasized by other therapists. Ann Jernberg (1979) indicates that the therapist must be in charge of the therapeutic activity or the child will manipulate the treatment to avoid becoming engaged with the therapist in any way that might be beneficial. Beverly James (1989, 1994) also stresses the need to be active and direct or the child will avoid all painful abuse and neglect experiences. While Stanley Greenspan (1992) is quite nondirective in establishing a fundamental engagement with a child, he stresses the need for mild directiveness when the child avoids two-way communication with the therapist and for even greater directiveness when the child engages in misbehavior. Greenspan also maintains that whenever the therapist must become more directive, she needs to balance this stance by increasing her efforts to maintain engagement with the child.

The therapist needs to direct the therapeutic process persistently, patiently, playfully, and relentlessly. She gradually moves the child into the emotional spheres of terror, rage, and despair that the child wants to avoid. The therapist makes it impossible for the child to maintain his maladaptive and repetitive control of situations. She directs therapy in ways that the child would never choose to do. With the therapist in control of the pace, themes, activities, and emotional atmosphere of the session, the child will haltingly, guardedly, but with a great deal of emotion, find himself being drawn into a close relationship with another human being. As the child reluctantly gives up control to another human being, time after time, and finds he is not abused in any way, he begins to rely on that person to define the process and content of the moment-to-moment interaction. He is unable to use his own maladaptive ways of relating and must begin to think and feel in ways that he has consistently resisted for years. In this setting, the child's anger, tears, and laughter are not techniques to manipulate but rather genuine human responses to a human interaction that elicits past memories, present experiences, and future hopes and fears. When these interactions occur again and again, the child gradually gives up moment-to-moment gratifications as he begins to experience a relationship, existing over time, with another human being.

Throughout each session the therapist will constantly be responsive to the child's moment-to-moment responses to the directive interventions and then modify the process and/or content based on the immediate affective experience of the child. Viewed in this way, the therapist can also be seen as being nondirective as well. The relationship quality that most closely corresponds to this form of therapeutic interaction is affective attunement between the mother and infant. The therapist is unconsciously aware of the child's moment-to-moment feeling state so that she can then modify her next response to more closely match the emotional/behavioral state of the child. While the therapist may have "preplanned" an intervention, it is quickly discarded if it does not match where the child is at that moment. While she notices and accepts the child's state of being and uses that state to help to formulate the next response, the therapist does not let the child dictate to her what the next response will be.

To what affect of the child is the therapist attuned? Just as the mother is attuned to her infant's vitality affects as well as to his categorical affects, so, too, is the therapist. Stern (1985, p. 156) indicates that most of the mother's attunements occur with vitality affects (level of intensity and degree of pleasure/unpleasure). By being attuned to vitality affects, the therapist is able to maintain an unbroken communion with the child at the most primitive, preverbal level. When the child gives affective expression to categorical affects (sadness, fear, anger, joy, etc.), the therapist's attunement is more easily experienced and accepted since it is part of a continuous intersubjective process.

Let me briefly describe Kate, a 4-year-old girl who had lived in her adoptive home for 1 year when her treatment began. During her first 2 years of life she had experienced pervasive neglect. This was followed by a year in foster care before moving into her adoptive home, where she demonstrated habitual anger, quick to be outraged over the slightest frustration. Of equal concern to her new parents was her apparent indifference about who took care of her. Often at nursery school she would show an interest in going home with other children's parents without any apparent regard for seeing her adoptive parents.

During the initial sessions with Kate and her adoptive mother, Barbara, it became apparent that Kate saw self-reliance as the only way to survive. In her world, her adoptive parents only existed to meet her wishes. When they failed, she wanted to trade them in for other parents. Her anger reflected her outrage at their failure to meet her wishes. At the same time, however, her pervasive anger reflected her response to her early years of neglect. She was able to deny the early experience of despair over being abandoned psychologically by adopting a tough and resentful attitude toward the past and toward her current relationships. She had spent day after day alone in her crib. She had little experience with the attunement that would have enabled her to experience union with a caring and protective adult. She would never be so vulnerable again!

In psychotherapy, Kate quite readily demonstrated her anger. She made various demands to engage in activities and when these were denied, her immediate response was to scream. I gave her empathy for her anger at not being able to do what she wanted and indicated that I would hold her to provide support, since she clearly felt so bad. I held her across my lap and her screaming only intensified. Not only was she not getting what she wanted, she also was being held! I expressed attunement with the intensity of her unpleasant affect by speaking more loudly and forcefully ("You are angry with me!") while leaning forward and waving my arm. My words expressed empathy for her distress ("This is so hard for you") while my nonverbal actions were attuned with her immediate feeling state. As she screamed louder, my attunement followed her and when she gradually became less intense my affective tone became more quiet and peaceful. I spoke more quietly, conveying a great deal of empathy for how difficult this experience was for her. I had to time my quiet comments with her brief pauses to catch her breath while she continued to scream. She then became angry over my speech. "Don't talk to me like that!" She was referring to my tone of voice, not what I was saying. She then screamed: "I am not sad! Don't talk to me like that!" I had not used the word "sad," but simply had focused on how hard the experience was for her. While she may have wanted me to be more attuned again with her intense anger, I continued to match the emerging feeling state that was tired and wanted peace and quiet.

Taking her word "sad," I concurred with her that she certainly seemed more "mad" than "sad" now. However, I added that the last time she had really felt sad was probably one of the days that she had spent in her crib when she was a baby. Her body became rigid and she screamed that she was not sad when she was a baby. Though still screaming, there was little intensity and her feeling state was one of passive acceptance. She appeared to be willing to engage me in a conversation. I quickly continued, again with a subdued tone of voice:

> But you spent so much time in your crib when you were a baby. And I know that when that happens, babies cry a lot because they feel so lonely. They so much want to be held . . . and played with . . . and fed . . . and rocked. I thought that since that happened so much to you, that you must have been so . . . sad . . . and . . . lonely. Kate replied now without screaming, "But I didn't spend a lot of time in my crib when I was a baby!" I quietly continued: Oh, you did. Joan (her case worker) told me all about those very long times when your birth mom left you in the crib while she was drinking. It's probably hard to remember because it made you so sad.

I noticed some tears in Kate's eyes. I rocked her in my arms briefly and she yelled, "Don't do that!" although with none of the intensity of her previous anger. I ignored her words and responded to her quiet and sad acceptance of my gently rocking her. Her tears flowed down her cheeks and I quietly said that she probably wanted her mom to hold her, not me. She passively consented as I carried her to Barbara, who quietly rocked her as they both cried.

This example clearly demonstrates the intensity of this work as well as the fact that the child is not given the power to structure the interaction as she wishes. I was quite direct with Kate and she was very angry that she could not control the interaction. I provided her with empathy for how difficult such interactions are for her. I also allowed myself to become attuned to her underlying feeling states so that I could match that state and enable her to feel a union with me. I gently led her into another feeling state that she habitually avoided. This example is not unusual nor do I regard the sequence described as being "a breakthrough." Countless similar examples, though possibly less dramatic, need to occur before Kate is likely to internalize such experiences and demonstrate therapeutic change.

Because of the directive nature of the treatment session, the therapist can lead the child to explore, rethink, and reexperience many past experiences that the child has rigidly denied and distorted. She also directs the child to explore, rethink, and reexperience his current relationships and discover that his current caregiver is not his previous abusing caregiver. The child is taught in numerous ways how to relate in a mutually satisfying way with his caregiver. He experiences attunement for the feeling states that underlie his sense of self. The child learns what trust and empathy really are.

A child may demonstrate that he wants to be left alone with respect to his relationship with me or to a particular theme. While I respect his desire to be left alone, I may well decide that it is in his best interest to continue to engage the child. My engagement will change slightly though as I incorporate his desire to be left alone. The child may tell me to quit touching him. I may express surprise at his annoyance about my placing my hand on his arm. I may wonder what makes him want that. I may gently touch his finger, ankle, ear, or hair and ask if he feels those touches any differently. I may choose to stop touching his arm and agree to leave my hand 4 inches away from his arm. (Then I would get a ruler to be sure of the distance!) If the pattern represents a chronic fear of closeness that has not decreased over time, I may give him empathy and preparation and leave my hand on his arm for 10 seconds, followed by a 5-second break, and then 10 more, and so forth. In making such a decision, I need to have confidence that I am matching his deep need to be touched while at the same time recognizing his resistance to it. I communicate empathy for his resistance and I express my commitment to meeting his deeper need, one that he has resisted and would most likely continue to resist with less intrusive interactions. However, I must not stop with that judgment. I must observe the child's state after I have chosen to touch him against his expressed wish and notice whether this intervention is leading to a deeper engagement or to increased resistance, dissociation, or fear. Being attuned to his new affective response, I have to make another immediate intervention, incorporating the new response and choosing among the new directions. If deeply engaged with the child, my judgment is much more likely to be correct than it would be if I followed either the child's verbal wish or a prescribed technique.

The nondirective nature of the interaction is based on attunement and empathy. The therapist experiences and communicates empathy for the child's emotional, cognitive, physical, and behavioral experience at the time. Whereas the therapist does not let the child habitually choose the focus and the activity, she nevertheless utilizes all aspects of the child's immediate functioning to determine the particular interaction at this time. The therapist chooses how to *utilize* the child's current functioning, finding the best match between a particular intervention or theme and the child's affective, cognitive, and behavioral qualities. In this manner the therapist is in the position to *pace* the presentation to enhance its impact on the child, and to *lead* the child to increased skills. The therapist may mentally begin each session with an outline of topics and themes to explore and develop, but this outline will immediately be discarded if it does not meet this child's unique affective experience at this particular time.

The therapist always uses the mother–infant relationship as her guide for the interaction. Just as the empathic mother participates in an intricate "dance" with her infant, constantly integrating cues from the infant into actions that meet the infant's needs, so, too, does the therapist "dance" with the child who fears attachment. When the therapist is so engaged, the child experiences attunement, empathy, and nurturance even at those times when the therapist is most confrontational. This affective experience allows the child to risk following the therapist's leads into new ways of feeling, thinking, and acting. The infant's tears and screams may serve as a message to the mother to intervene in a certain way (i.e., feed me before changing the diaper), but the mother does not simply obey these wishes. She shows empathy, not rejection, for the child's anger and then continues with her intervention against the child's wishes when she thinks that it is in the child's best interest to do so.

Too often in therapy as in life, empathy is given in response to another's enjoyment, sadness, or fear but not toward his anger. Too often we adopt a serious, somewhat stern, rational, and possibly mildly annoyed tone when we are focusing on a "misbehavior" or the child's resistance to our interventions. When we are able to give empathy for these behaviors, too, it changes the entire experience for the child. He is now much less likely to disengage through dissociation, resentment, and withdrawal, since our consistent and persistent emotional tone invites continuing engagement.

Relationship-Centered

The focus of the treatment session is on both the child's relationship with the therapist and the child's relationship with his parent. For that reason, all three are present. Any games or activities will be used only if they help to further explore these relationships from another perspective. Such focusing on another person and having that person focus on the self is hard for the poorly attached child. He will inevitably search for distractions but the therapist must consistently bring the child back to the present experience of the therapist and parent. The focus on the relationship between therapist and child is also central in the therapy of Jernberg (1979). The activities employed in Jernberg's Theraplay (i.e., elbow trophies, pillow push, hello-good-bye) facilitate playful and emotional interactions which focus on the here-and-now therapeutic relationship.

The therapist brings the relationship into focus quite directly by expecting that the child maintain eye contact with her. Without eye contact the child is so much less responsive to the therapist's questions, emotions, confrontations, and support. The poorly attached child feels vulnerable when he maintains eye contact in an emotionally charged relationship and he will invariably avoid it whenever he does not feel in control of the situation. Thus, the therapist must become quite alert to noticing eye contact and maintaining it. In the same way, when the child interacts with the parent during therapy, eye contact is expected.

Physical contact is also very important if the therapist is to be able to maintain the child's emotional connection to the interaction that is being directed by the therapist. In the course of therapy, she often touches the child's hand, arm, shoulder, hair, back, puts her arm around him, briefly tickles, gently pokes, wrestles, places her hands on the child's chin, on either side of his eyes. The therapist holds the child as he screams in anger, shakes with fear, or cries with profound sadness. As this contact is occurring, the child's thoughts and feelings about the contact are explored, with his receiving empathy of the difficult moments and many smiles and much laughter for the lighter and more mutually enjoyable moments.

Allan Schore (1994) also indicates that in therapy for psychopathology that has its origins in the preverbal attachment sequences of self development, the therapist needs to develop a relationship which is established and maintained at the preverbal, unconscious, "primary process" level of relatedness. To maintain such a relationship, visual modes are more important than auditory ones, just as they are for the young child. Eye contact, facial gestures and responses, body movement and posture, all communicate affect and mirror qualities far beyond the ability of words. Schore stresses that therapy, just like the infant's early development and attachment with his mother, is fundamentally a process of the right hemisphere of the brain and of the communication between the right hemispheres of the therapist and patient.

Because maintaining a mutually satisfying relationship with the therapist is going to be quite difficult for the child, he often searches for ways to distract the therapist. When that fails, the child frequently becomes actively or passively resistant to the treatment process. The therapist must be quite adept at working with that resistance so that the resistance itself becomes simply a new way to maintain the focus on the relationship. Paradoxical interventions often help, where the resistance is encouraged and actually becomes a unique way to cooperate. For example, the child who closes his eyes is praised for his sensitivity to his eyes' need to rest, and his ears are then engaged in any number of ways, such as quietly whispering in his ear how special he is while the therapist holds his head in her hands.

Many an angry child will giggle when the therapist whispers in his ear, speaking to his stomach, lungs, heart, brain, and so forth, telling each its unique role in maintaining the child's welfare. It is hard for the most mute child to resist protesting when the therapist tells his stomach that it must learn to like beans and dislike candy so that the child's elbows can get softer and not bruise the therapist's arm. At other times it may be best for the therapist to encourage the child to express his anger more loudly and directly, praising these expressions and giving empathy for how difficult the work is.

The relationship with the parent is frequently the focus of the interaction. The therapist or parent may initiate a topic and expect the child to respond to the parent. The therapist may suggest words for the child who is reluctant to speak. If the child still refuses to talk, the therapist may role play the child and enter into a conversation with the parent. If the therapist chooses to convey thoughts or feelings that the child is not willing to accept as being part of self, then the child may choose to speak for himself. This is done deliberately, though playfully.

At other times the therapist may choose to convey a thought or feeling that the child recognizes and accepts but fears to express. The child may sigh, present a few tears, nod, or smile. For example, the therapist may loudly say to the child's mother, "Mom, I got real mad at you when you wouldn't let me watch TV because right then you seemed to be so mean, and I just couldn't imagine that you really did love me!" The mother then would respond with empathy by saying something like: "After all that you've been through, it must be so frightening to think that you got stuck with a mean mom who doesn't love you at all. I'm glad that we're working to help you to see and feel my love for you even when we're angry or when I give you a consequence that you don't like." After pausing to let that sink in, or to see if the child will respond verbally, the therapist may again speak for the child and say: "Mom, when that day comes, I'll probably want to hug you so much, I won't have time for TV." The mom might respond by giving the child a quick hug and saying: "Let's practice now!" Such a sequence would only occur, however, if the child was engaged in a meaningful way, even if primarily by listening. If the child disengages, that becomes the new focus.

A parent recently told me that she had been struggling with her own response to her child's continuing angry and oppositional behaviors. She was becoming caught by the child's emotion and beginning to respond in kind. It occurred to her that she might try my therapeutic stance. She said that she was able to do so and found that she could then positively affect her child rather than allowing the child to negatively affect her. This led me to attempt to detail what the central therapeutic attitude was that facilitated this change. There are three underlying ways of relating that consistently enable the therapist to engage the child under just about any situation or emotional/behavioral state of the child. I believe that the same three qualities build upon the attunement between the mother and infant. These qualities are:

1) *Empathy.* This has been addressed already and will be again and again as I consider it to be crucial for any therapeutic relationship as well as for effective interventions in the home. Not only can the child accept more conflict and stress when it is experienced with

empathy, the child will also learn what empathy is and begin to show it to others. Engagement with empathy is certainly harder to resist.

2) *Curiosity and Interest.* The child's moment-to-moment gestures, voice tone, words, movements, choices, emotions, and so forth, are interesting and constantly tell us if we are engaged with the child and how we can continue the engagement. If those qualities of the child are important to me, eventually they will be more important and seen as more worthwhile to the child. If I struggle to understand why the child chooses to be angry at that moment, the child may struggle to understand why too. The child then may become aware of other options. Also, if I am busy communicating interest, I am less likely to be communicating evaluation and criticism and the child will be more likely to feel accepted.

3) *Playfulness.* As I relate in a playful manner, the child will be more likely to respond in kind and less likely to continue to try to elicit anger. If we are smiling and laughing, the child will be more engaged and less bored. The child will also be more able to explore the areas of his life about which he experiences shame if we are maintaining a playful connection. Laughter and shame are essentially incompatible.

Emotional Richness

For therapy to reach the child who is a master at avoiding genuine human interactions, it must be emotionally very full and rich if he is to begin to experience a deeper relationship with an adult. These children habitually experience little emotion in their interactions with adults because past emotional experiences were so painful. In therapy, the child is exposed to a great range of emotion and, consequently, discovers that this entire range has a place in close relationships. He also must discover how to integrate his mixed, complex emotional responses to close relationships and gradually carry these emotions into a more fully developed identity. The child learns that he can feel intense rage toward someone he loves. He also learns that his rage is part of him; it need not be rejected and he need not hate himself for having it. The child learns that he can experience sadness without dissolving as an integrated self. He can show his sadness without being rejected. He can be vulnerable and show dependent feelings and have them acknowledged and accepted by a nurturing parent and therapist. He can also engage in reciprocal laughter. He can experience true mutual pleasure and comfort. When his mom says quietly and firmly, "John, try to notice it. I am loving you right now!" he can remain quiet, too, and let the meaning of such a comment take hold of him.

The four categories of therapeutic interventions developed and described so well by Ann Jernberg (1979) in *Theraplay* are also basic interventions in the treatment now being described, although the range of techniques and the focus of treatment described in this book differ in significant ways.

Jernberg's categories of treatment are based on descriptions of four qualities of maternal behavior that are seen as promoting both attachment and autonomy. She describes these maternal characteristics as Structuring, Challenging, Intruding, and Nurturing. By Structuring, Jernberg speaks of how the mother limits, labels, holds, and restrains the baby. In Challenging, the mother teases, encourages, dares, and varies the baby's experiences. When Intruding, the mother tickles, surprises, swings, and bounces her baby. The mother is Nurturing when she rocks, cuddles, hugs, and feeds her baby.

In working with the poorly attached child, the therapist and parent *structure* the session by directing and restricting the child's activity and by focusing and/or utilizing the child's attention. The therapist and parent *challenge* the child by focusing on stressful and frightening past and present experiences that he has habitually avoided or acted out in a compulsive manner. Such experiences may be traumas but they may also be experiences of emotional intimacy that are very difficult. (Theraplay however focuses on the present and does not direct the child into the past.) The therapist and parent *intrude* by moving into the child's physical and psychological space so that the child must deal with a close relationship in a new and more satisfying and productive manner. The therapist and parent *nurture* the child through hugs, stroking his hair or shoulders, holding, and speaking softly with empathy and communicating that he is "prized."

In working with the poorly attached child, the therapist and parent must constantly be sensitive to whether the current interaction is emotionally rich and meaningful. If it is not, discussions of past abuses or current difficulties will not be therapeutic. If it is not, activities such as drawings, games, or role playing will have no felt connection to the child and no lasting effect on his inner life or behavior. I discontinue relevant therapeutic content before completing it when the emotional atmosphere does not feel genuine and rich. During therapy it is not enough that the immediate here-and-now is the core of my experience. It must also be the core of the child's and his parent's experience. The child needs to share the focus with me and/or his parent and be emotionally engaged in the process.

Focused on Attachment Sequences

A central ongoing pattern in the development of an attachment between infant and parent is the sequence of the child feeling close to the mother, experiencing a break in the relationship, and then reestablishing the emotional connection. This pattern is crucial to understanding the nature of attachment, infant development, and the pathology of poorly attached children. Countless research studies have used this model (Strange Situation) in deepening our understanding of secure attachments as well as variations of insecure attachments. In these studies, the break in the engagement is physical with the mother leaving the young child's presence. While this is important for children who have been abandoned and neglected, it is equally important to understand the effects of psychological breaks in the mother–child engagement, although the mother may still be present physically.

As noted in previous chapters, during the first year of the child's life, the mother–child attunement is the center of the child's complete development and his attachment to his mother. This leads to the early Practicing Stage (10 to 12 months) in which the child, while still feeling a primary union with the mother, begins to explore the world with interest and joy. He has his mother and the world, too! Life will never be better!

Then, as the child develops into the later Practicing Stage, the dictates of reality and socialization cause the mother to direct and limit his behavioral initiatives. The child immediately feels that the mother is now a "stranger," and the connection is broken. He feels shame over his choice and mentally withdraws from her. He does not want to be seen, and so he avoids her gaze. This process is healthy and necessary not only for socialization and safety but also for the child to begin to integrate separateness into his sense of self and to develop his autonomy. For the child to do this well, it is crucial that the shame experience be accepted as a natural part of life and development and that it not be associated with humiliation and rejection by the caregiver. When shame is healthy, the break is brief and the child experiences a reunion with the mother fairly quickly. The direction or limit to his behavior in no way placed the relationship with the mother at risk. She assists the child in experiencing the strength of their relationship through "interactive repair" actions, namely empathy and support, while reestablishing attunement.

With poorly attached children, the initial engagement is often weak, unpredictable, and inconsistent. The normal breaks, relating to shame experiences, are associated with rejection, anger, and humiliation. The reunion experiences either are not present or are a long time coming. It is crucial for the therapist who wants the child to begin to understand and trust the value and satisfactions of a strong attachment with his new caregiver to give the child the opportunity to experience all phases of this sequence in a healthy manner, over and over again, rather than in the ways that he has lived it in the past.

Allan Schore (1994) indicates that developmental psychopathology has at its core a working model of poor attunement, pervasive and unregulated shame, and an inability to reestablish an emotional bond with a significant other person following a shame-inducing experience. He stresses that the therapist must first become closely attuned to her patient's internal state. From within this context, the therapist induces stress by focusing on shame inducing topics. She then works to enable the patient to tolerate shame more adequately so that these experiences can enter his consciousness. Shame is separated from the humiliation and rejection that were originally associated with it. Shame temporarily disrupts the therapeutic relationship and the therapist works to restore the relationship through mirroring and comforting behaviors. Schore's treatment model is very applicable to the treatment of the poorly attached child.

In reenacting the attachment sequence, the therapist first adopts an attitude that fosters attunement with the child. Qualities of empathy, interest and curiosity, and playfulness are crucial. The child needs to become fully engaged with the therapist and parent. In therapy there will be frequent experiences of breaks in the engagement. Whenever the therapist directs the child in ways that the child resists, the child will briefly disengage. At times, the child will deliberately try to break the engagement because it is so stressful. When the therapist and parent explore some of the child's poor choices at home, the child will most likely feel shame and immediately break the engagement. At that point, the therapist and parent must be available to the child to re-engage. Since the child usually cannot or will not take advantage of this availability, the parent and therapist must actively facilitate the reunion with the child.

Slowly the shame experience will be open for exploration and integration. Slowly the child will see that he is not rejected or held in contempt for his actions. Slowly the child will see that breaks in the engagement are temporary and neither destructive to the relationship nor to his well-being.

Very significant therapeutic work can occur when this sequence is reenacted in therapy. The pathological sequence that the child had experienced when he was younger needs to be challenged so that it does not play a central role in his current relationships. Children with very negative self-concepts, as these children certainly have, are very resistant to exploring the same themes that fostered their self-hatred in the first place. For this reason, the treatment needs to be directive, within a context of great empathy and support. With the therapist directing the interaction, the child first experiences an engagement based on attunement with his immediate feeling states. As the therapist continues to direct the action, the child experiences a break in the engagement, with shame associated with the past memories or actions that the therapist is exploring. However, there is no humiliation or rejection! Then, with the therapist directing the action, the child again is engaged. How can this be? The child questions at the core of his being if he is worthwhile and liked and valued by the therapist and parent. Past experiences are reviewed because they have made and continue to make his life more difficult. They are being explored to help him have a better life—not to humiliate and reject him! The relationship is still felt and enjoyed after merely a pause. The child's rage at this sequence is not a problem! His fear and rage are simply absorbed.

Further thoughts emerge from within the child's new experience of shame-within-engagement rather than shame as rejection-and-contempt. Possibly lies, deception and sneaky behaviors are not necessary. Possibly tantrums in response to consequences for behaviors are not necessary to hide the pain of apparent rejection. Possibly poor choices with their subsequent limits, directions, and even consequences are simply minor irritations, frustrations, and even opportunities to learn rather than attacks on the relationship and the child's core sense of self.

Recently I was holding 4-year-old Jack in therapy. He was laughing in my arms as I made a fuss about how many teeth he had while I briefly and gently tickling his ribs. I then paused and made a facial expression suggesting that I had just remembered something. I very quietly said:

Your Mom and Dad said that you are often very mad at them! You
scream and kick and scratch them. I wonder why.

Jack immediately became very tense, started to scream, and tried to
get out of my arms. I continued:

Oh, you don't want to talk about this! You want me to stop talking
about how mad you get at your mom and dad. But I need to talk
about this because I'm mixed up about why you try to hurt them.
I'll bet you're mixed up too.

Though still screaming. Jack was listening to what I was saying and
he was more willing to stay in my arms. I slowly said:

I know you love your mom and dad.

Jack nodded yes and looked at his adoptive mother. Just as slowly I said:

Your mom and dad love you.

Jack suddenly screamed, "Noooo!" again looking to his mother for a
response. His response immediately suggested a crucial theme that
ran throughout his constant outbursts of rage toward his parents. He
did not want them to love him. He did not deserve it. He did not want
to trust it. If he wanted and needed it, he would certainly lose it. His
rage served to try to prevent them from loving him and it further
convinced Jack that he did not merit their love. He could love them,
but he could not let them love him. I said:

You don't want your parents to love you. I didn't know that. Now
I understand why you try to hurt them. You want . . .

Jack interrupted and screamed: "Don't tell them!" I replied:

You don't want your parents to know why you don't want them to
love you. But they need to know, Jack. It's hard for you but it will
be good if they know. You don't want their love because you think
that you're bad and shouldn't be loved. You might also be scared
that someday they might stop loving you and that sure would

hurt. When they say no to you, you think they don't love you! They do love you, Jack, and they won't stop.

Jack again looked at his mom, with some fear. She nodded yes and I continued.

You think that you're bad when you try to hurt them. Your mom and dad and I know that you're not bad. It's just hard to get used to loving your parents . . . and their loving you.

Jack was now much quieter. His mom hugged him. As she did, I briefly talked about how he thought he was bad when his birth mom abandoned him and again later when his birth father abandoned him.

During that session Jack had two additional rage outbursts toward me, although they were shorter and less intense. He had further outbursts in therapy during the next month. However, at the same time, his outbursts toward his parents at home were decreasing. These outbursts represented his experience of acute shame and rage within the maladaptive attachment sequences of his past and present life. Within the context of continuing positive engagement with his parents and me, his shame greatly decreased and his attachment to his adoptive parents developed. While my words were important in helping Jack to reexperience his shame and self-contempt, they were effective only because of the emotional context in which they occurred. Jack's intense affect was matched, accepted and absorbed. His adoptive mom and I engaged him with a great deal of physical contact. Eye contact was present throughout the sequence. I spoke slowly and quietly, in a manner to encourage him to anticipate every word.

GOALS OF DIFFERENTIATION AND INTEGRATION

When there is a pervasive disturbance in the developmental attachment patterns such as were described by Stanley Greenspan, Margaret Mahler, and Allan Schore, the therapeutic goals need to address the major areas of the child's development. These goals must include the following:

1) The child needs to begin to trust that his current caregiver relates to the child in a manner that is in the child's best interests;

2) The child needs to begin to take pleasure in interacting with the caregiver in a reciprocal fashion. Acts of pleasing, identifying with, having empathy for, and being able to resolve conflicts with the caregiver gradually must emerge;

3) The child needs to begin to recognize, regulate, integrate and appropriately express the wide range of affect that forms the core of his sense of autonomy;

4) The child needs to develop appropriate behavioral skills, falling between impulsivity and inhibition, which serve the needs of self and other; and

5) The child needs to develop the cognitive abilities to reflect on his inner life, learn from new experiences, and redefine his self as being worthwhile and capable.

In working to achieve the above goals, the therapist must keep in mind that the normal developmental process of differentiation and integration, described well by Greenspan, Cicchetti, and others, has not occurred within the child whose developmental attachment patterns have been significantly compromised. Traumas are dissociated, denied, and reenacted in compulsive ways. Early working models of mother–child relationships contain much self-rejection, mistrust of one's caregiver, and a pervasive obsession with maintaining one's own safety in a frightening world. The child is left unable to differentiate old experiences from new. He is unable to experience pleasure and manage conflict within close relationships. He is unable to manage his poorly understood emotional eruptions. He is unable to reflect before acting. He is unable to see himself as having any worth in the face of his "bad" acts and his experiences of abuse and rejection. In addressing these problems, the therapist must constantly recall the need to help the child to differentiate all varieties of his inner and external experiences so that he can then integrate these experiences into a more positive and coherent sense of self. Therapeutic gains will last only if they occur within the context of the child's ongoing development. These therapeutic experiences must first be differentiated from his countless negative experiences so that they can play an integral part of a new definition of self.

This process of differentiation and integration must occur in these four crucial areas of the child's experiences and development if they are to be effective.

Past, Present, and Future

Given the traumas which these children have experienced, it is critical that these *past* traumas be understood and explored with the new caregivers within the context of the child's new life. If they are not, the lingering effects of the trauma will tend to distort his current relationships and make it very difficult for him to seek help from his new parents. The parents, in turn, will have difficulty understanding and responding appropriately to their child. When his parents are able to help him come to terms with past trauma, this activity becomes one of the more powerful means of helping him to differentiate the past parental sources of abuse from the new parents' beneficial and healing influences.

At the same time, it is not enough to focus on the past traumas and simply assume that if they are resolved, the child will spontaneously begin to relate well with his new parents in the *present.* He is often lacking the skills to do so and must be taught how to do it. This is true on many levels, from taking the child's arms and showing him to hug his parent to showing him in specific ways how to verbalize his thoughts and feelings. Also, the process of helping him to differentiate routine family stresses from past experiences of abuse and neglect is very critical and often very difficult. It needs to be done over and over in many different ways if it is to become a part of the child's cognitive and affective world view.

Finally, the *future* cannot be ignored. Poorly attached children commonly have not had a future that they can anticipate with confidence and pleasure. Abandonment, rejection, disruption, and sudden, unpredictable, or repetitive experiences of various forms of abuse rob a child of any hope for a good life to come. He needs to identify predictable positive experiences and to develop confidence that his parents will provide the opportunity for these experiences. The child also needs to learn to anticipate surprises, having the confidence that surprises are usually delightful rather than something to be dreaded. He often thinks that he does not deserve a good experience and sabotages his birthday and holidays. These responses need to be anticipated, with the child's self-definition challenged and then enlarged. His ability to manage the anxiety associated with excitement will then be enhanced.

Cognition, Affect, and Behavior

The poorly attached child often has extreme difficulty being able to identify and express various aspects of himself. Entire parts of his cognitive view of himself are labeled as "bad" and are not explored and understood. As a result, they cannot be relabeled as a normal part of a child who has had various traumatic experiences. They are not integrated into the whole self. At the same time, certain emotions are not claimed as one's own but rather are alien sources of turmoil for which the child does not feel responsible. Often, an all-pervasive sense of shame makes other affects inaccessible to the child. Many children are indeed helpless to understand and integrate both their rage, which is so evident in their behavior, and their despair or terror, which is generally minimized, distorted, or denied. In therapy, the child's behavior may be confronted intensely, while his thoughts and feelings are identified, supported, and encouraged to find expression. The child learns that discipline is directed toward behavior, not toward thoughts and feelings. These are to be understood and integrated into the self but are not the subject of discipline.

Therapeutic interventions for the poorly attached child need to draw upon cognitive-behavioral techniques as well as affective, psychodynamic, and Gestalt techniques to help the child to access these various parts of self as he develops from the past through the present to the future. Some of these techniques may help the child with one aspect of himself and with one segment of his past, present, and future. They must all be put to use if the intervention is to be intensive and comprehensive enough for the child to genuinely improve his readiness for attachment. The infant's attachment to his mother is a total cognitive, emotional, physical, and behavioral experience. For the abused child to be able to approximate such an experience as far as is possible and necessary, therapy must also be as all-encompassing as possible.

Self–Other Duality

The original infant—mother attachment develops within a cyclical process of differentiation and integration at ever more mature and complex levels. The duality that defines this original relationship incorporates a joint awareness of the needs of both mother and child. The development of empathy, conscience, identification, and autonomy all emerge within the original secure attachment relationship. The poorly attached child has a limited and distorted perception of both self and other: Empathy occurs infrequently, conscience is weak, and the child is slow to identify with the new parent.

Since the parent is present during the therapeutic session, the parent and child are jointly participating in the emotionally rich and intense atmosphere. Laughter, confrontations, hugs, tears, shared thoughts and feelings facilitate the developing relationship. They perceive each other in a more complex and positive manner. Since the child is not able to use his general tendency to control interactions, he is more receptive to the initiatives, teachings, expectations, and affection of his parent. As the parent sees the more vulnerable, genuine aspects of her child, her motivation to continue to facilitate the bond increases. As his sensitivity to both self and parent increases, he begins to notice that his needs are best met within the relationship rather than through maintaining solitary control.

In therapy there is an alternating flow from the child's inner life to the child's relationship with the parent and back again. This relationship is shown as facilitating and supporting the child's thoughts and feelings. As the thoughts and feelings become better defined, integrated, and expressed, their development enables him to access more fully the benefits of the relationship. In such a setting, he feels empathy for self and then begins to experience empathy for the parent's thoughts and feelings. The therapist encourages and treasures this healthy duality. For example, the therapist may comment:

You seemed so proud when you told that to your mom!
Your mom sure understands you better than I do. Must be that love again!
Your mom thinks that you did a good job with that. What do you think?
I notice some anger between you and your mom. How does that affect
    what you think about each other?

Problems and Skills

For the sessions to be fully therapeutic they must focus on both the pain and the hope, the problems and the talents, the limitations and the opportunities. These children generally experience life from a very negative perspective with few positive expectations. They resist understanding the abusive roots of their negativity and find it very difficult to view themselves or their world in a positive manner. Both assumptions must be challenged. The child needs to learn about and be responsible for all aspects of the self. He needs to really notice profound differences between "good" and "bad" parenting.

These children experience themselves very negatively in part because of the frequent negative responses that they receive to their very poor behavioral choices in the present. While these behaviors are certainly explored, the exploration occurs in an atmosphere of great empathy and with a great deal of hope that the child can learn to take advantage of his excellent home, begin to form a deeper attachment, and develop the inner resources and behavioral skills needed. Successes and their meanings are reviewed. Progress is acknowledged and strategies are developed for further progress. Practice is expected and homework to make the gains observable to all is assigned. The child needs to think that he does in fact have the capacity for change. He needs to feel that he is a good kid who is very special to his parents. Gradually he will understand that their expectations are not punitive, rather they reflect his real potential to become a responsible, loving, and joyful individual.

The poorly attached child experiences himself as both "good" and "bad," the "bad" being primary, and he has little ability to allow one of these aspects of self to influence the other. The child's past, in which shame led to contempt and rejection, needs to be explored again within an atmosphere of empathy and support. Therapy needs to help him to fully experience both aspects of the self so that he can gradually integrate the two.

Too often, therapy provides empathy primarily for the child's "good" functioning or for his past traumas. He then experiences empathy only superficially because it is just directed toward one aspect of the self. Since the child is split into "bad" and "good" with little integration, the empathy directed toward the "good" self has no effect on the "bad" self. In fact, he probably experiences the "good" self as being superficial or phony and thinks that he has tricked the adults into liking this superficial aspect of the self. He is convinced that the adult has no empathy for the "bad" self, which he generally experiences as more basic and genuine. The empathy from the therapist and parent must be directed toward both aspects of the experienced self if the child is ever to become integrated. If his negative self-concept is to be modified, he must experience the adult's intense involvement as being directed toward this aspect of self, too. Confrontations and themes that elicit anger and resistance provide opportunities for him to be angry at the therapist. He then experiences how the therapist relates to his "bad" actions. The therapist's continuing empathy for the child is crucial if he is to feel accepted by the therapist for his whole self, not just the charming and often manipulative "self." When the whole child is accepted and engaged in therapy, he can begin to integrate and accept all of himself.

With an anxious and sad child who has a good attachment history and who does not have a rigid split within the self, the therapeutic relationship can and does generalize to all aspects of the self. He can use the relationship to resolve the trauma and get on with his developmental tasks. Oppositional or distancing behaviors at home may then become much less prevalent even though they are not directly dealt with in treatment. These children have a fundamentally integrated self so that therapeutic empathy affects the entire child.

However, the poorly attached child, with a self that includes a rigid core of "badness," needs to have the therapeutic relationship enter into that core as well. Persistent, profound empathy, along with readiness and initiatives to reengage regardless of whatever rage he manifests, are necessary if we are to reach that child. He needs to expose the whole self to the therapist and parent for integration to occur and to begin to fully attach to his parents.

PARENTAL PARTICIPATION

A crucial and central feature of the treatment of the poorly attached child is the active participation of the parent with whom he is expected to learn to form a secure attachment relationship. Our treatment goal is to facilitate the development of basic attachment patterns within the child's functioning, and these patterns will not develop in isolation from his parent. Since this attachment relationship is our focus, both members of the relationship need to be full participants in the treatment. For a variety of reasons, the involved presence of the parent brings a depth of meaning to the therapeutic focus which greatly facilities her child's progress. The child's new parent becomes a co-therapist whose abilities and commitment are necessary components of the therapeutic process.

REASONS

Emotional Attunement

Emotional attunement between parent and child is crucial for therapeutic success. By having the parent present in the session, attunement with her child can be encouraged, supported, and reinforced. Through her attunement to many of his feeling states, he is able to achieve a degree of self-integration that would otherwise be lacking. Her child is able to experience his worth as a whole person. A full range of vital and categorical affects is accepted within the immediate experience of attunement. Frequently the therapist sits back and observes the parent and child being so deeply engaged with each other. By giving this experience such a central place in the session, the therapist is reinforcing its value and increasing the likelihood of similar experiences at home.

Often when a parent is fully attuned with her child she becomes engaged with him as if he were much younger than his chronological age. This is quite understandable in that he is often fixated at an earlier developmental level in his psychological functioning and in the nature of his attachment abilities. This degree of attunement will allow and support a level of regression that is very beneficial to the eventual development of the poorly attached child.

Emotional Support and Empathy

A parent provides emotional support and empathy to her child beyond what the therapist is able to offer. This enables the child to engage more fully in stressful themes either from the past or present. Her empathy provides him with a sense of feeling understood and being secure. When he is asked to explore past experiences of abuse, he is often able to do so at a deeper emotional level when he is being held and comforted by his parent. This enables him to achieve greater therapeutic resolution of the event. It also makes him more likely to spontaneously express memories of abuse and neglect to his parent at home, since he has had a positive experience doing so in therapy.

When the child is asked to process recent events and conflicts involving his parent, he is more likely to fully explore the situation when she is present and communicating empathy for his fear or anger. This enables him to quickly re-engage with her rather than feeling isolated and rejected or blamed. It also makes it more likely that this exploration will generalize to similar situations in the future at home. Finally, with his parent present, the child will not be so likely to try to create a split between his parent and therapist since it is obvious that they are working as a team to help him.

At times when a theme is very difficult for the child, his parent and therapist can assist him in working on it by talking to each other about the theme so that he only has to listen. If the therapist thinks that the child will not be ready or able to indicate what he feels when his parent is angry with him, she instead can turn to the parent and ask her what she thinks that the child is feeling as well as what she is feeling and what she hopes he will begin to think or feel. The child can listen or respond as he wishes. This will give him the opportunity to know what his parent thinks about his inner life before he reveals it. After feeling supported, he is more willing to express himself.

Differentiation

A central goal of treatment is to help the child to differentiate his interaction with his current parent from the experiences of abuse and neglect that he had with his birth parents. By having the parent present when the child is exploring past instances of abuse, the therapist is given many more opportunities to help him to see that his new parent is not the same as his birth parent. He is shown how discipline is not abuse, conflict is not rejection, and periodic separation is not abandonment. In making these important distinctions between his current and his abusive parents, the child is removing a crucial impediment to taking the risks necessary to develop a positive relationship.

Increased Similarity between Therapy and Home

With the parent present in the session, there is greater similarity between therapy and life at home. The therapist is supporting and modeling the various ways of interaction between parent and child. Consequently, these are more likely to occur at home following the sessions than if the parent were not present or were seen separately from her child. The central therapeutic role of the parent in the child's life is made obvious during the session and parents relish such a chance to be a central part of their child's development. Their motivation and their skills are greater when they are directly involved in their child's treatment.

Frequently in therapy there are discussions about the child's life at home. The therapist may choose to give "homework" to the parent and child regarding strategies to employ at home for practicing skill development or for modifying consequences. Both of them are more likely to follow through with these interventions if they both are part of the initial discussion of their merits.

Expert Knowledge

By participating in the treatment session the parent is able to bring her expert knowledge of her particular child into the therapeutic interventions. She can assist the therapist in identifying key themes that interfere with her child's functioning from day to day. She can help to devise strategies that are uniquely suited to her child's needs. Through her awareness of various anecdotes from her child's life, she can make the session more relevant to his daily experiences. Also, if her child is trying to manipulate the therapist through distractions and lies, she is in a good position to aid the therapist in reducing these tactics.

Parental Authority

With the parent present in therapy there are numerous ways to communicate to her child the value and importance of parental authority. The therapist shows the child how she respects his parent's judgment and skills and how she defers to the parent in decisions about the child. She never questions the authority of the parent in front of the child, never tells her what to do or criticizes her decisions and actions. When the therapist has a suggestion, the approval of the parent is directly sought and the parent's decision is final as far as the child is concerned. If the therapist has reservations about the parent's decisions or actions, she discusses them outside his presence. Any major recommendations to the parent are made without the child being present so that the parent can easily reject the suggestion without the child being aware of any important conflict between parent and therapist. This attitude toward the parent's authority is very clear to both parent and child during the session.

Safety

The safety of both the child and the therapist is enhanced by the presence of the parent. Because of the intense emotions generated by this treatment, along with the frequent physical contact between the child and therapist, the issue of safety cannot be overlooked. There is danger that the child may feel or perceive a situation as being abusive, either physically, sexually, or emotionally. His parent's presence will reduce the risk of a false allegation about the therapist's actions. Her presence will also help him to feel more secure when he is being confronted, directed to explore painful themes, or held by the therapist. This reduces any risk that the child might be traumatized by the therapist, either deliberately or accidentally.

Clearly, the active participation of the parent is necessary to the overall effectiveness of this form of treatment for poorly attached children. We are not assisting this child to "attach" in the abstract. We are working to facilitate his attachment to his current parent. By interacting with them both in treatment and observing their interactions with each other, the therapist has a much greater chance of succeeding.

SPECIFICS

There are a variety of activities and interactions between a parent and child in therapy that can facilitate his attachment to his parent. The therapist is always looking for concrete ways to assist the child in experiencing his parent in a positive manner so that his trust in the relationship increases. As he practices ways of talking, relaxing, resolving conflict, showing affection, and having fun with his parent in the treatment session, he is more likely to risk engaging in similar ways of relating at home.

Emotional Attunement

Emotional attunement between parent and child has an important place in most treatment sessions. Early in therapy the parent and therapist discuss what this experience entails. Most parents will respond with obvious understanding when given examples of the mother–infant bond. Parents need to fully comprehend how crucial this experience is for the poorly attached child, regardless of his age, if he is to become attached.

In fostering attunement, the therapist stresses the need for the parent to interact with physical contact, eye contact, smiles, laughter, facial expressions, and movements. Numerous concrete activities in therapy lend themselves to emotional attunement. For example, the parent may hold her child, rock him, sing him a lullaby or a loud "happy" song, count his freckles or the hair on his eyebrows, or give him a bottle. She may also play "peek-a-boo," "mother, may I?" or "I went to California and brought an *alligator, book, cow,*" and so forth. Specific activities provide the content within which attunement is experienced. The activities make it easier for the parent to match her child's immediate feeling state, establish an affective union, and then, in small, subtle preconscious ways, lead the child's affective experiences into more regulated and integrated forms.

The parent may sit close to her child, hold his hands, or hold him in her arms and communicate empathy for all the pain and sadness that he experienced in the past before this parent ever knew him. I have seen many parents cry as they show their sadness over their child's past. Invariably their child will stare intently at their parent's tears. Some children have wiped their parent's tears just as their parent had done for them at other times. Often children will hug their parent closely and cry in turn. Sometimes a child and parent imagine together what life would have been like for them both if this mom had given birth to him. Many of the activities described in Ann Jernberg's (1979) *Theraplay* are excellent means of achieving attunement.

One 4-year-old boy asked his foster mom if she would pretend that she was giving birth to him. She agreed with pleasure. She put on her winter coat, buttoned it, and covered her son with it as he curled up in her lap. She spoke quietly about how happy she was to be ready to give birth to her new child. She opened her coat and spoke with joy as she took her "newborn" into her arms, made eye contact, and delightfully explored his face and hands. She "showed" him to me, taking obvious pride in her wonderful new baby boy. This habitually angry and oppositional 4-year-old became quiet and peaceful as well as giggly and joyful in my presence while in his mother's arms. They reenacted his "birth" many times at home and this experience helped him to truly accept her as his mother.

When parent and child are attuned to each other I usually remain quiet and simply observe their mutually rich experience. At times I get my camera and take a picture so that they can recall the experience together at home. I encourage the child to keep the picture in his room for those times when he needs to remind himself how nice it is to feel close to his mom.

Directives

There are numerous directives that the therapist can give to the child that will address specific difficulties in his daily interactions with his parent. The therapist is restricted if she simply discusses with him areas of difficulty that he has in his relationship with his parent. It is much more productive if the therapist directs him into immediate interactions with his parent and then processes the results of that intervention. There are many examples where such interactions are highly beneficial to the developing attachment, including the following:

1) The child has difficulty expressing his fears and sadness;
2) He is reluctant to ask for help;
3) He is reluctant to verbalize his anger at his parent;
4) He is reluctant to express his affection for his parent;
5) He has difficulty receiving affection from his parent;
6) He has difficulty maintaining eye contact in conversations with his parent;
7) He has difficulty resolving conflicts because of his intense shame and rage;
8) He has difficulty remaining relaxed when embraced by his parent; and
9) He becomes anxious whenever he is having fun with his parent.

In these and similar situations, the therapist directs the child to practice with his parent through words, hugs, games, and activities the various interactions that will address his difficulty and facilitate the relationship. Invariably he will make greater progress, more quickly, when he is guided in ways of relating with his parent during therapy than when he is left to his own resources to initiate the activity at home.

For example, when a child has difficulty asking his parent for help, the issue is first discussed with empathy. He is told how hard it must be when a person has great difficulty learning a skill, accomplishing a task, or even coping with a fear and is not able to rely on someone for assistance. He is shown understanding for why he finds it hard to ask his parent for help since he was so seldom given any help in the past. He had to rely on himself and if he was not able to manage a situation, then he failed. If he ever asked for help, he might have been ignored, ridiculed, or rejected.

After communicating empathy for the source of the difficulty, the child's parent expresses a willingness and even enjoyment of being able to offer to help him when he is having trouble. He is told that an important part of her role as his parent is to help him in various ways. At that point the therapist suggests that he might practice asking his parent for help doing something right then. Rarely has a child refused this suggestion. Among the various activities I have used are the following:

1) The child is told to read a book to his parent and to ask her for help with any word that he does not know;
2) He is shown a card trick or puzzle. His parent helps him to learn how to do it;
3) He is directed to ask his parent for help in learning how to tell the truth at home when he does something wrong; and
4) He is told to imagine that he feels lonely. His task is to tell his parent and ask for help in dealing with the feeling.

One child frequently hit and screamed at his mother but he would never talk about his anger toward her. During the session I positioned him directly in front of her and told him to tell her that he was angry at her because she would not let him ride his new bike. I stressed that he needed to express his anger with intensity so that his mother would have some idea of exactly how angry he was with her. I modeled for him how he needed to speak more forcefully. When he did so, I directed him to tell her why he thought that she was unfair in not allowing him to ride his bike. From there I told him to tell her that he thought she often did not care what he felt and that it really did not seem to matter to her that her restrictions made him mad . . . and sad. His mother responded by expressing empathy for his feelings about not having the bike as well as for his thoughts that she did not care about what he felt. She indicated to him that when she limits him she does know how hard it is for him to accept her limits and she hoped that someday it would get easier for him. She then thanked him for honestly expressing his thoughts and feelings to her and she gave him a hug. She did not justify her decision to limit his bike riding nor did she give any long talk about his need for discipline. Her response validated his inner experience and supported his initial communications. We gave him many similar directives in the weeks following that session and gradually he began to be more expressive at home. Her excellent initial response to his directed expression greatly facilitated this process.

Directives serve as excellent means for beginning to address a difficulty. They are often followed by specific tasks at home that will reinforce the directive. In the example about asking for help, the therapist might have directed the child to ask his parents for help five times before the next therapy session and to write down each request and his parents' response.

Differentiation

Parental participation in therapy is an excellent way of assisting the child to differentiate between those parents who abused and neglected him and his current parents, with whom he is being asked to form a secure attachment. When his parent is giving him empathy for the difficult task he has in exploring his past, he is made very aware of a fundamental difference between this parent and his previous one. The same is true whenever he screams his rage at his parent and experiences his parent's commitment to him.

During a session the therapist remains aware of the value of taking advantage of opportunities to contrast his new parents with those who abused and neglected him. Comments such as, "Is that something that (abusive parent) would have said?" or "Did you ever get put to bed in the past the way your mom puts you to bed now?" help the child to become aware of the differences. This awareness will facilitate his readiness to risk trusting that this relationship is, and can be, different from his past ones.

When the therapist uses *psychodrama* to assist him in resolving past traumas with his abusing and neglecting parents, the child will often move strongly toward his parent for support and affirmation. The psychodrama itself will bring out clear differences between the past and present families. The therapist might choose either to have the abusive parents criticize the new parents or else have them recognize the excellent way that the new parents are raising their child. Either way, the child is able to experience their fundamental differences in caring for him.

Current conflicts between the child and parent are explored during therapy with the parent showing patience and empathy. Differences will be acknowledged, reasons given when appropriate, and natural consequences presented. Throughout the process, the relationship is nurtured and available to the child. This process contrasts sharply with the experience of abuse, rejection, and humiliation that he experienced repeatedly when he lived with the abusive parents. Through discussions and drawings, the therapist works to help the child have some insight into this difference as well as into the damaging effects that the prior experiences had on his development and readiness to attach.

Parental Authority and Knowledge

The parents of the poorly attached child must be the most important adults in his life if he is to learn to form an attachment with them. It is crucial for the therapist not only to believe this reality but also to give it central importance in developing practical means of helping their child. Interventions, developed by using the knowledge and values of the parents, are enacted with the participation of the parents. The success of the intervention is determined by the parents' judgment of their child's daily functioning. There is constant communication between the therapist and parents regarding the best interests of their child and the means of achieving it.

The parents need to see how much the therapist trusts them to know their child the best, as well as to know his attachment problems and the effects of these problems on the family. The therapist needs to get to know the family relationships, values, interests, communication patterns, routines, strengths, and weaknesses. She needs to discover the unique features of this family so that she can have a better understanding of the realistic goals that this child must have if he is to fit into this family. Features of a family that would be "good enough" for the healthy development of a child who had no significant difficulties in forming an attachment may have to become stronger and be communicated more fully to this particular child. Qualities that worked well for their other children may have to be modified a bit for this poorly attached child to be able to benefit from them. The therapist consults with the parents about such family interventions while always respecting the parents' position of knowing what is best for the family as a whole.

During much of this consultation, the child is not present since parent and therapist must resolve any potential differences before presenting an issue to the child. If there are differences between parent and therapist, the therapist will state clearly that his parents will decide what is best and that she trusts the parents' choice. I might joke about a difference, telling the child that I would really be hard on him if his parents' love didn't stop me or I might express relief that the parents' knowledge of the child saved me again from doing something wrong and looking foolish.

During the course of treatment, I constantly communicate to the child the importance of the family and the need to preserve its overall well-being. I also communicate to him my confidence in his parents' judgments, memory of recent events, knowledge of him, and ability to act in his best interests. He is told that I consult with his parents frequently about ways that they can respond to his needs even more effectively. Also, I communicate to the child the reality that progress will be measured in large part by his functioning in the home and, especially, in his relationships with his parents. He knows that what I am observing are his choices to "get close to" his parents or to "push them away." I am evaluating his trust in his parents by determining how well he is able to comply with their judgment about what is best for him to do. I also evaluate his choices in light of how well they reflect his commitment to work hard to become a part of the family. I communicate that his resistance to receiving "fun and love" from his parents might represent his difficulty in loving himself enough to be able to relax and enjoy such experiences.

Generally, I tell the child that since his parents know him much better than I do, we need to ask his parents why he may have chosen to do a certain thing. We also need to ask his parents if such a choice is acceptable in their family and, if not, what consequence may be needed. The child needs to see very clearly how much I trust the judgment, motives, intentions, and commitment of his parents. At times, I say directly to the child: "Your parents love you and I don't. I like you, but there's a big difference between the two." I want the child to wonder about this difference since probably he has never given it much thought. What are the implications of their love for him? Since I place so much meaning on their love, perhaps he might do the same.

At times I suggest that the parents give a firm consequence for a behavior and then inform the child that this consequence resulted from my suggestion. The parents, in turn, imply to the child that probably they would not be quite so strict in choosing a consequence but that they trusted my judgment in this situation and would follow through with my recommendation. They are doing this because of their love for the child. We then discuss the issue in therapy and I ask the child to thank the parent for this sign of "love." That tends to evoke some laughter, but it also lays the groundwork for the child to accept the consequence at home with less anger or with some of the anger directed toward me. The parent might be encouraged to show empathy by saying: "I trust Dan's judgment that this consequence is helping you. I'll be glad when he thinks that you don't need it anymore so we can drop it. Until then, how about a hug?"

Homework

Commonly, the child is given homework to emphasize something emerging from the session or to develop certain personal and relationship skills. Also, I want him to think about the goals between sessions. I want him to know how much I stress the need to work on attachment issues in the reality of daily family living. I may use homework to serve as a setting for the parent and child to experiment with new, mutually enjoyable activities. At other times, I may assign homework hoping that the child will "fail" and have this experience as a source of new learning about his motivation and about the work to be done. Whatever the reason and content of homework, the parents need to be consulted as to its appropriateness for the child and family. Whether the parents should intervene in the homework through a reminder, assistance, consequence for not doing it, or recognition for a good job needs to be discussed. Homework is routinely reviewed during the next session.

There are as many forms of homework as there are unique problems, skills, and family routines. Here is a brief list of random homework assignments:

1) In therapy, the child makes a list of ways to communicate love to his parent. He needs to do each item on the list once or twice before the next session;

2) The child practices, three times a day, telling his mom calmly what he feels when given a limit or a chore;

3) The child asks for help, information, and a favor, each one daily;

4) The child gives his parent a note each day containing a thought or feeling that his parent did not know;

5) The child finds five things that are funny and sees if his parent can guess what they are;

6) The child reviews one of his poor choices daily with his parent and gives a recommendation for a natural consequence to that choice;

7) The child and parent take turns selecting a 30-minute activity that they can do together at home each day. On a scale of 1 to 10, they each secretly rate how much they enjoyed the activity;

8) The child is given a list of ten different feelings. He is asked to keep a journal of when he experienced each feeling;

9) The child notices when the parent experienced five different feelings. After writing them in the journal, the child checks with the parent as to the accuracy of his perception;

10) The child keeps a list of five times he liked himself and five times he did not like himself; and

11) The child will immediately do what he is told by his parent, without any excuses or arguments. He keeps a list of his successes on the day before the next therapy session. I guess how many times he was successful.

Homework assignments must not simply focus on "good behavior." They should cover a variety of situations to communicate to the child that all aspects of his functioning and his relationship with his parents are important. Certain assignments are given simply to stress that the child's enjoyment and happiness are very important to the therapist and parent. Others are provided to stress the value of mutual enjoyment. Working together at home on a puzzle, learning to sew, building a model, or fixing a chair provides a very focused, shared activity that leads to enjoyment. Still other "tasks" are given to simply recognize the work that he has done and to give the parent and therapist a chance to show their enjoyment of him.

To facilitate the child's acceptance of his homework, it is often helpful to assign his parent homework as well. This makes it evident to him that his parent is willing to work to help him to have a better life in her home. When she calmly accepts her homework and carries out her commitment, he will be more likely to manage his in a similar manner. The parent should agree with doing specific "homework" before it is presented to the child. Examples of homework given to a parent include keeping lists of her thoughts and feelings in response to specific situations, surprising her child with certain activities or gifts, identifying and developing a plan to manage a specific problem, and responding to her child's behaviors in specific ways. She might occasionally fail to do her homework and demonstrate appropriate means of dealing with her failure.

Regression

Frequently with poorly attached children, the child must be allowed and encouraged to regress and relate to his new parent as if he were a much younger child, one that actually reflects his psychological age. This enables him to relate with his parent in a way that more effectively meets his psychological and attachment needs. The parent who frequently "gave birth" to her 4-year-old boy in my office and at home is one dramatic example of such regression.

Numerous therapy and home activities support the child's regression, both in areas of nurturance as well as in discipline and skill development. They include the following:

1) Holding, rocking, feeding, giving him a bottle, combing his hair;
2) Movement, music, touching, and "make believe" games;

3) Making many choices for him, including what to wear and what activities to engage in;

4) Supervising and being physically close to him throughout the day; and

5) Discipline consists of teaching. He is shown how to practice doing something the right way. Hugs and support go with teaching.

In almost every case in which I have recommended and a parent has established a comprehensive routine by which she relates to her child as if he were much younger (i.e., an 8-year-old "becomes" 4 and a 4-year-old "becomes" 2), her child has accepted and enjoyed this intervention. Parents report that the child is more agreeable, content, and willing to accept directives than he has ever been. Most children show no embarrassment about being treated this way. They seem to relish the opportunity to experience their new parent as a younger child. Children request bottles and diapers with no hesitation. One 5-year-old calmly told his visiting aunt, "Mom gives me a bottle every day because I need to be her baby right now."

I originally thought that the oppositional child would greatly resent the increased supervision and the reduced freedom to make choices that this routine involves. I have repeatedly found that such children often feel more content and secure in having less opportunity to make poor choices. They do not get into nearly as much trouble and they seem relieved not to have the responsibility of making good choices. Importantly, the increased directives and supervision are not given as a consequence of poor choices but rather they are presented as a natural part of the child's life since he is "younger" now. The parent and child often demonstrate to the therapist the various activities that they engaged in at home and the new learning that the child achieved.

Regression can only be encouraged in this comprehensive fashion if the parent is committed to the concept and willing and able to provide the high degree of time and involvement that such a routine requires. This degree of supervision and one-to-one engagement and teaching represents a total commitment that the parent must be ready to make. She also must be confident enough to engage her child in this manner regardless of the questions and criticisms that she may face from friends and relatives. She must understand that such extensive regression proves to be much more effective in facilitating a child's movement through the development of the self and the attachment with his parent than isolated acts of regression such as giving a bottle or rocking and singing to him occasion-ally.

In summary, with the parent actively involved, each treatment session has numerous possibilities for facilitating the child's attachment to her. The experiences and learning that occur in the session are shared by both and are easily generalized to events at home. The stress that comes from focusing on abusive themes and memories is made more bearable when his parent is present to share his pain and comfort him. With the parent present, the central message being conveyed to the child is that he has much to learn about trusting and forming an attachment with his parent. His parent is present to assist and teach him because she loves him.

6

THERAPEUTIC INTERVENTIONS

Within the context of the therapeutic principles described in Chapter Four, there are numerous therapeutic interventions that are quite suitable for structuring the session to maximize the therapeutic benefits for the child. These interventions are taken from various therapeutic frameworks such as psychodynamic, Gestalt, cognitive-behavioral, family, Ericksonian, and Theraplay. They are never ends in themselves; they are most effective within the context of the type of relationship described in the previous chapters. The therapist might anticipate using certain interventions prior to the onset of treatment, but she must be ready to discard them all if other interactions are necessary to maintain the emotionally intense, relationship-focused nature of the treatment. When an intervention has become mechanical, it is discarded. When the child asks for a certain activity in a manipulative fashion, it is set aside. Some of these interventions I have used with every child in many sessions. Others I have used on some occasions with certain children.

ENGAGEMENT AND LEADING

Crucial to the therapeutic work is the need to maintain an emotional engagement with the child so that he will be receptive to the various therapeutic interventions employed. Maintaining an engagement with a child who resists such engagements especially when he is under the direction of an adult can be a difficult task.

Being attuned with the child's vitality and categorical affects is crucial if the therapist is to maintain a continuous affective engagement with him. Because of the intense affective demands of therapy, the child is certain to experience extreme variations of affective intensity in his feeling states. He also is likely to move rapidly from intense feelings of pleasure to comparable feelings of displeasure. If the therapist is not attuned to the affective background of his therapeutic experience, the interventions will be ignored, discounted, and ineffectual. Through attunement with the "explosions and fading" of his feeling states, she is assisting the child to regulate and integrate the feeling states that underlie his emerging sense of "self." Through the attunement experience, the feeling states become less extreme and the feeling shifts less abrupt. Certain feeling states that have frequently been rejected and avoided are more able to be explored and integrated.

The level of engagement that characterizes affective attunement occurs through eye contact, physical contact, facial gestures, movements, posture, and breathing. Through these nonverbal modalities, the therapist's awareness, interest, and affirmation of the child and their immediate interaction is experienced by him at the most primitive level and incorporated into his most fundamental sense of "self."

It may well be impossible to "teach" a therapist or parent how to be attuned to a child in therapy or in the home. What one can do is help the therapist and parent to be receptive to their instinctive attunement abilities so that they will understand their central role in working with the poorly attached child and, consequently, allow their appropriate expression. To relate with the child at the level of affective attunement, the parent and therapist must have experienced attunement themselves as infants and young children. It also is helpful if they have parented healthy children of their own or have observed attunement experiences between mothers and their very young children and regularly participated with healthy young children in that manner.

In the more usual therapeutic stance, the therapist is detached and does not facilitate the attunement experience with the child. She communicates empathy in traditional therapeutic endeavors, but stops short of affective attunement. Such a stance is indicated with children who have sufficient attunement experiences in their histories with their primary caregivers since they are able to benefit from empathy and maintain an affective bond with the therapist while doing their therapeutic work. With the poorly attached child lacking an adequate history of attunement experiences, empathy is not able to reach the "self" of the child and he does not engage in any depth with the therapist.

Hypnotic induction techniques developed by Milton Erickson (Erickson and Rossi 1979, Erickson 1980) can be very useful in maintaining a continuing engagement with the child. These techniques direct the child's attention into the therapeutic areas selected by the therapist. They also assist in maintaining the emotional connection between child, therapist, and parent that is so necessary for therapeutic work to occur. The child needs to be receptive to the therapist's directives, to be curious about what is occurring, and to be anticipating what might occur next. This engagement exists both on a conscious and an unconscious level as the child slowly internalizes and integrates the therapeutic "messages" that the treatment attempts to convey. As is the case in Erickson's practice, these interventions work first to *pace* the child's psychological reality and then to *lead* the child to areas that will facilitate change. This process is similar to aspects of affective attunement, in which the mother *matches* her infant's feeling state and in very small increments encourages his development.

Doing the unexpected is often highly effective in maintaining the child's attention. During a session I might leap off the couch and leave the room for a minute then rush back and express satisfaction that what I just did will be of help to the child. When the child has made a good choice, I might scream in annoyance that such choices will shorten the length of our treatment or I might take fifteen tissues from the box, throw them around the room and tell the child to order me to pick up every tissue. If the parent reports that the child was quite defiant this week, I might shake the child's hand while expressing satisfaction that the child is showing his fear of attachment so directly. Each of these actions is likely to leave the child somewhat perplexed, possibly amused, and ready to respond to what comes next.

Voice modifications also tend to elicit an alert focus on what is being said. Frequently, I will pause, stare, and put a very serious look on my face before saying something. This might be used when the content is something that I want the child to recall. At other times it is used simply because I notice that the child's mind is beginning to wander. Often I will speak loudly for a sentence or two and then speak quite softly while slowly changing my facial expression, or I will whisper in the child's ear something quite relevant to our intervention. This might be especially effective when the message relates to his parent, who is present. The child takes some pleasure in that the parent cannot hear what is being said. I might speak very quickly while describing a recent angry incident experienced by the child and then follow this by speaking softly and slowly as I set the tone for the child to feel some sadness over the isolation that he felt from his parent after the event.

Touch is an excellent means of maintaining a responsive and focused engagement with the child. I might gently touch the child's shoulder while giving empathy regarding how hard the work is that we are doing. To make a point, I might tap my finger in rhythm with my voice on the palm of the child's hand. I might hold a child who is very resistant and wants to leave while giving empathy and encouragement for his difficulties. I might direct a conversation between a child and parent while having them hold hands and periodically embrace. Touch often greatly facilitates a child's readiness to focus on the task at hand while fostering a sense of being supported and engaged.

One child insisted that I get his permission before touching him. While usually I would not give such control to a poorly attached child, in this instance I decided that he wanted a power struggle that I might easily avoid. I praised him for his honest expression of his wishes, and then asked him for permission 10 to 15 times over the next 20 minutes, each time getting assent. Finally, the child spontaneously gave me permission to touch him in the future without permission. I utilized his need to control being touched while communicating how important it was for him to be touched. I was willing to get his permission hundreds of times, if necessary, to provide him with what he needed. Since I completely accepted his wish, he fairly quickly gave it up. If I had resented it or had a power struggle, the treatment would have been much more difficult.

The *manner in which a theme is presented verbally* is also crucial in helping a child to interpret, or reframe, a situation in a more favorable light. For example, I often want a child to begin to question the interpersonal meaning of his behaviors in order to reduce the driven, compulsive quality of certain symptoms. Thus, I might suggest that the next time the child becomes angry at his mother, he's likely to begin to notice how his anger serves to disguise his love for her. In fact, he may even see how he is tempted to feel even angrier as his love becomes stronger until he discovers himself becoming more comfortable with the love. Such a comment reframes his anger. It is no longer a sign that he is "bad" nor is it a sign that he hates his mother. Rather, his anger proves his love and his fear of this love. His anger will help him to notice his love more. The inevitability of his getting used to love so that he needs anger less is also presented for both conscious and unconscious consideration. This is done not by insisting the child change nor by telling the child to try harder to love. Rather, confidence in the child's inner wish to accept his mother's love is shown with patience and curiosity as to the speed with which this will occur. Thus, I lead the child to rethink who he actually *is*, now. He and I can accept his basic self; he does not have to hate his present self to become "better." Such a process would be an impossibility since his current self-hatred is central to his current symptoms.

Double binds are a favorite intervention of Erickson that are effective with children. I will direct the child to do any one of a number of options and then create the interpersonal meaning of the child's act. For example, I might tell the child to show his mother that he loves her by screaming, smiling, or by doing something entirely on his own. I then congratulate the child on his choice for demonstrating his love. The child, thus, cannot refuse to do what I ask since whatever he chooses to do has been defined as communicating love. At the same time, the child's love for his mother has been validated and supported. Rarely will a child say that he does not love her and, even then, I am likely to suggest that I know that it is hard for the child to show love with words. That is why I gave him a nonverbal alternative.

Another effective double bind is to tell the resistant child to refuse to do what I tell him to do. Whether he does it or not, I praise his choice to comply with my request. When I repeat it and he does the opposite of his first response, I praise him again. I then acknowledge how important it is for him to oppose me. I tell him that as long as it is important for him to oppose me, I will attempt to make his opposition helpful to his treatment and to our relationship. Thus, when he opposes me quite forcefully, I might give him a hug with enthusiasm. When he opposes me tentatively, I might give him a hug with even more enthusiasm. Again, I want the child to question the meaning of his actions, to become more receptive to my directives, and to start to frame his thoughts and feelings and actions in a way similar to mine. This will reduce his rigid, negative self-concept and help him to rethink his definition of his "self."

I might also ask the child if he is going to be angrier at me than at his mother because he loves her or if he is going to be angrier at his mother than he is angry at me because he so much wants my help to learn to love his mom more. If the child says that he is angry at us both the same, we then have a great opportunity to maintain his engagement by rating his acts of anger during the session from 1 to 10 to find out if he is accurate. If the child refuses to become angry, we praise his ability to manage it in the session and we wonder if he is likely to control his anger toward us much longer.

I provide an unconscious *therapeutic suggestion* by expressing confidence in the child's healthy changes through casually speaking of therapeutic movement as if it is inevitable. I wonder if the changes regarding learning to playfully joke with his mom, for example, will occur very slowly or all at once. Will he notice each laughing exchange or will he be surprised when his mom comments about his playfulness? I tell the child that some kids begin to notice that they are less angry before they notice that they are more relaxed while other kids notice that they are more relaxed first. I wonder in which of those groups he belongs.

Often children who are poorly attached lack a sense of *humor*. This may be due to various factors in their interpersonal, emotional, and cognitive development. They often are fairly concrete in their thinking, being weak in the conceptual flexibility and abstract abilities used in humor. Also, humor requires a relaxed playfulness in one's relationship with another. When effective, both the giver and recipient are sharing an enjoyable moment, one that enters the history of the relationship from whence it can be recalled again and again.

There is also an intimacy about humor that is frightening to the poorly attached. Humor often occurs with a smile, eye contact, and possibly a playful pat or poke that recognizes what is occurring within a shared warm tone. There is intimacy in the private meaning created between the two individuals to be shared later. When another person notices and asks about it, it has to be recalled again with fondness and gentle teasing.

I look for opportunities to be teased by a child about my ignorance of his youth culture, my clothes, choice of words, or my physical condition. I might feign an outraged response to the teasing, which gives me an excuse to grab the child, pull some hair gently, or do something else likely to cause a scream. Later in that session or the next, I will "accidentally" get around to that topic, give the child an "evil eye," and repeat the sequence.

I may also introduce humor into my efforts to facilitate the child's attachment to his parent. If the child has engaged in some behavior that I interpret as "pushing away" from her, I might praise him for his choice—tell him that it most certainly would be awful to feel close to or actually be hugged by his mom and compare it to his worst nightmare. I might then discipline the child by dragging him screaming to his mom for a quick hug. The next time that behavior occurs, the child can be confident that another such sequence will occur.

Frequently I suggest consequences to the parent for the child's behaviors only after first building up the suspense about what the consequence might be. I might exaggerate how much the child will dislike it or present it as a "gift" for which the child will most certainly experience considerable gratitude. The consequence then is associated with surprise, laughter, or a loud "No!" accompanied by both a scream and laughter. After such a buildup, the consequence is less likely to be forgotten as well as being less annoying in itself. The child is liable to experience my role in the consequence with ambivalence rather than simple negativity.

As the child makes progress toward a stronger attachment, the parents often report that he is developing a sense of humor. Fewer things are taken as seriously as they were initially. Gentle teasing is occurring with regularity, going in both directions between the child and parent. There is more laughing in the home and the overall atmosphere is more relaxed. Conflict and consequences lose some of their bite for the child; he can moan and complain somewhat and then move on to more relevant things to feel strongly about.

These and other interventions serve as the context in which therapeutic changes can occur. It is important to engage the child emotionally and cognitively if one is to be able to lead him into areas of greater psychological health. He is so used to hearing others evaluate and criticize his behavior that he goes into a trance at the first hint of a "sermon." This protects the child from an attack on the self and it detaches him from the adult's efforts to become engaged. The therapist must avoid such lectures, sermons, and "commercials." She needs strategies for maintaining the engagement, for undermining the rigidity of the child's cognitive, affective, and behavioral self and for introducing healthier views of both the self and parents. She then places these views at the child's fingertips.

CONTRACT

Given the directive and intensive nature of the treatment, it is very important to have a contract with the child and parent regarding both the goals of treatment as well as the general framework of treatment. The child is asked to commit himself to the contract at the onset and then to do so again throughout treatment. Reasons are given, goals that clearly should benefit the child are developed, empathy for how difficult therapy will be is provided, and the need for the therapist to determine what happens in therapy is explained. Foster Cline (1991) asks the child five questions which serve as a basic contract. They are:

Are you *happy?*
Are you partly unhappy with yourself?
Do you want to work on it?
Do you want to work hard?
Do you want to work hard my way?

I have found these questions to be very effective in eliciting the child's motivation to engage in therapy. The questions need to be presented in a curious, serious, but relaxed manner, with obvious interest in the child's responses. I usually prepare the child for the final question by emphasizing in a dramatic way that it is the hardest one of all. Rarely has a child refused to agree to this format. Often, during or after particularly difficult sessions, I will recall this agreement with empathy about how hard he is working while gently teasing that if he had known what he was getting in for, he might not have agreed.

With younger children, the contract with the child may be less verbal, but it still has some value in communicating respect for the child's thoughts and feelings about the process. The contract might simply be for the 4-year-old to learn how to have more fun hugging mom and less fun hitting mom. Being directive does not mean ignoring what the child thinks and feels about what is happening in therapy. These children have such a hard time giving up control, and in therapy they are being expected to give up a great amount of control within an intense, emotionally rich, but demanding relationship. The child's basic security is enhanced and his motivation is increased when his thoughts and feelings about the treatment are elicited and understood with empathy and respect.

I approach the need for a contract with a great deal of patience and tact. These children are so sensitive to being blamed for the family problems that they will not agree to anything that might be seen as blaming them. Also, they may see the contract as confirming their own fear that they are "bad." They strive to maintain a strong defense. At the same time, however, it is necessary for them to deal with the reality that it is their fears of closeness, perceived rejections, and self-doubts that contribute in significant ways to their own negative, rejecting behaviors that are impeding the developing attachment. These issues are maintained primarily in the child's thoughts, feelings, and expectations that originated in the past, not in the current family. If we engage the child and parent with the traditional family therapy assumption that the pathology lies within the system and not within the traumatic past, then we validate the child's need to blame the parents for his difficulties to protect himself from profound shame. This family is not the source of the child's weak attachment nor is the child "bad" because it is hard for him to form an attachment with his new parents. The child and parents need to be very clear on the therapist's position on this issue.

In motivating these children and adolescents to accept the contract, I often acknowledge that at times their parents are angry and do ignore them. I suggest that these responses reflect normal family life and that such happenings occur in all close relationships. I then state that their perceptions of such behaviors as being abusive, neglectful, or rejecting make the interactions especially painful for them. These perceptions become the basis of their own subsequent rage at their parents and their own increased guardedness about emotional closeness. I further suggest that such perceptions are very understandable given the extent of their own abusive and neglectful histories. I indicate that they have had little exposure to good family living and are now being asked to learn some very hard matters that relate to living in a good family. I affirm that their parents need to realize that what is being asked of them is hard and that their parents need to work hard, too, if they are to ask their child to do this work.

In making this presentation, I make it clear that my commitment is to facilitate the child's attachment within the family since this is what they all want and this is what the child needs. I ask if all the family members are committed to the work while making it clear that the child has the most work to do and needs the most support. It is his traumatic history that is making this new learning about healthy relationships so difficult. I give examples of why the child will be able to do the work if he is willing to become engaged in the treatment. He needs to follow my leads, initially on faith if necessary, to achieve this new understanding and way of relating. When he agrees, I express pleasure with the decision because of my anticipation that he will be happier (and closer to his parents). What is clearly implied, and at times stated, is that while the child will have to work the hardest, the child, not the parents, will also benefit the most.

In past years in my practice, I can remember many poorly attached children who were fairly neutral about traditional therapy and, at times, were resistant to it for various reasons. Even though the therapy that I am now describing is much more intense, demanding, intrusive, and challenging, the children I treat are generally very willing and ready to come to their sessions. This is probably because there is a great amount of affection and support along with the strong expectations. Parents report that the child might complain a bit but without any genuine resistance. Many children are clearly very emotionally involved in their therapy and refer to it in various ways during the week at home. I recall one girl who was told to show and explain to her father (who was not present during that session) a drawing I gave her that demonstrated how her past abuse affected her and how she would be changing. With much pride she not only showed and described the drawing in detail to her father but also to other members of her extended family. She showed great pleasure in thinking that she would soon know how to be close to her parents.

When a child entering adolescence or later years refuses to participate in this therapy, I do not recommend forcing the child to do so. This work is so difficult that for it to be successful, there needs to be some motivation for change on the part of the young adolescent. Also at this age, the child's desire for closer family relationship is usually less. To attempt to force the young adolescent to work for such closer relationships is likely to be very frustrating and nonproductive for all members of the family. In these situations, I recommend either more traditional individual or family therapy or consultations with the parents alone. I then focus on ways for the parents to safeguard their family life while maintaining appropriate choices, consequences, and empathy for their child.

HOLDING

When thinking of an infant's attachment to his mother, one immediately envisions the infant in his mother's arms. There is eye contact and their faces are alive with emotional meaning. This picture is quickly expanded to include acts of the mother stroking her infant's hair or cheeks. She rocks him and sings quietly with his hand wrapped around her finger. She laughs and holds him away from her before bringing him wiggling to her lips and kissing his belly. She gives him a quick hug and murmurs something unintelligible while poking his nose. There is a great deal of laughing and shouting as well as smiling and gentle touching. In this dance, the infant is participating in a great range and depth of emotional experience that is the foundation of his attachment to her. These are the interactions of emotional attunement, the foundation of this work.

The therapist also employs ongoing physical contact with the child to develop his ability to form an attachment to his parents. Foster Cline

(1991) and Gregory Keck (1995) use therapeutic holding as a central component of their treatment of poorly attached children and adolescents. Their work is closely associated with the treatment philosophy of The Attachment Center, in Evergreen, CO and it differs in various ways from this work. Martha Welch (1988) provides a different treatment paradigm which is directed toward both the mother and child in an effort to strengthen the attachment bond. In her treatment, practiced at The Mothering Center in Greenwich, CT, it is the mother exclusively, and not the therapist, who holds the child. Viola Brody (in James 1994) uses touch in a variety of forms as a central component of her treatment of children with weak attachments. Tiffany Field (1986, 1992) has shown through considerable research that children ranging from premature babies to children and adolescents in a psychiatric facility benefit significantly from receiving regular massages.

While holding the child, the therapist or parent is able to "dance" with him and elicit a great range and depth of emotional experience and expression. While being held, the child is very receptive to experiences of sadness, anger, curiosity, fear, humor, shame, pride, and affection. He is more able to seek and accept support, affirmation, affection, and encouragement and is more playful and alive in his movements and expressions. At the same time, he shows his profound sadness and rage at various life experiences with clarity and genuineness.

The therapeutic stance of holding the child is often the most important intervention in the therapeutic process. Numerous intense and complex emotions emerge from within it. During the time that the child is being held by the therapist or parent, he will have many attunement experiences where his feeling states are being matched by the adult. Some of the feeling states involve laughter, excitement, or peacefulness. Other states involve rage, sadness, or fears. Any state that emerges will be matched. Commonly, the therapist or parent will lead the child into a feeling state and then match it. The resulting interactions enable the child to process and integrate important aspects of the self that are defined as "bad." These traits have habitually elicited uncertainty, annoyance, separation, or punishment from the important adults in his life. While he is being held, the child is able to access these qualities of himself and his life in ways that are more emotionally rich and relevant to him than he otherwise could.

Attachment sequences of union-separation-reunion occur repeatedly when he is being held. The feelings associated with each aspect of the sequence is matched. Throughout the process, the child is experiencing unconditional acceptance of his affective, cognitive, and behavioral expressions at that time. The experience of shared affect between him and his parent or therapist is at the core of the therapeutic benefits for the child.

Many children have screamed and screamed at me while being held but ended the interaction laughing, hugging, and just feeling "good" in ways that their parents had seldom seen. Other children quickly move into experiencing and expressing despair or terror. Later, they may move into strong expressions of anger. My affect matches the child's. As it is more integrated than is his, the shared affect leads him into greater integration of his own. At other times, I may lead him into expressing his affect more intensely before attending to the need for increased integration into his sense of self. During this process I am increasingly empathic. I reflect on the child's expressions—whatever they are—try to understand his experiences, and try to guide his experiences into realizations that include greater self-acceptance and increased trust of his parent. The child undergoes considerable catharsis, but the interaction does not stop there. He also experiences increased reflection on his inner life, greater affect regulation, a more coherent sense of self, and a deeper attachment to his parents.

Generally, the child willingly accepts the experience of being held during the treatment session. At the onset of a session, he might complain about being held, just as he might complain about taking his dirty plate to the sink. On these occasions there is no real opposition to the experience. The child simply may not want to appear to enjoy it or even to admit to himself that he likes this degree of contact. He also knows that therapy is essentially hard work, no matter how much laughter might occur, and he is not looking forward to beginning. If the therapist adopts a relaxed, matter-of-fact attitude of expectation that the child will be held and that this is simply one standard part of treatment that children experience, then resistance tends to be minimal. If, however, the therapist communicates in his attitude that the child should be afraid of being held and that this will be a very difficult experience, then the child is likely to strongly resist. He will very often take his cue from the therapist as to the psychological meaning and impact of the therapist holding him.

In order for the child to understand what to expect, he is told that he will be held a lot by me and by his parent, and he is given a brief reason for this plan. His history of physical and/or sexual abuse will be mentioned so that he knows that the therapist is aware of his possible anxiety about physical contact. Such abuse truly makes appropriate physical contact more important. I might say to the child when I first hold him: "You might have a thought that I might hit you or touch you sexually. If you do, I will understand such thoughts, given your past. Tell us if you do and we'll discuss it." After a few such acknowledgments of his past and his feelings, it is seldom an issue. During the first or second session, the child is briefly shown how he will be held in future sessions. This is done in a matter-of-fact manner, giving him an opportunity to express his thoughts and to ask questions. His parents are also given a chance to comment on the therapist holding their child. If the child knows that his parent understands, supports, and has confidence in this intervention, he will be more relaxed and accepting himself.

The standard therapeutic position is for the child to be lying across my lap with his head and sometimes his legs supported by pillows. One of his arms is behind my back; I hold his free hand. In this position, it is considerably easier to maintain good eye contact with him while exploring difficult themes. He is much more attentive when my face is directly above his as I speak with emotion. He is inclined to feel more ready to address a trauma when I stroke his hair, pat his shoulder, squeeze his hand, or give him a quick hug. In this position, the child feels somewhat younger and more vulnerable and is more apt to reexperience the emotion associated with past or recent experiences. When I lead the conversation with an emotion similar to what he might have felt in the past, he is likely to have the same feeling state again. Thus, I might yell, "You must have really been mad when he pulled your hair and threw you down." If I think that the child felt more fear than anger, I will begin by bringing out the fear, giving ample empathy: "You were so young! How scary that must have been! How could a grown-up do that to you? You might have thought you were going to die!" The same approach is used to help the child express his sadness: "That must have been so hard for you. You were so alone. If only someone had held you then and told you that you were safe and loved."

If the child does not talk, I might talk for him; or I might tell him what to say and ask him to repeat it with the appropriate emotion. This might eventually lead to my quietly reflecting on how sad and lonely a young child must feel during and after such experiences of abuse. When loud, intense anger about an event is followed closely by such a quiet cue for sadness, often the child is allowing himself to be led into recognizing and acknowledging the painful reality of his inner life. This then becomes the ideal time for the parent to hold the child and relate with a great deal of tenderness to the child's pain. Such experiences facilitate attachment.

Commonly a treatment session will begin with my having most of the interactions with the child and the parents taking a quieter, secondary role. While I engage the child in emotional themes from the past, the parents offer support and understanding. They may sit closer and hold his hand. If we are exploring themes relating to their current lives together, I model ways for him to express his thoughts and feelings more directly to his parent. While I hold him, the child maintains eye contact with his parent and follows my cues. At some point, the parent is asked to hold the child. Nurturing eye contact, quiet talking, and strong hugs occur with the parent taking the initiative. When the child is not being receptive to the parent's attachment-facilitating behaviors, I may ask the parent to take another seat while I again become more actively involved with him. At other times, I may ask the parent to speak directly to the child about his resistance to the nurturance. I may suggest to the parent that she encourage the resistance and frame it as reflecting his just beginning to learn how to receive such warm feelings. What I want to have happen is for the child and parent to remain engaged regardless of whether the child accepts the nurturance or not. The child, then, does not thwart a basic emotional connection with his mother. He cannot make his mother stop nurturing him, whether it be directly or indirectly.

Frequently, when a child is being held as part of therapy, he is ambivalent about aspects of the intervention. He may scream that he does not like me and that he does not want to be held. This occurs most often when we are exploring a shame-related event involving his current behavior and relationships. His anger at processing this event is displaced onto my holding him. I provide him with the empathy both for being held and for exploring the event. I encourage him to fully express his emotions about each experience. If he refuses, I speak for him, validating his anger and leading him to explore his sadness, fears, and self-doubts as well. Some children try to hurt me at these times. They may try to hit, kick, or even bite me. I respond with: "You really are mad at me! You don't want to talk about this or have me hold you at all! I'm going to keep both you and me safe while you're mad. I won't let you hurt me, but it is sure OK for you to be mad about this."

Such a sequence is eventually resolved as the child's emotions are respected, the event has been explored without humiliation or rejection, and the work that the child has done is recognized with comments and affection. The child is still being held and he begins to relax again and engage me and his parents with some light conversation and humor. Such sequences occur a number of times during many sessions and the child is often held throughout the whole process. Ambivalence, with associated anger, is frequently an inherent component of the intervention. However, the context in which the child is held during this intense work strengthens his relationship with both his parents and the therapist. The overwhelming emotional experience is one of affection and support along with playfulness and a sense of pride in having done a hard job well.

The child is held by the therapist or parent in other ways also. He may sit in his parent's lap as she reads him a story. He may sit in his parent's lap with his back to her as they chat with the therapist. His parent may hold him in various ways as they sing or play hand or finger games. His parent may rock him or whisper in his ear as he "sleeps." Physical contact that involves pleasurable feeling states must have a central role in the treatment session if the child is to remain engaged in experiencing the unpleasant feeling states.

I have been asked if I would hold a child if the overwhelming emotional response to being held was hatred or terror. I have never experienced such responses in my work with poorly attached children. With the child whom I have held, there has always been a positive engagement with the child before, during, and following the experience, in spite of his ambivalence. If I did not experience such an engagement, I would not hold the child. If the parent reported that the child demonstrated strong fear about our sessions, I would immediately adopt a more traditional therapeutic stance. If the child was completely negative about his therapy, I would review what was happening and try to engage the child in a more traditional way. However, this has not been necessary for the children with whom I work. They show a willingness and ability to engage in this difficult work. They do so because of the great amount of support and affection and playfulness that they receive from their parents and me.

Some adolescents have refused to agree to be held and I have accepted their decision. If an adolescent does not want to be held, it is going to be very difficult to do so without restraining him with the help of other adults. I do not believe that such interventions would be therapeutic. In these cases, I have used other interventions, with varying degrees of success. In a few cases, the adolescent did eventually agree to be held, and greater progress was evident.

In holding a child during therapy, the therapist needs to continually recall the model of the mother holding her infant. This model serves to remind the therapist of the high degree of affection, interest, playfulness, and empathy that is necessary if the experience of being held is to be therapeutic. The therapist and parent need to be highly attuned to the child's experience of the moment-to-moment therapeutic engagement. As is the case for the infant, only in this way will the child benefit from being held, the benefit being developing an attachment with his parents.

ATTACHMENT SEQUENCES

As was indicated earlier, attachment is understood as a developmental sequence in which the successes of the early stages are important, if not crucial, for further development in later stages. The infant's first 10 months of attuned interaction lead to the practicing phase that is first characterized by vibrant exploration. When the mother places limits on the child, a psychological separation occurs and her child then experiences shame. This is followed by a reunion with the mother at a more mature level of engagement. The reunion integrates both the child's autonomy and attachment needs as well as the "good" and "bad" aspects of self and mother.

When the shame experience contains humiliation and rejection, the child becomes convinced that he is worthless. I recall a young boy who told his foster father that his birth mother did not keep him because he was trash. I brought up his comment while I held him during a session. I communicated interest in his thinking about his rejection by his mother and he immediately withdrew into shame. I then shouted, "You are not trash!" He responded with instant aggression toward me. Over and over I repeated, "You are not trash!" while his rage intensified. Gradually his rage subsided, he became very sad, and he allowed me to quietly show empathy for the pain of his self-contempt.

The basic model of attachment research, "The Strange Situation," (Crittenden and Ainsworth 1989) involves the sequence of the child initially being with the mother, then being separated, and finally being reunited. This sequence also is central in the psychotherapy whose function is to facilitate the child's attachment to his caregiver. He needs to repeatedly experience, at a deep emotional level, the aspects of engagement, separation, and reunion with the therapist and with his parent. This sequence enables the child to experience and integrate varied and complex emotions within the context of a relationship modeled on the mother–child relationship of the first 1½ to 2 years of life. The therapist is first affectively attuned to the child and, later, directs the child to experience past and present shame experiences, separating these experiences from the contempt and rejection of the past. The therapist continues to give empathy and reengages with the child. The child becomes aware that autonomy and attachment can be maintained and developed while integrating shame experiences. His worth remains positive and constant as does the nurturing and mutually meaningful relationship with the therapist and parent.

The therapist begins each session by communicating pleasure at seeing the child again. This message begins with the first eye contact in the waiting room. I greet the child, expect eye contact and a return greeting, and then communicate that I'll be looking forward to seeing him as soon as I speak with his parents for a while. If the child does not acknowledge me, I go to him, take his head in my hand if necessary, and again, with a smile, greet him and wait for a return greeting. From this first contact, the child must know that our mutual engagement is necessary if I am to be of any help to him in this work. I cannot let his ignoring me in the waiting room be overlooked. I may express empathy for his resistance: "Boy, you sure don't seem to be very excited to see me today! But I am glad to see you! Hi!" If he does not respond, I might say something like: "The silent treatment! Great! Well, if you choose not to say 'Hi,' then I need two quick hugs. Your choice!" Most often, the child will quickly yell, "Hi!" and I will insist on a smile along with it. If not, two quick hugs and I'm off to see his parents.

After I review notes of our interactions in the last session, receive an update on aspects of the child's functioning and experiences since then, and consult with his parents about possible interventions, I am ready to invite the child into my office. He knows where he is to sit on the couch. I sit near him and we begin to chat. I begin with small talk about recent events, giving him ample opportunity to speak with me about meaningful events of his life. I am interested in anything and everything, not just problems. If the child is fairly nonverbal, I ask his parents for details and maintain my focus on the child as if he were giving me information. I usually comment on his clothes, haircut, expressions, posture, general emotional tone, or anything else that might elicit further communication. I am communicating constantly an acceptance of whatever he might be feeling, thinking, or doing. Whatever aspect of self he chooses to show is fine with me. Opposition and withdrawal are as valid as friendly cooperation. I accept what he gives and then relate with him. I show empathy for the aspect of self that he reveals. I am interested in the thinking and feeling that may be reflected in his current words and behaviors, and I show enjoyment over our engagement. Usually, I move in a playful direction next, finding topics about the immediate past or present to laugh about. I might recall something that we enjoyed in a previous session and elicit the feeling state that was present then. The child will be given opportunities to tease me or his parent, just as I tease him or his parent and his parent teases me or the child. Laughter is a powerful means of feeling close to the person with whom you are sharing the laughter. The child who is smiling and laughing is becoming engaged in an intensely emotional way, often in spite of himself. Certainly, if he chooses to directly relate with me about a theme of sadness, anger, or fear, I would not negate the expression in order to find something to laugh about. Most poorly attached children are very unlikely to begin the interaction in such a direct and personal way. Laughter frequently gets the session and our engagement off the ground. At other times, we might begin by discussing something exciting that has happened or something about which the child is proud and happy. When this occurs, infrequent though it is in the early stages of therapy, I structure the engagement around this theme.

Usually I have established a relaxed and playful atmosphere during the first part of the therapy session. I sit very close to the child, probably with an arm around him or gently touching his hair or hand as we talk. I may have him lie across my lap with his head on a pillow. As I take the child onto my lap and establish some comfort and eye contact, there is commonly a brief intermission where the child might fuss, yell, challenge me, or laugh and try to distract me by teasing me about something. I show empathy for whatever feeling that he is showing, help him to intensify the feeling if that seems indicated, and establish an engagement that includes my holding him. In general, the child is engaged, fairly relaxed, and somewhat playful or only mildly annoyed with me within a few minutes. I then move into some difficult areas of discussion. I might alert the child to this by saying: "I need to talk with you now about something that is likely to be hard for you to discuss. We need to do it, though, so we can work out ways for you to handle it that are better for you and your mom. Are you ready? Take a deep breath. Let's begin." I then tell the child the event that I would like to discuss. At other times, there is no need to prepare the child in this way. Stressful conversations simply have their turn among various things that we discuss.

Commonly, as the stressful theme is introduced, the child immediately disengages! The eye contact is gone. The child's emotion is one of anger, anxiety, or sadness, or a combination of these. He pulls away from me and is now silent. So much for our mutual laughter and engagement! But I do not change my way of relating. I remain accepting, expressive, empathic, interested, and mildly playful. I might say:

I can see that you don't want to talk about this! It must be hard. You don't seem to like thinking about how you swore at your mom. Maybe you think that she hates you for it. Maybe you think I hate you. Maybe you think that you're no good because you swore at her. Yes, we really have work to do about this. It's hard for you to be close to me now or look at me. But it's important that we stay connected. I'm holding you so it will be easier for me to help. It will also help you to know that I like you even though you swore at your mother.

    I ask the child to give me the context and facts about what occurred. I focus on what he felt at the time, what he thought, and how he acted. I ask him what he thought his mother thought and felt before and after he swore at her. I am very interested in what he tells me without evaluating or criticizing what he says. Again and again, I show empathy for how hard the experience was for him. I summarize the feelings and thoughts that he reported as well as those that he felt that his mother had.

    If the child has not volunteered such information, I guess what he was thinking and feeling prior to and immediately after swearing at his mother. I imagine what he guessed about what his mother felt and thought. I assume my guesses are accurate and I communicate considerable interest and empathy about his inner life at the time that he swore. I maintain eye contact and say with feeling:

That must have been so hard when you thought that your mom wouldn't let you watch TV because she didn't care that the TV show was important to you. You thought: "Another mom doesn't care for me! Why bother? Well I don't care either! I'll show her. I'll hurt her too!" And then you swore at her. . . . Then you probably thought that she really didn't care. She might even hate you! You probably thought you'd give up then. She'll never care for you. Nobody will! You figured that you're not worth much to anyone . . . or to yourself. What a rough time that was for you! So hard. So hard . . .

    As I speak to the child, my voice first communicates his intensity, anger, and fear. Then, I speak more slowly and quietly to elicit some sad and lonely aspects of the experience. Initially, I place my face closer and hold him tighter. As I elicit sadness, I relax more, stroke his hair or arm, or maybe give him a quick hug. Most children follow my emotional and cognitive lead and reexperience the event differently. Their original shame and rage experience has been elicited but modified by other emotions within the context of an engagement. This time, the shame experience contained much less of the anticipated contempt and rejection and the child was able to reengage fairly quickly.

Since the child's birth parent was a central part of the original shame and rage experience, it is very beneficial to bring his current parents into this therapeutic activity so that he can experience shame over his action without the humiliation and rejection that he had experienced earlier. He is directed to maintain contact with his mother and to tell her about his thoughts and feelings before and after swearing at her. I have him tell her what he guessed about her thoughts and feelings toward him. I tell him to ask her what she actually thought and felt at the time. What does she think and feel now about his swearing at her, about their relationship, about his worth? When the child has been reengaged with me and his mother, he is much more receptive to what his mother has to say to him than he was when he was disengaged, defensive, and angry.

If the child does not speak to his mother, I speak for him. He sits on my lap facing his mother. I put my head directly behind his head and speak for him. His mother responds to my comments as if they were her child's. I then respond to his mother in ways that I would hope that the child will eventually be able to do. I might say:

> I am sorry for swearing at you, mom. It's so hard at times to think that you really do care and aren't being mean to me. It's hard to feel your love for me. Thanks for telling me again; someday it will sink in, and I might even start to like myself more.

Mom and I will interact with the degree of emotion that we would have if the child had said this himself. I then will hug the child for taking the chance to say this and mom will hug him, too.

There may be a series of sequences like this in most therapy sessions. We establish a mutually enjoyable engagement, focus on a stressful—and probably shameful—experience, and then reengage fairly quickly with empathy and support. Through such sequences, many children begin to process their shameful experiences without having to react with such rage and without having to disengage to such an extreme. They begin to rely more on the relationship, to trust its constancy, and use its curative qualities following shame and stress.

Frequently, the same experiences involve the parents who are present in the session. However, we also explore past shame experiences associated with the child's history of abuse and/or neglect. The child is aroused as we explore these traumas and self-negating experiences. In the context of our supportive and empathic engagement, the arousal is not too extreme. As the engagement continues, he learns to rely on it to aid him in calming down and experiencing himself without contempt. We help the child to surmise what he and his abusing and/or neglecting parent felt or thought at the time. We help him to express his thoughts with the level of intense emotion that he was likely to have felt at the time. We encourage and model such expressions. We affirm his experiences, his rage, terror, and despair. In reexperiencing these original abusive events, we are helping the child to reframe the events without the overwhelming emotion of the time and without the pervasive self-contempt. We are also using the experience of a positive engagement with the therapist and a deepening attachment with the parents as a secure base for this exploration. The child can return, again and again, to this experience in therapy and at home.

CONFRONTATIONS

There is a need to focus on the second aspect of the attachment sequence, since some may object to this manner of exploring with the child his poor behavioral choices. Such objections may stress the need to "confront" the child for his misbehaviors by adopting a stern, serious, mildly annoyed attitude to convey to him our belief that he needs to take this behavior seriously and to learn from us alternatives so that he does not repeat the behavior. If the child does not respond with appropriate earnestness, the adult, from this perspective, should become more annoyed since the child's behavior now reflects a lack of motivation to take the situation seriously. This viewpoint suggests that the more playful, relaxed, and casual approach that I propose would reinforce the child's misbehavior or treat it as if it were not important.

Yet, the lectures that commonly are considered to be "confrontational" too often only elicit dissociation, passive resentment, and a general lack of motivation to deal with the misbehaviors more appropriately. The child may say a few things to appease the adult but is probably thinking about the satisfaction that will come from the next misbehavior which will show the adult who is really in charge. When we "confront" the child in this manner, he is much less likely to work to accept and understand this aspect of himself so that it can be integrated into a more comprehensive positive self-identity. At the core of his being, he already has a profound contempt for himself. Such confrontations are often experienced as being a basic rejection of self, so the child responds with increased denial, more rigid fragmentation of self, and rage at the adult who threatened his defensive posture. Consequently, he is not ready to learn about this aspect of his "bad" self so that he can become truly autonomous. He is not likely to trust the therapist or the parent to assist him in exploring his "bad self" since he experiences the confrontation as critical and mildly rejecting. In this case, to say to the child that we are angry with the behavior but not with the child is not likely to have an affirming effect at the affective core of the self.

The therapist must assist the child in being able to integrate his poor behavioral choices by helping him to experience himself without the pervasive self-contempt that he is likely to habitually feel. As he feels acceptance from the therapist and parent, he begins to experience shame, although, initially, the experience may be too threatening to allow him to interact enough to discuss the incident very well. Gradually, with further empathy around other incidents, the shame will become manageable and the child will be receptive to integrating the experience into the self. He also will be able to reattach to his parent fairly easily, having the trust that he is still valued and cherished.

When I confront a child about his poor choice, I do so with any emotion as long as it is not annoyance. I might be surprised at the choice he made. I smile slightly and say with mild shock: "You what! How could this be! Were you having a bad hair day?" or "Is your mom exaggerating again? How can we help her not to say you did it five times when you certainly only did it four times?" I am showing the child that my attitude toward him has not changed. I enjoy interacting with him just as much when we explore a poor choice as when we talk about how much I wish he had saved me some of the pizza he had for lunch. His poor choice is explored because it probably led to a consequence that he does not want and because it may have stimulated some doubt about his relationship with his parent. It is also explored because the behavior probably reinforced his feeling of self-contempt. I might even say: "Are you more mad at yourself or at your mom over what you did?" or:

> You might think that we think you're a no good, rotten kid. You probably think that about yourself and presume that we must feel the same way. You have trouble imagining that your mom . . . still . . . cares . . . more for you . . . than you care for yourself and that what you did has . . . not . . . changed . . . her thoughts and feelings for you."

When I suggest to the child that his poor choices are not helping his situation and that he might consider changing them, I do so in a playful, dramatic way. I constantly check to see that the child has not "spaced out" but, rather, is fully engaged with what I'm saying. The following "lecture" is typical of what I commonly say:

> So you actually refused to do your chores again! My, you must hate your chores. Or is it that you hate your mom telling you what to do? I can see why. It would take you 10 minutes to rake the grass! How mean can she be? Does she think that she's the boss? Do you want to trade her in? Maybe you really didn't want to be able to watch the movie that you lost because you would not rake the grass. It would have been too much fun. (Here the child might seem distracted.) What! You're not listening to me? Here I am trying to help you find ways to let yourself have more fun and you're not listening! Maybe you do hate fun! Maybe you want to say to me: "Shut up, Dan, I don't want your help!" Well, you got my help, like it or not. I will teach you that it's OK to have fun. And it's going to start now! (Here I might quickly tickle the child.) Now you're ready for even more fun. (I might then rock and hug the child, as he laughs and screams.) Now maybe you'll let yourself have fun and rake the grass the next time you're asked. Or maybe you won't, in which case you're going to get even more fun practice the next time I see you.

After such an interaction, I might become more quiet and reflect with some sadness on how the child tries so hard to not let his mom get closer to him. Doing what she tells him would help him to trust her more and laugh with her more. I might drop the issue and move to another topic. Many of the parents who are present during such "lectures" have indicated that the child might not refer to the poor choice or my response for many days after a session, but then the child might spontaneously say something to suggest that he heard much of what was said to him and it had some meaning for him. For example, in response to the above example, the child might say a few days later after doing a chore, "I thought that Dan said that this would be fun. Wait till I tell him it's not." The child and parent then laughed about it. On one occasion a child did what he was told and then came to his mother and told her that he *did* feel closer to her. Another child started to defy his mother and then, instead of his usual tantrum, he stopped and said, "Don't tell Dan what I just said!" He then smiled and did what he was told. At times, the parent has reported that the child remembered what I had said word for word. Some children have even "taught" their parents about their differing motives for past and present behaviors by using exactly what I had taught them, with little conscious awareness that I had used the same words.

Such "lectures" seem to have a more positive impact on the child's subsequent behaviors than do traditional confrontations. I believe that this is because the words are embedded in enjoyable interactions that keep the child's attention, are nonthreatening, and allow him to frame his own behaviors differently. The child is also given little to oppose in the lecture so there is little reward in defying me. He can experience future behavioral choices with some of the detached, playful acceptance that I manifested. He need not be so self-critical. Any compulsion he feels to reenact a "bad" aspect of self is lessened. The child has a greater sense of autonomy in choosing alternatives. Positive choices leading to a more positive identity and a more secure attachment now are more accessible to him.

INFORMATION AND EDUCATION

Specific interventions facilitate the integration of the affective, physical, or behavioral components of the child's functioning. The use of information and education focuses on the child's cognitive life and aims to develop these skills. However, this intervention does not ignore the affective and behavioral aspects. Information is not given in a boring, dry manner with connotations of criticizing or belittling the child. The information is only offered after the child has first been engaged emotionally. He needs to see how the information may be of benefit to him. It is also given in a matter-of-fact manner, removing any stigma or negative implications from the discussion. It is helpful to preface the information with phrases such as:

Sometimes children who have been abused feel or think . . .
Some kids who are learning to trust their new mom need to . . .
When you hug this way, your mom is likely to feel good about it.
You might have some fears about it. If so, you could . . .
Because of your years of abuse, you probably haven't learned . . .
After you learn to ask with words, you'll probably get . . .

Let me describe one therapeutic intervention that shows dramatically the power of information given in the context of the treatment relationship.

I was asked to treat an 8-year-old boy who, among a number of significant psychological issues, had the problem of repeatedly touching his foster mother's breasts under a great variety of circumstances. In his previous therapy, positively reinforcing abstaining behavior had had no effect, nor had giving him "time out" for his behavior. After getting to know the child and foster mother in the first two sessions, I decided to begin treatment with some focus on this symptom since it was most damaging to the placement and since this child seemed to be giving expression to a strong desire for physical contact with his foster mother.

I indicated to the child that he seemed to want to touch his mom a lot but that the way he was touching her was not a way that she wanted to be touched. I suggested that since he had not been hugged very much in good ways when he was younger, but, instead, had been sexually abused by his birth mother a lot, he probably never had had the chance to learn how good parents hug and are hugged by their children. I offered to help him to learn. He quickly agreed that he would like to learn. I suggested that the best way to learn would be to practice good hugs. However, since he might have a hard time practicing with his mom, and since he needed some confidence that he would not touch her breasts before I could ask her to help him to practice, he first had to learn while practicing with me. I then gave him a great deal of empathy for being stuck with hugging me when I could tell that he certainly preferred hugging his mom. I suggested that he was a bright fellow and probably would learn the basic ways of hugging fairly fast. He agreed.

Andy was then shown how to stand, position his arms and hands, and squeeze as we hugged each other. Minor adjustments were suggested with enthusiasm and enjoyment and we repeated the procedure 3 times. I then had him ask me for a hug a number of times, with me responding positively. Finally, I suggested that he might be ready for one practice hug with his foster mom. He agreed, and they hugged with success. I gave him the homework of hugging his foster mom the way he was taught once each day until the next session, during which we would review his progress. Andy returned the next week with considerable satisfaction that he had had 7 appropriate hugs with his foster mom and no sexualized touches. We practiced hugs a bit more and then they decided that during the next week they would have 3 appropriate hugs each day. During the next 6 months Andy touched his mom inappropriately only twice. In the same period, his appropriate hugs had occurred spontaneously and often. Before the intervention, he had been touching her breasts at least 5 times each week. His behavior changed immediately with the education. Also, nurturance was being provided in a meaningful and mutually satisfying way, while in therapy we actively worked on issues of his sexual abuse. Andy demonstrated that he could engage in appropriate physical contact prior to the resolution of the issues of sexual abuse. In fact, I believe that if we had waited to teach hugging until after having first resolved the sexual abuse, we might still be waiting. Children are less likely to give up sexualized physical contact if they do not have satisfying appropriate physical contact.

I often give information to the child visually by drawing a picture for him of a reality with which he is struggling. I might draw a cartoon to depict a difficult situation in his life. The child in the cartoon is doing something (behavior) similar to what the child does. "Thought bubbles" are drawn coming out of his head which describe what he is thinking at the time. "Feeling arrows" are drawn coming out of his heart to describe what he is feeling at the time. In subsequent drawings, different thoughts and feelings result in different behaviors. The child is asked to participate in deciding what the cartoon character is thinking and feeling and what his future options are. This is done with much humor, suspense, and some excitement as we root for the cartoon character to improve his situation. The drawing goes home with the child to be shared and/or pinned on the wall.

Information may also be given by developing lists that are ideal for taking home as a homework assignment. Often I have asked a child to make a list of the things he could do that would show his mom that he loves her. We struggle together to make the list and then check with mom as to whether she would feel loved if he did what was on the list. The child is told to do each item on the list "no more than" twice, to make a note of what he did so that we can review it during the next session, and to have mom tell him if it had the desired result. Such an activity can be very therapeutic since these children do not often feel that they are capable of showing love and bringing pleasure to their mother's life.

Cognitive-behavioral therapy has developed many techniques which serve as means of providing information about changing various aspects of oneself. (See Finch and colleagues 1993, LeCroy 1994.) Some interventions emphasize a "broad spectrum" of techniques to address issues involving assertiveness, relaxation, self-regulation, and conflict resolution. They may each have an important role in the overall treatment when presented within the context of the emotionally engaging treatment relationship as well as the general goal of developing a meaningful attachment to the primary caregiver.

VERBAL DIRECTIVES

When a child is able to give expression to important thoughts and feelings about himself and others, the therapist attends to what is being said to facilitate its continued expression, while also being alert to the child's integration of what he is saying. However, as was discussed in Chapter Two, the great majority of children who are poorly attached to their parents are very reluctant and often unable to give expression to their inner lives. With these children, it is generally very beneficial to tell the child what to say to the therapist or the parent during therapy. Through repeating such a thought or feeling verbally, the child, at times, becomes aware of thoughts and feelings that were outside his awareness. The awareness then often elicits the feeling that he was told to express.

For example, if I notice that a child appears to be annoyed at something I say in treatment but will not express his anger, I may tell him to say, quite firmly: "I don't like what you said, Dan." This might be followed by, "I'm mad at you now, Dan." If I notice that the child is annoyed by this intervention, I might then instruct him to say: "I'm really mad at you now, Dan!" followed by: "I hate doing this!"

This process:

1) Helps the child to become more aware of his inner life;
2) Communicates that it is acceptable to express his inner life verbally;
3) Communicates that, if he feels anger or any other feeling during the session, I will understand and accept the feeling;
4) Helps him to be more emotionally engaged during the session;
5) Reduces resistance that may be forming during difficult moments during the session;
6) Increases the child's receptivity to the therapist's initiatives, empathy, interpretations, and directives during the session;
7) Facilitates the expression of more intense emotions which may lead to a more genuine and therapeutic level of emotional expression; and

8) Changes the context in which the child is expressing himself. He is relying on the therapist's direction. This is necessary if he is to move into new areas of psychological experience and ways of relating.

Frequently, the purpose of a verbal directive is to modify or intensify an emotional expression. This is necessary because the child's emotional expression is rigid, restricted, and repetitive. He needs to become more aware of what feelings he does have and then integrate them into the overall meaning of the situation and relationship. For example, after telling a child to say that he's mad at me, I might say, "Say it again!" "Louder!" "Again!" "Look in my eyes and say it like you mean it!" This commonly leads to a level of emotional honesty and intensity that the child seldom shows, while still remaining emotionally engaged in the relationship. Also, the child has unwittingly allowed me to assume the direction of the interaction.

After the child has repeated what I told him to say, it becomes obvious to him that I have not abused him. He is accepted and encouraged, and his hard work is recognized. It is a confusing experience for a poorly attached child with a history of abuse to express his rage so openly at someone with whom he has a relationship and to discover that the relationship has become stronger! On countless occasions, such an intense expression of anger toward me in therapy has led to tears and then to his willingness for me to comfort him while softly giving empathy for how hard he was working. On many other occasions the child is told what to say to his parent, does so, and then participates in a conversation with his parent about something that is truly meaningful to him.

Verbal directives about the child's past may also be very helpful. I may briefly discuss with a child a past experience of abuse and then have the child visualize the abusive individual in the room. I might then say: "Tell him he had no right to punch you!" "You're mad at him for what he did." "He hurt you very much!" "You did not deserve to be treated that way!" If the child struggles with such a sequence, I might say it for him with great affect. I then ask his parent to make similar comments to the abusive individual. The parent's emotion while confronting the image of the abusing individual often has a powerful effect on the child. The parent's anger and/or tears vividly demonstrate her depth of feeling for her child and the person who hurt him. The child may then be asked again to confront the individual. Most children who initially had difficulty confronting the image are soon able to do so.

Directives toward the parent present in the session may be quite beneficial. I have the child maintain eye contact with his parent while telling her of his thoughts and feelings about something in their relationship. Generally, children who are quite capable of intense verbal and nonverbal expressions of rage at home have difficulty in the therapeutic process accepting responsibility for and expressing these feelings while maintaining eye contact and an emotional engagement with the parent. Through this process, the child is more likely to integrate his thoughts and feelings with his overall experience of the parent–child relationship. He is less likely to split the parent and himself into good and bad parts. Consequently, there is a reduced need to express rage at home.

I may direct the child to speak to his parent about how he confuses his new parent with his prior, abusing or neglecting parent. I might say to him with intensity: "You must still get confused and think that Judy (new parent) is Penny (old parent). But Judy is not Penny! Tell your mom that you're sorry that you sometimes get her mixed up with Penny. Tell her that you're glad that you can begin to trust her not to hit you. Ask her for help in realizing that she is not Penny." Such directed interaction leads to considerable emotion on the part of both the parent and child.

One 9-year-old boy showed in his constant defiant and challenging behaviors toward his adopted mother that he had little trust of her love for him. I directed him to tell her that he did not trust her. He initially refused and denied his mistrust. I firmly told him to say: "Mom, I have a hard time trusting that you really care for me." He repeated that directive to her without affect and I directed him to say it again. This time there was more affect and he began to cry when he added on his own: "And I never feel that you love me like dad does." I asked his adoptive mother to respond to this statement. She began to cry as well when she told him of her deep sadness over trying to communicate her love for him over the years and how she often felt that he did not want it. As they both cried (and this was a rare event for him) I quietly told him to ask his mom for a hug. He did and she held him. He then cried with the intensity that one might expect from a 9-year-old boy who had felt extremely alone for most of his life.

A directive may begin with an emotion such as anger and lead to a series of thoughts and feelings that need to be understood and experienced as being connected to and, possibly, more basic than the anger. For example, I might direct the child to say:

I got mad when you wouldn't take me to the store with you. I thought you didn't want me around. I thought that you're getting tired of me. I feel sad when I think that you don't love me very much anymore. I think that you might want to get rid of me. I get scared when I think that you might not want me. I get really scared.

In suggesting thoughts for the child to consider as relevant for himself, the therapist is leading him toward other emotions that his anger may often conceal. He may be more likely to experience similar situations in the future in ways that are less repetitive reenactments of past abuse and more appropriate to his current relationships. When the therapist gives these words, she presents them with the appropriate emotional tone. Thus, the sequence might begin with the therapist yelling and end with her barely whispering. Emotions are contagious, and when the therapist emotionally enacts what the child may be experiencing, the child is more likely to feel the same emotions. They also may be intensified by having the child hold the parent's hands while having eye contact, with the therapist speaking from a position directly behind the child.

The therapist needs to be sensitive to the reality of mixed feelings and ambivalence while facilitating such verbal expressions. This is true not only with the child's relationship with his current parent but also with his past relationship with his abusive or neglectful parent. The child who has been abandoned may well experience both rage and intense sorrow when thinking of the parent who did this. He may recall both the anger and the pain associated with certain experiences. Again, to facilitate the child's ability to integrate all aspects of his past and present psychological life, he needs to become aware of each and every significant feeling about his important relationships. In a given session, the therapist may choose to elicit one aspect of the child's experience of a relationship, but she must not lose sight of conflicting and complementary experiences, too. She needs to facilitate their expression also—if not during the session, then certainly at a later date.

What if the therapist guesses wrong in giving a verbal directive for the child to say about his inner life? This is not likely if the therapist restricts his comment to what she clearly observes in the child's nonverbal communication or to what the therapist knows to be true generally about children's thoughts and feelings as they relate to significant events and relationships. The therapist might also qualify what the child is to say, by saying: "*Sometimes* I feel mad at you when . . ."

If the therapist is wrong or if the child is not ready to face a well-defended thought or feeling, the interaction may not be therapeutic but does not appear to be detrimental to therapy or harmful to the child. Often

I have said to the child: "I'll be guessing what you think or feel. If I'm wrong, say it anyway. If you want to tell me what you really thought or felt, you can do so later and I'll be glad to understand."

At times, the child will resist repeating what he is told to say. That resistance is simply utilized by the therapist without annoyance. The therapist might say: "You don't want to do what I tell you. No problem. Say, 'I don't want to say what you want me to say.'" If this gets no response, the therapist could say, "No problem, I'll talk for you." The therapist, then, speaks for the child with much emotional intensity. This might be followed by whispering in the child's ear how that experience helped the therapist to understand what the child felt in an even better way than if the child had said it himself. The therapist might then suggest she will speak for the child regarding the next few situations, too, so the child should remain quiet.

The resistance might also decrease if the parent responds to the therapist who is speaking for the child as if the child spoke for himself. Sometimes I position myself between the child and parent so that the parent can see neither my face nor the child's face. I then try to imitate the child's voice, "tricking" the parent into thinking that the child has spoken. When the parent continues the conversation with the "child," the child himself will often try to interrupt and deny responsibility for what he supposedly said. The parent will, of course, say that she heard the child speak, and that she is glad that the child chose to say such important thoughts and/or feelings. Such a sequence usually leads to laughter among us all, followed by a brief, quiet discussion about the theme of the "trickery."

PSYCHODRAMA

Psychodrama is a most effective way to deeply engage the child in the process of therapy. It helps the child to reexperience his relationships with the parents who abused or neglected him as well as with his current parents. Children enter this drama with a great deal of intensity when it involves significant people and events in their lives and when the adults present become fully involved in it as well. Again, the adults' emotion is contagious and the child often begins to experience these past and present relationships and situations with a new range of emotion.

Generally, psychodrama focuses on the abusive and/or neglectful parent from the past. The child is encouraged and often directed to convey to that parent his memories about what did or did not happen, his complex thoughts and feelings about what happened, and the effects of those experiences on the child's current life and relationships. When the intervention is developed primarily for the child's expression, he may be told to imagine that the parent is sitting in a chair in the office or the therapist and/or child may draw a picture of the parent, with the child looking at the picture while speaking. Using an actual picture of the parent is often quite effective. Often, however, psychodrama is used to stimulate interaction between the child and the past caregiver. In those cases, it is usually best for an adult to play the part of the abusive/neglectful person from the past.

The therapist may quite adequately fill the role of the absent parent. When this is to be done, the child is made fully aware of the "make-believe" nature of the interaction. He is informed that what the therapist says is meant to reflect what the abusive/neglectful caregiver may have thought and felt and does not represent what the therapist thinks and feels about the child. To help with this differentiation, I first leave the office before coming back in the new role and habitually sit in a different chair when taking the part of the past caregiver. I change my voice tone and posture and may put on an article of clothing to further differentiate myself from myself-as-therapist. At the conclusion of the drama, I again leave the office and come back as myself. Then, I review with the child and his current parent what had occurred as if I had not been present. I might add that I "saw" the abusive individual outside the office as they were leaving and told them not to return.

The parent with whom the child now needs to develop an attachment is not asked to take the part of the past caregiver. Since much of treatment is aimed at helping the child to differentiate the current from the past caregiver, such a role might be counterproductive to this goal. Equally of importance is the parents' role during the psychodrama. The parent is asked to sit with the child and support his efforts to speak. The parent may whisper things that the child might say to the past parent when the child is at a loss as to what to say or when he responds in a way that does not affirm his basic experience of having been abused and neglected. Then, when the "abusive caregiver" leaves the office, the new parent continues to sit with the child in a nurturing and supportive way while praising his work.

At times, I have used a female assistant to play a maternal caregiver from the past. At those times I have either observed or adopted a parental role.

A common psychodrama sequence is for the past abusive/neglectful caregiver to deny responsibility for the maltreatment of the child and even to blame the child for what occurred. The caregiver makes excuses and possibly suggests that if the child had been "good," there would have been no problem. The child is encouraged to take a firm stand that the abuse was not appropriate, that it was the caregiver's problem and not the child's problem that caused the abuse. The child might add that he is quite angry about what had happened as well as telling about the negative effects it has had on his current relationship.

The "abusive individual" might then attempt to get the new parent to agree that this is a bad child. The new parent strongly supports the child's position that it was not his fault. The "abuser" then verbally attacks the new parent as lying and also as spoiling the child. The "abuser" tells the child that the new parent cannot be trusted. Commonly, the child then defends the new parent with considerable emotion. He makes statements such as "She's a better parent than you ever were," or "I do trust her. She'll never abuse me the way you did!" In fact, some children have a much easier time asserting themselves in defense of their new parent than in defense of themselves. When this becomes apparent, the "abuser" initially focuses more on the new parent than on the child. A dramatic and therapeutic way to end such a sequence is for the "abuser" to take the child's arm and say: "You're coming back with me; I'll teach you who's right!" The child most certainly then pulls back and the new parent holds the child tightly and both the child and new parent order the "abuser" to leave. This is followed by the new parent hugging the child and celebrating their alliance.

Since the child usually has ambivalent feelings about the primary caregiver from the past, further psychodrama sessions are often indicated that will better facilitate the child's expression of affection for the past caregiver and/or profound sadness of the loss of that early relationship. Such sequences are often structured with the child being told that we will imagine the past parent has come to accept responsibility for the abuse/neglect and wants to help the child to get on with his new life with his new parent. The child is clearly told that we are imagining that the parent now feels this way without any evidence that it is so. (Unless, of course, we do know that the past parent has this attitude about the past.) In this session, the "abuser" recalls for the child what had occurred, accepts full responsibility for it, acknowledges the terrible effects it had on the child, and apologizes. The "abuser" then indicates that he/she still is not able to adequately care for a child and may never be able to do so. The "abuser" then asks the new parent how the child is doing, and after briefly "getting to know" the new parent, tells the child how glad he/she is that the child has this parent. The "abuser" gives a "blessing" to the developing attachment between the child and the new caregiver. When appropriate, the child is encouraged to express his sense of loss that the old relationship with the "past parent" is over and had not been healthy. When appropriate, the child is encouraged to forgive the "past caregiver." Here, the therapist must not force a "happy ending" when that reality does not exist psychologically for the child. There are often tears at the conclusion of this sequence; it becomes an ideal time for the new parent to nurture the child as he experiences more fully the profound loss of his first significant attachment.

Other psychodrama sequences may be developed depending on the unique history and needs of the child. The purpose of the drama is to help the child to work through the experiences of abuse and/or neglect and loss while affirming the child's worth, differentiating the past parent from the present one, and making the child receptive to the support and nurturance of the new parent. These sequences are also emotionally quite intense and help the child to remain emotionally engaged in the treatment. Months later, I have heard children tell me word-for-word what was said during a psychodrama. The drama itself also facilitates the integration of the affective, cognitive, and behavioral aspects of the past trauma and relationships as well as the current developing attachment. Such integration is crucial if insight and behavioral change are to be lasting.

PARADOXICAL INTERVENTIONS

For children who attempt to reduce both the negative affect that might emerge from within as well as the uncertainties of the external world, maintaining control is often the most important goal in their lives. They cannot relax and accept the adult's directives since that could lead to a flood of inner turmoil or imagined experiences of abuse from the world. Thus, the child resists directives for no other motive than to maintain control of the interaction. With these children, our engaging in repetitive power struggles is of little therapeutic value. In such struggles, no one wins and the child loses his opportunity to take advantage of the adult's actions which might have led to increased attachment and psychological growth. In these situations, which are permeated with substantial emotional stress, paradoxical interventions can be very therapeutic.

Since much of the therapy to facilitate attachment is quite directive, the child has many opportunities to resist in order to maintain control of the interaction. When the child does resist and is encouraged to be more resistant, he must either stop resisting or else give control of the resistant behavior to the therapist. If he ceases resisting, the therapist has not "won." She simply and respectfully accepts the child's decision to follow the initial directive and so continues with the intervention. When the child continues to resist, the therapist simply and respectfully accepts his decision to follow the secondary directive to resist and proceeds with the new intervention. Either way, the control of the momentum of the interaction resides with the therapist and the child has, in effect, given up control of the interaction to the therapist *and has not been abused.* This may well be anxiety provoking. The therapist gives the child a great deal of empathy and acceptance so that he can begin to more fully experience the process of giving up control to the therapist and parent. This is framed as being an acceptable level of anxiety for the purpose of psychological development and attachment.

For example, when the child refuses to tell his mother that he is angry with her for not letting him ride his bike, I might encourage him to remain silent so that I can speak for him in a way that conveys what I want better than the way he might say it. A crafty child might then talk loudly while still not saying what I want. I encourage him to talk even louder and I model how he might do it. This might lead him to begin to hum, so I begin to hum with him and hold him closely as if we are dancing while we hum together. Finally, the child might yell at me "Stop it." This leads me to tell him to say it again and tell me how mad he is at me for doing this. During this whole process, my intensity and emotional engagement is congruent with his. The child often imitates me in my emotional expression, tone, posture, or statements, even if he is not complying with what I want on the surface level. I then verbally or nonverbally briefly note with enjoyment his compliance on the deeper level. The child has remained engaged with me even though his initial refusal was an effort to break the engagement. He is also aware that I know he has remained engaged and that I am pleased at his "choice" to remain so engaged. After a few such interactions as this, the child usually follows my directives more easily since the success of his resistance has been minimized. In essence, the child may choose the particular content of our engagement, but he will remain engaged. This is the core of what I wanted—and what he did not want—in the first place. However, I do not suggest that I won anything. The child simply needs to remain engaged with me if he is to benefit from treatment. I work to ensure that he gets what he needs.

Let me describe another child's resistance. With me, as with many others, this girl was quite negative, grumpy, and habitually moaning about something. I quickly noted this trait with pleasure and called her "Miss Sunshine." During each session, I would search for something new that she was grumpy about or a new way she was showing her displeasure. When she began to enjoy her grumpiness with me, it became hard for her to maintain her negativity while we were both taking pleasure in it. The highlight of our reciprocal enjoyment came on a morning when she brought a piece of hard candy as a gift for me. Clearly something was up; it was a wonderful therapeutic opportunity. I quickly put the candy in my mouth, only to discover that it was the most sour object that was ever invented. I groaned, screamed, and ran out of the office to the bathroom, where I proceeded to make awful sounds at the sink, all the while listening with delight to the howling coming from my office. I then faked outrage over her treachery, ran back into my office, grabbed her, and yelled how awful she was, while she roared with laughter in my arms. This is a child who seldom had showed joy and happiness and even less often laughed. Her sour manner had been her way of holding others away from her. I had utilized it to be close to her. She and I began to tease each other quite openly after this incident. Miss Sunshine became known as having a good sense of humor and her foster mother reported how much others enjoyed her newfound ability to laugh.

In treatment, the child should have to really struggle to find ways to resist the therapeutic engagement and progress. Anger is not a good resistance since it is very clear how much I accept him expressing his anger, especially at me. Silence tends to be ineffective, since I then use his silence to devise interactions that elicit even greater emotional involvement than the initial directive would have elicited. Silence elicits the child's passivity, which is an open invitation for me to create imaginative, memorable engagements. The child might choose to distract me by changing the subject. I might "catch" the child in his effort to disengage and then "punish" him by a tickle or hug. Or I might follow his distraction and develop it therapeutically until the child wishes that he had not brought it up in the first place. When he successfully distracts me, I might give him a reward for his quick thinking.

Whatever he does, I must, and I will, remain engaged with him and the process will be therapeutic. Such engagements, no matter how brief, are the building blocks for the active process of forming an attachment. Affective attunement is the model that I continually bring to mind. The parent is brought into the engagement and often will learn how to maintain a similar interactive style at home. This, of course, is a primary therapeutic goal. Paradoxical interventions are ideally suited to keep the engagement alive during the emotionally difficult and painful process of both therapy and becoming attached.

ILLUSTRATED STORIES

Children find stories and drawings to be very effective means of both communicating their own inner life and understanding information that the therapist wishes to convey. Stories and drawings go beyond verbal communication to give him a fuller understanding of the concept that the therapist wants him to grasp. They also hold the child's interest at times when the spoken word is becoming boring. I often rely on stories and/or drawings to make a point, to hold the child's interest, and to engage the child with a medium that holds some intrinsic interest. Frequently as I draw, I will elicit comments about the drawing from the child and encourage him to elaborate on my basic drawing. We both may laugh about the quality of my drawing, while I present content in the drawing that might be threatening to his self-concept. Drawings also are useful in that the child can take them home, put them on the refrigerator or the bedroom wall, or use them to explain to another family member or case worker what he has learned in therapy.

One illustrated story that I use with many poorly attached children who have experienced abuse and/or neglect is the *Wall-around-the-heart,* a drawing that I learned from Foster Cline. In this drawing, I begin by drawing a picture of a baby. I give it the child's name and write "one-day-old" under it. After a brief discussion of the child's birth, I draw a heart in the baby picture and ask him what the heart is for. Most kids will say that the heart is necessary to keep you alive. I agree and ask how it works. I then tell him that it keeps the blood in the body moving but that it also is for loving and receiving love. I suggest that at birth his heart worked quite well and he was quite good at giving and receiving love. Next, I draw a larger child, again with his name, and label it with the age at which I know he had begun to experience abuse or neglect. I speak briefly about the pain of being treated that way and indicate that such pain hurts the heart. I then draw cracks in the heart.

Drawing a third picture of the child, again older, I indicate that the pain in the heart is so great that the child worked out a very bright way of saving the heart from further pain. I draw a wall around the heart. I direct arrows of pain at the heart but they bounce off the wall and cannot cause any more cracks. I praise him for saving his heart from breaking further by creating that strong wall. I then draw another picture of him and date it at a time when he was living in his current foster/adoptive home. I again add the heart. By now the cracks have healed and are very small. The wall is still around the heart. I indicate that he no longer needs the wall, and in fact, the wall prevents love from reaching his heart.

His new parents, who do not abuse him, show love often to the child but he cannot experience the love because of the wall. As a result, he often doubts that his new parents do love him. The best answer to this problem is to find a way to take down the wall. I might elaborate further to suggest that the wall has changed from being the wall of a fort to keep pain out and has turned into a prison wall that keeps him from love. I then suggest that his new parents and I are willing to help him to learn how to take down the walls if he wants such help.

This image of a wall around the heart has proven to be very vivid for many children. They listen very attentively, at times with tears, as they feel that it fits their experience quite closely. Children have taken this drawing home with a great deal of interest, described it to others as being very real to them, and spoken often about how they are working to take down the wall around their heart. They have begun sessions with pride, telling me that they have taken down two bricks, or three boards, or half of one side of the wall. They have recalled with joy how they were beginning to feel some of the love that their new parents were showing, love that previously had bounced off the wall.

Another drawing, again which Foster Cline demonstrated, involves drawing a picture of a child with a large hole in his body. The drawing represents the child; the hole represents the empty feeling inside that he often feels. Since that feeling is so unpleasant, the child tries to fill up the hole and so feel complete. Foster Cline used this for a child who was a compulsive eater. He was trying to fill the hole with food to feel complete and happy. However, food never works. The only things that can fill the hole are signs of love from the parents such as hugs and smiles. I also have used the image of the hole for other symptoms with some success. The child is said to steal or break things and fill up the hole with those objects. Also his lies are an effort to cover over the hole so that it cannot be seen. But of course, it still causes that empty feeling. The only way to fill it is through attachment to his new parents. We then can refer back to this image and review progress by asking how far up the hole has been filled with love.

Cartoons that involve actions, words, feelings, and thoughts also are quite good at conveying important concepts to the child. I use cartoons for both contrasting the past experiences with the present and for understanding his response to the present and developing alternate ways to think, feel, talk, and act. The words are drawn in a circle coming from the figure's mouth; the feelings are in a similar circle with a line connecting it to the heart; and the thoughts are in a circle connected by small circles to the head.

For example, I might draw a picture of the child being abused, with the adult saying something verbally abusive in combination with neglect or physical/sexual abuse. The child's behavioral response is minimal and he is saying something to appease the parent. He is feeling a combination of rage, fear, and/or despair, and he is thinking that he is bad and/or the abuser is mean, or hates him, and so forth. Thus, his thoughts and feelings are likely to be at odds with his speech and action. He has learned to conceal his inner life and to deceive others. I then draw a picture of the new parent disciplining the child for some misbehavior. The action of the parent is appropriate, as is her verbal statement. The child's response, however, is similar to what it was when he was being abused. The child is given a great deal of empathy for why his response is the same. At the same time, it is suggested that he might handle the discipline much better and feel much happier if he would choose to respond differently in his speech and action. His thoughts and feelings are explored, and alternative ways to think and feel about the situation are considered.

In another cartoon I draw a child's destructive behavior and relate it to his rage at being denied something that he wanted by the parent. His thoughts reflect his rage and his thinking that the parent is mean to him or that the parent does not like him. The child "doesn't care," but he still wants to pay his parent back. I question those thoughts, erase them, and write in alternative thoughts, for example, "Mom wants me to take better care of my toys." Using these new thoughts, we explore related, alternative feelings, for example, sad but resigned, and then change what the child might say or do. When these drawings appear to be having an impact on the child, I ask him and his parents to make similar drawings at home following some situation that was difficult for the child. He then brings the drawings to the next session and shows me how he originally responded to an event and how he reframed the event through the second cartoon.

Another picture that is useful involves drawing the child as a circle that is divided into parts. At times, I draw the child as two parts, which he experiences as the "good" and "bad" parts of himself. We fill in the circle with various behaviors, thoughts, and feelings that he considers to be part of his identity. Many children have many more qualities in the "bad" part than they do in the "good" part. We then reframe these qualities, one at a time, possibly over a number of sessions, until he can come to see them as reflective of past experiences, judgments, choices, and so forth which are not proof that he is "bad." When we review progress, we note that some qualities no longer are evident and that others simply are present, but are not "bad." The goal of the intervention is to help the child integrate the "good" and "bad" parts into one self.

One 8-year-old boy was convinced that his stealing was so bad that there would always be a "bad" part of his self that he would always hate. We framed it in various ways over four sessions. First, his stealing represented his effort to fill up the "hole" in him. Then it was seen as resulting from his thoughts that his mother disliked him as well as from his anger and desire to hurt her back. Then it was seen as resulting from his fear of his mother's love and his hope that she would stop loving him if he stole enough. I was not committed to any interpretation; I wanted the child to be aware of different possibilities, any of which might disrupt his sense of being "bad." This boy was convinced, however, that he was not afraid of his mother's love. I expressed some surprise at this since he was not used to getting much love in his life. I suggested that at home his mother could help him to accept her love by giving him some hugs while she read him a story. She then was to leave a pen on the kitchen table for him to steal. He was to bring it to the next session and sneak it to me without his mother seeing it. The mother and the child both cooperated and we did this for two more sessions. I subsequently asked the boy where he would put stealing in the circle of himself. He replied that he was not sure because, other than the three pens, he had not stolen anything for a while. Mom agreed but added that there was another quality of himself that he had not listed earlier. She was referring to his enjoyment of hugs. We all agreed that this quality might best find a place in the "good" part of himself. As the "bad" part began to empty out and the child seemed to have greater self-acceptance generally, his mother and I began to have more confidence in his future. Later, I offered to return the pens. Both the child and his mother told me to keep them.

Sometimes I divide the circle of the child into various emotions. The emotions that he expresses the most take up larger pieces of the circle. We use this as a guide for which pieces he wants to enlarge and which he hopes to reduce. I might have the child review the circle three times a day and check what feeling he is experiencing then. This sometimes results in the child realizing that he is happier or having fun more often than he might recall. At a minimum, this helps him to have some sense of how frequently he feels a given emotion. We then can contract to work on that emotion with various other techniques.

Another story, best illustrated with role playing rather than drawings, involves developing a fantasy in therapy about another child who has a strong attachment to his mother. The child plays the part of that other child, presenting thoughts, feelings, and behaviors different from his usual manner of relating to his mother. In this story, the mother holds the child and talks to him about times they had together involving mutual enjoyment, learning, affection, and so forth. The mother also comments on her current feelings about the child. Later, the child is asked what he thought and felt while pretending he was the other child who had successfully attached to his mother.

In another fantasy, the mother and child keep their own identities but play a role about a time in the future together. The fantasy may involve going on a vacation together, the child graduating from high school, the child getting married, the child becoming a parent, or the parent being on her death bed. As in the prior fantasy, the child often is able to explore ways of thinking, feeling, and relating to his mother in this "pretend" context that are not accessible to him in the here-and-now.

ADDITIONAL PROPS

The therapist is always searching for ways to place added emphasis on an emerging attachment. External ways of both facilitating an attachment and demonstrating it are helpful supports for the therapeutic work. The following have been beneficial for many of the children with whom I have worked. Other therapists may well make use of other "props." It is crucial that these aids do not become sterile by being used in stereotyped ways as fillers for boring moments in therapy. If they are to be beneficial, they must emerge naturally from within the context of a deeply engaging therapeutic relationship. They must have meaning to the child and parent and capture the essence of the therapeutic movement.

Children's Books

There are many excellent children's books that focus on the parent–child relationship. Frequently, I will ask the parent to read a book to the child as they snuggle closely on the couch. The parent and child might each read their own parts. They might discuss it afterwards or take the book home. At times, the parent is asked to read a different children's book on a particular theme such as fears, insomnia, anger, or death. Some of the books that I have found to be helpful for some poorly attached children include the following:

Even if I Did Something Awful, Barbara Shook Hazen, Aladin Books, 1981;
Mama, Do You Love Me?, Barbara M. Joose, Chronicle Books, 1991;
The Way Mothers Are, Miriam Schlein, Albert Whitman & Co. 1963;
The Runaway Bunny, Margaret Wise Brown, Harper Trophy, 1942;
Jafta's Mother, Hugh Lewin, Carolrhoda Books, 1981;
On Mother's Lap, Ann Herbert Scott, Clarion Books, 1972;
Love You Forever, Robert Munsch, Firefly Books, 1986;
Through Moon & Stars & Night Sky, Ann Turner, Harper Trophy, 1990;
So Much, Trish Cooke, Candlewick Press, 1994;
Mama, If You Had a Wish, Jeanne Modesitt, Green Tiger Press, 1993;
What Do Bunnies Do All Day?, Judy Mastrangelo, Ideals Children's Books, 1988;
Grandfather's Lovesong, Reeve Lindbergh, Puffin Books, 1993;
The First Song Ever Sung, Laura Krauss Melmed, Puffin Books, 1993;
I Love You As Much . . . , Laura Krauss Melmed, Lothrop, Lee, & Shepard Books, 1993;
You're My Nikki, Phyllis Rose Eisenberg, Puffin Pied Piper Books, 1992;
Jonathan And His Mommy, Irene Smalls, Little, Brown, & Co. 1992; and
Guess How Much I Love You, Sam McBratney, Candlewick Press, 1994.

Photographs

The treatment sessions often involve very intense moments with the child and parent laughing, crying, yelling, hugging, role-playing, or simply having mutual fun. I sometimes highlight such moments with my Polaroid. The parent and child might be hugging or smiling at each other. Both parents might be holding the child, who is laughing and struggling to get loose. The parent and child might be sitting together, holding a sign saying, "We survived therapy!" or "Yes, mom! No, Dan!" or something they both design. As the film develops, parent and child usually giggle and tease each other. The child, then, has something to take home to show to the rest of the family and keep in his bedroom.

Pictures are also useful for visually capturing an interactive pattern.

One 6-year-old boy had difficulty allowing himself to become emotionally close to his mother. We had difficulty exploring the problem with him. I took a picture of him pushing his mother away and another of her hugging him as he held her. He became deeply engrossed in the two pictures and in subsequent weeks took pride in identifying whether he was "pushing away" or "getting close" to his adoptive mother.

Stuffed Animals

Sometimes I use stuffed animals or puppets in the traditional manner to assist the child in giving expression to a trauma or other relevant theme. At other times, I use a stuffed animal to represent his early years. The animal is given the child's name, "Little John" or "Little Sue." I ask the child to talk to this part of himself while holding the stuffed animal. He is asked to nurture, teach, play with, and essentially provide it with those experiences that he had wanted and needed as a young child but had failed to receive. The child can vividly see that the young self was not bad, not deserving of abuse and neglect. He comes to want that part of self to be safe, understood, and cherished. He is told to ask his parent to hold "Little John" and nurture him the way he had wanted to be nurtured when he was much younger. The parent and child may both interact with this symbol of the young child, sharing their care and concern.

The child knows that sometimes he rejects the young and vulnerable part of himself. At those times, he cannot adequately protect "Little John." The parent and I will not let "Little John" be hurt again. Therefore, until John is able to consistently keep "Little John" safe, the stuffed animal will remain in my office, or possibly in his mother's care, with John caring for him only under supervision. This symbol has been very powerful for some children. One boy who was very reluctant to acknowledge and express his strong wish for nurturance was able to provide very adequate "mothering" to the stuffed animal. Gradually, he began to accept that this part of himself still needed such nurturance from his mother.

Music

From time to time I have employed music to foster a mood of closeness between the parent and child. Different lullabies and songs of love between parent and child serve as background when I ask the mother and child to hug after a difficult session. The most difficult hugs for the poorly attached child involve having them maintain eye contact and refrain from talking for an extended time. The mother might gently stroke the child's face, arms, or hair while smiling into his eyes. The music enables mother and child to maintain this intense degree of engagement without breaking it with lighter talk and laughter. At other times, the lighter ways of relating and relaxing together are fine.

I also frequently use music that was part of my own affective attunement experiences as well as those of my children and millions of other children. Parents and I have often sung such songs, including the following:

Row Your Boat	Rock-a-bye, Baby
Kum-Bah-Yah	All Through the Night
Twinkle, Twinkle Little Star	Pease Porridge Hot
	If You're Happy and You Know It
Hickory, Dickory, Dock	
Sleep, Baby, Sleep	Pop Goes the Weasel
Eentsy Weentsy Spider	Pat-A-Cake
Are You Sleeping?	Jack & Jill
Mary Had a Little Lamb	I'm a Little Tea Pot
Old Macdonald Had a Farm	Tora, Lora, Lora

In selecting a song, I have not yet needed to be concerned about the age of the child to whom I was singing. With no evidence of being self-conscious, many 12-year-old children have enjoyed experiencing these songs. I sing while holding the child and I involve him in the song through touch or by assigning him key words and phrases. The song is selected to match his mood or to facilitate a mood.

Miscellaneous

Various other specific interventions may be useful at times. Those presented by Beverly James (1989), Michael Durrant (1993), and Ann Jernberg (1979) can be quite therapeutic. Now and then, especially when I am working with younger children, I review Thoman and Browder's *Born Dancing* (1987) and Lansky's *Games Babies Play* (1993) for ideas. I have noticed that at times when I am deeply engaged with a child, I have spontaneously said or done something that I had done with my own children over the past 22 years.

7

MATTHEW

After lunch one day a professional friend mentioned that she was very concerned that one of the children whom she was treating was making no progress and she thought that my treatment interventions might provide another means of trying to assist this boy. Later she informed me that she had been treating Matthew, age 7, for the past 18 months but had seen no evidence of therapeutic benefit. She is a skilled and experienced child therapist who is not quick to give up on her cases. She indicated that in therapy Matthew engaged in play in a very compulsive, repetitive manner. Invariably he moved to a theme of conflict and aggression and he showed no response to her modifications of this theme, her interpretations and empathy, or her introduction of alternative themes and activities. The more direct she became, the more resistant Matthew was. She did not think that she had established a therapeutic relationship that held significant meaning for him. She did not want to "abandon" him since he had experienced considerable abandonment already in his short life. Her conviction that her treatment of him for another 18 months would be of no significant benefit to him led her to conclude that she had no other option but to consider referring him to someone else.

Her greatest concern was Matthew's placement. He was now in his third foster placement and his foster mother had indicated that his aggressive and defiant behaviors left her discouraged and at times exhausted. My friend feared that this placement might well disrupt as had the others. I agreed to consider treating Matthew but only if his foster mother, Betty, would first meet with me and commit to working with Matthew and me for at least 6 months. Betty met with me and agreed to make that commitment, so I began to work with Matthew about a month later. His lack of response to the termination of his therapy with my friend, both with her and at home, convinced her that her decision had been correct.

As is true for so many foster children, Matthew's first 2 years had been characterized by chronic neglect, periodic physical abuse, frequent moves, and various temporary caregivers. He was the youngest of three children being raised by a single mother, Donna, who periodically abused alcohol and who had various dysfunctional relationships with men who might or might not abuse her and her children, At 32 months of age, Matthew entered protective custody because his 5-year-old brother received a broken arm from abuse. Matthew and his siblings initially were placed in one foster home but their numerous problems ended this placement in 2 months. They were then placed separately, and Matthew remained in his second foster home for 18 months. He had to leave that home for reasons related to his behavior as well as other sources of stress to the family. He had now lived with Betty for over 2½ years. She and her husband, Joe, had two adolescent birth children and two other foster children, a 10-year-old girl and a 4-year-old boy. Betty was an experienced foster mother who had cared for eight different foster children over the past 10 years.

When I first met Betty she immediately impressed me as being an idealistic and religious woman who definitely wanted to make a difference in the lives of the children who came into her home. She indicated that she had never before "given up" on a child and she hoped that Matthew would not be the first. However, she expressed the fear that he had "beaten" her. She found herself becoming increasingly tense and angry toward him because of his very frequent and unpredictable aggressive and defiant behaviors. At the same time she indicated that she did not feel that she meant very much to him. She thought that he was comfortable in her home and probably would not want to leave, but if he had to leave, she did not think that he would really miss her. She had not seen any indications that he missed his mother or his previous foster parents.

Matthew's aggression was primarily directed toward Betty and toward her 4-year-old foster son, Jack. When she limited Matthew or refused a request, he would usually scream at her and call her names. At times he would throw things, either to break them or to hit her, and periodically he had hit and kicked her. If unsupervised, he might well knock Jack down, pinch him, take and break his toys, or call him names that would leave Jack crying. Although Matthew did not show much interest in affection for himself, if he saw Jack being held or played with by Betty, he would insist that he be included and he would try to disrupt the activity. As a result, Matthew had to be supervised a great deal, and this added significantly to Betty's responsibilities. He also had hurt the family dog and two cats, resulting in the need for additional supervision.

Joe and the two adolescent children were becoming increasingly annoyed with Matthew. Betty's 17-year-old son had originally spent a lot of time playing with Matthew, but now he was Matthew's greatest critic. Betty defended Matthew against the rest of the family, but she was now questioning her ability to help him.

During my first meeting with Betty I summarized for her my methods of treating children who show symptoms similar to Matthew's. I indicated that my impression was that he had significant difficulty forming an attachment to her, just as he had had similar difficulties in his prior relationships. I indicated that the chronic abuse and neglect that he had experienced left the inner resources that he needed to begin to trust his caregiver poorly developed. Lacking the experience of consistent nurturance and protection, he was left to rely on himself for protection through his attempts to manipulate and control others. Finally, I told Betty that if I were to work with Matthew I would need her to be present and actively involved in each session. I also would have many specific recommendations regarding her daily care of Matthew that were necessary because of the severity of his problems. While her maternal skills were more than adequate for her own children and the other foster children, his unique needs required more specialized child-rearing approaches. I wanted Betty to realize that my specific recommendations to her were not due to any deficiencies in her parental abilities but rather to Matthew's extreme difficulty forming an attachment with any mother. I wanted to contract with Betty to be willing to try other approaches in raising him that would complement what she already was providing. Finally, she needed to know that if Matthew was to make progress, her role in his treatment was central and his continuing in her home was crucial. Betty agreed to this contract more on faith and determination than on actual confidence that we would make a difference.

Before meeting Matthew I also spoke with his caseworker at the Department of Human Resources. I obtained more specifics of his history including past evaluations. Matthew's cognitive functioning was average, although his academic functioning in first grade was delayed and he received special services for both academic and behavioral difficulties. I also learned that during his first 2 years, his maternal grandmother had been a frequent caregiver. She had been the primary caregiver for him and his siblings for almost 14 of his first 32 months. Although she had not been able to assume their care when they entered protective custody, she had remained interested in their welfare and Matthew had visited with her 8 to 10 times over the past 4 years.

Because of Matthew's predominantly oppositional and defiant behaviors, his resistance in his past therapy and the daily tension, annoyance, and discouragement that he must have been feeling in his foster home, I decided that I would structure my initial contact with him to be very directive and goal-focused. I would attempt to elicit a contract from him in which he would agree to work with me and his mother to learn to both stay out of trouble more and to increase his happiness. He needed to see quickly that this was for his benefit, not mine or Betty's.

Matthew greeted me by refusing to talk or to leave the waiting room. He clearly was not happy about beginning treatment again and he might also have been angry over no longer meeting with his previous therapist. I accepted his decision to stay in the waiting room by closing the waiting room door and sitting down with him and Betty. I immediately told him that he probably was mad that he had to see another therapist and that it was not his choice to do so. I had spoken with his previous therapist about her termination sessions with him and I quoted her as to what she had told him. I indicated that I was not trying to replace her since my treatment was quite different from hers and the only reason she had discontinued his treatment was her concern over his lack of progress with her. I added that both she and I wanted to know what he thought and felt about this decision, although we could not let him make it. I indicated that he probably did not like being excluded from this decision. I conveyed empathy that this pattern had happened a lot in his life and that it often had led to his moving and ending relationships.

Matthew's first words for me then were "So what!" This told me immediately that he did not want to discuss the past, he did not want my empathy, he certainly was not going to acknowledge issues of abandonment and loss, and he was not likely to be very friendly with me. The odds of getting a contract at that point appeared to be slim. However, he had spoken to me and his words were connected to what I was saying. He had been listening. I replied that some kids would rather not move a lot because that makes it harder to know what to expect and it also makes it harder to get to know someone well. I was not ready to suggest that it also made it harder to learn to trust and love someone. Matthew again said "So what!" My reply was met with a third "So what!" so I turned to Betty and told her that I was very impressed with Matthew's telling me three times how much he disliked what I had to say. I expressed satisfaction with his decision to use two words to express all of his anger.

He then said "Shut up!" I replied, "I think that you want me to be angry with you too, then we'd both be mad. But I don't think that your getting people mad at you is good for you." I turned to Betty and asked her if Matthew found ways at home to get people mad at him. When she replied that he did, I asked her if she often got mad at him. Betty admitted that she did get angry with Matthew and she also said that she probably was angry with him a number of times every day. I asked her how she felt about getting angry with Matthew so often. She replied quietly that she felt sad about her frequent anger toward him. I asked why and she replied that she wanted to get along with him and give him a good home and she feared that her anger made this hard to do. I asked her if she wanted to learn how to be less angry with Matthew. She immediately replied, with feeling, "Yes!" I asked her if she would consider ideas during Matthew's work in my office that she could do at home to make it easier to be mad at him less often. She agreed to do this. I added that it would be hard for her since Matthew seemed to expect people to get mad at him and he might be more comfortable with mad feelings than with relaxed and close feelings with her.

During this interchange between Betty and me, Matthew listened intensely. At one point, when Betty demonstrated her strong feelings, he looked at her briefly before looking away again. He made no comments.

Not wanting to encourage Matthew to reject me again, I continued my conversation with Betty. I also thought that he might be quite interested in this discussion since we were exploring her anger, not his. I asked Betty for an example of an incident in which she became angry with Matthew. She recalled a recent time when she saw Matthew walk past her sleeping cat and lightly kick him. She yelled at Matthew to stay away from the cat and leave the room. Betty said that she felt responsible for her pets and that she could not allow anyone to hurt them. I agreed that both her children and pets were her responsibility and I was sure that she would not allow her cat to scratch Matthew while he slept. She agreed. I suggested that if one member of the family hurts another, restitution seemed to be indicated. We explored possible consequences and she thought that feeding the cat, changing the kitty litter, or buying the cat a toy were appropriate consequences. Such consequences might help Matthew work harder at leaving the cat alone. Betty said that she also would keep a list of how many times she got angry with him about the animals as well as what consequences she gave him for bothering them. We discussed the possibility that he had never learned how to touch or play with a pet. Betty agreed that three times each day she would briefly invite Matthew to learn how to touch, pet, hold, and play with the cat or dog. Apart from these times, all interaction with any pet was prohibited.

Matthew remained silent during this discussion and I did not want him to commit to sabotaging this plan so I avoided asking him for agreement. I continued to talk with Betty. We discussed her pleasure for Matthew when she watched him learn to swim. She also mentioned his Nintendo skills and the fun he seemed to have riding with his foster father on a snowmobile. I then ended the session and recognized the good job Matthew did listening. I considered it to be a successful session even though Matthew did not engage with me verbally. He was a silent participant in my conversation with Betty and I believe that he was less threatened and more motivated to work by hearing Betty acknowledge her difficulties and commit to trying to improve both her relationship with Matthew as well as his relationship with the pets.

The second session again began in the waiting room. Betty expressed pleasure that she had not gotten angry with Matthew even once about the pets. She had seen him throw something at the dog one time and she had him feed and water the dog for 2 days. She had remembered to offer to allow him to touch and play with a pet every day under her supervision. Three times he said that he did want to play with the cat. Twice the cat was resting and Betty showed Matthew how to gently stroke and hold him. The third time when the cat was alert she demonstrated how to have fun with the cat by pulling a toy on a string around the room. She felt he seemed to enjoy these occasions. Matthew then spoke to Betty, adding that she had also shown him how to carry the cat. I asked Matthew if he thought that he might want to learn to play with the dog too. He actually replied "Yes," without anger. I also asked him if Betty was accurate when she said that she had not gotten angry with him about the pets. He again said "Yes." I praised Betty and I indicated how pleased I was that she was willing to work hard to have a better relationship with Matthew.

I suggested that Betty ask Matthew if he would like them to have a better relationship. He told her that he would and I asked them both if they were interested in having me give them more ideas "and other help" to be able to get along better with each other. Betty immediately agreed and

Matthew followed her lead with less enthusiasm. I indicated to Betty that since she had had more successful experiences in her life getting along in a family and since as the parent she made the rules, she would have an easier time learning to "get along better" than would Matthew. He would have to work harder than she would and I wanted her to acknowledge that. Betty turned to Matthew and said: "I know that this is harder for you than for me. You've had a much harder life already than I ever had. I do make mistakes sometimes with you, but I want to maker fewer of them." She reached over and briefly touched his shoulder and he passively accepted this gesture of support. I suggested to Betty that we all go into my office and make up a contract that she and Matthew would sign. I led the way and Matthew followed without protest. I led them to my couch and Matthew headed toward the puppets and dragons on the bookshelf. I directed him back to the couch, indicating that I would show him my "stuff" if we had time after finishing the contract. He consented although I could feel his resentment toward me.

When I began to discuss what I thought should be in the contract Matthew said that he did not want to do it. I did not want to challenge him, try to convince him of the merit of doing this, nor "give in" to his oppositional statements. Instead I again focused on Betty and worked with her on what she might agree to do at home for Matthew. After we finished I acknowledged his annoyance with me and suggested that Betty and Matthew might best work on his part without me. I asked Betty to tell me when they were finished, and I left the office. Ten minutes later Betty asked me to return and she informed me that Matthew had agreed to a number of things to do at home.

In the contract, Betty agreed to greatly reduce her anger at Matthew, to continue to teach him how to "get along" in the family with all living creatures, to give him appropriate consequences for good and bad choices, and to give him one popsicle and one candy bar of his choice each week. Matthew was pleased with Betty's list and he was willing to agree to learn how to greatly reduce his anger at Betty, to learn from her how to "get along" in the family, to learn to understand and accept the consequences that she had given him for his choices, and to give her two 30-minute Nintendo lessons each week. Finally, I added that they both needed to agree to follow my directions in each session, and I promised not to tell them to do anything that was too hard, too funny, or too boring. They agreed and we signed the document, with Matthew choosing to write his name in red ink. I immediately told them both to clap their hands three times. Matthew smiled and watched Betty as they clapped together. I told them to tell each other "good job" and they did. I then directed Matthew to get the cat puppet and show his mother how to hold, pet, and carry it. He grabbed the lion, and when I redirected him to the cat, he complied. He showed her correctly and complemented her success. I then said "good job" to them both and ended the session, promising to send them each a copy of our contract.

I have described these first two sessions in detail because I believe that they were crucial to all of our later success. This angry, resistant, and solitary boy needed to be engaged successfully within a context in which I, not he, directed our activities or we would have had countless hours of oppositional behaviors and two frustrated adults. I needed to engage Betty initially so that Matthew could simply watch and listen and let Betty take the risks to reveal herself and commit to working in therapy. Both he and Betty had things to teach, to learn, and to give to each other. I avoided verbal arguments and all power struggles with him while not allowing him to dictate the focus and activities of the sessions.

I have found that in focusing on the initial engagement and ground rules of the sessions it is not too difficult to establish a therapeutic structure without power struggles with the child. I often am able to elicit some meaningful engagement and even some enjoyment from the child. It is much harder to elicit and maintain such interactions on a consistent basis. If I fail to start the process well, it is much more difficult to do later. However, it is not necessary, and it is even detrimental with the poorly attached child, to initially engage him by being nondirective and allowing him to determine what we will do and what we will discuss during the initial sessions. If one approaches him in that way, he is likely to be very resistant to giving the control back to the therapist and he is very likely to strongly avoid the necessary therapeutic work.

In the contract there was no mention of the past, although I fully intended to interpret for him at a later time how experiences from his past were making it difficult for him to meet the terms of the contract with both Betty and me. By having the contract, I was hopeful that Matthew would be willing to remain engaged with therapy in spite of the intense affect that was certain to arise in later sessions. By the end of the second session, I had established an initial working control of the treatment while setting a slow pace, being sensitive to Matthew's fears and defenses. I also focused initially on his difficulties in the home from a cognitive/behavioral per-spective. Could I maintain this control when Matthew began to express rage, sorrow, and fear? Would he accept efforts to relate his present to his traumatic past?

During the next three sessions I worked to establish a routine with Betty and Matthew in which we would review their interactions with the animals at home, the terms of the contract, and the candy bars that Matthew chose. We used the puppets that he seemed to enjoy but Betty and I chose the themes. I asked Betty to mention some of Matthew's choices and the consequences that she gave. I asked Matthew to mention how he responded to these consequences. I wrote down their responses without any comments. I checked on Betty's Nintendo lessons that were going slowly.

At the beginning of each session I spoke with Betty about the situation at home while Matthew waited in the other room. She was discouraged as she spoke of his continuing and possibly increasing aggression toward her and Jack. I reassured her that I did take these behaviors seriously but that I did not yet want to focus on them in therapy because his fairly weak engagement and compliance might dissipate and be hard to reestablish. She acknowledged her continuing anger at Matthew and her frequent struggle to enjoy him. I spoke with her on the benefit of giving him empathy along with the consequences to increase his readiness to accept them while not experiencing them as rejection by her. Betty agreed, but I sensed that she was feeling some frustration with me that I was not treating his behaviors with the level of concern that she felt they merited.

In the sixth session I decided to begin to deal more directly with those aspects of Matthew's current functioning that were undermining his placement. I reviewed with Betty a recent incident in which he had refused to turn off the TV and then pushed and screamed at her when she turned it off. I outlined for her how we might process this incident in the session and she agreed. With Matthew present we discussed the contract just as we had done in the previous sessions. This time, rather than simply describing the incident for me to record, I indicated that I would like to explore it. I told Matthew that this might be hard for him so I would pretend that I was him and guess what he might have been thinking and feeling. He agreed and loaned me his baseball cap to perch on my head. Betty then told me to turn off the TV, and I said quietly but loud enough for Matthew to hear, "Why won't she let me see this show? She never lets me do anything that I want. She seems to like bossing me around. She's not fair. She probably just doesn't like me." When Betty pretended to turn of the TV, I got out of my chair, approached her and said, "Why did you turn it off? I just wanted to see this show. I don't think that you want me to ever be happy. You just don't seem to like me." She responded. "Thanks for telling me what you think and feel, Matthew. I know that it's hard for you to do what I say when you're having fun. I'm sorry that you think that I don't like you when I tell you to do something. I do like you and I want to teach you how to have fun *and* how to follow our family rules." I turned to Matthew and asked if my guesses about his thoughts and feelings were right. He nodded that they were.

During this sequence I demonstrated only mild annoyance with Betty, fearing that Matthew would not acknowledge having more intense anger and more critical thoughts about her. I hoped to both model for him how to verbally express his anger and communicate understanding for the thoughts and feelings that might have led to the inappropriate behaviors. I was not yet ready to deal with his actual behaviors as I was convinced that these were very shameful to him and that our considering them would most likely elicit rage. I asked Matthew if he wanted to play himself and I would be Betty and he declined. I then asked Betty to be Matthew and I would be her. We reenacted the same sequence in a similar fashion, again eliciting agreement from Matthew that Betty had represented him adequately.

Immediately after this sequence I asked Betty to read Matthew a story of parent–child conflict. Matthew replied that reading was "no fun" and he indicated that he would rather play with my magnets. I sat motionless for a moment, then went to him and whispered in his ear, "You must think that I'm like Betty and only want you to learn stuff and have no fun. You'll probably want me to get a TV soon." When he smiled I replied that after she read him the story we would see how many magnets it took to pull a metal toy across my desk. The session ended well. We had now added a bit of emotion and conflict into our very directed sessions and Matthew was still engaged.

In the seventh session we enacted another incident in a similar manner. This time Matthew did agree to play Betty's part and he demonstrated more anger toward "Matthew," played by me, than she had done. He enjoyed the activity and was actively cooperative while his cooperation had been more passive in the previous sessions. At home, however, there was no change.

In the eight session I again focused on an incident in which Matthew had become very angry with Betty. I prepared him for the fact that this time I would be screaming at Betty the same words that he had said at home. I communicated empathy for how hard it might be for him to listen to me because part of him probably felt very bad for what he had said, although another part probably felt fine about it. With Matthew watching intently, I screamed at Betty and she replied with the same words and anger that she had used at home. I turned to Matthew and quickly acknowledged how well he listened in spite of how hard it probably was. I told him that Betty and I would enact the sequence again, and this time I would guess what he might have been thinking and feeling when he and Betty expressed their anger. After doing the scene again, I held my head in my hands and said, "She's always mad at me. She hates me! I'm no good! No one has ever loved me. My mom, Donna, didn't love me and no one ever has since." Betty quietly got up, came to my chair and placed her hand on my shoulder, saying, "Sometimes I do get mad at what you do but I don't hate you. I'm sorry if Donna didn't love you, but I do care a lot for you. You're a good kid and it's hard for you now to learn how to live in our home, but I'll keep teaching you and loving you." We looked at Matthew and saw some tears in his eyes. Betty went and sat next to him and gently put her arm around him. He let a few more tears come before regaining control and becoming restless. I commented "good job" and directed the session to a less intense interaction.

In the ninth session, for the first time we explored in some detail Matthew's early history of severe neglect and periodic abuse while living with his birth mother, Donna. Matthew remembered little of those first 32 months and his memories of his mother primarily were from the numerous visits that he had had with her during the first 2 years after he entered protective custody. After that, her parental rights had been terminated and he no longer had any contact with her. He had ambivalent feelings toward her. I read to him various statements from his file that described aspects of his early life with her, being careful not to criticize her. I did express sadness that he had not experienced good parenting during the first 32 months of his life. I turned to Betty and asked her to describe for us various interactions that she had had with her birth children when they were infants and toddlers. She described numerous incidents and activities that she had had with them. She recalled that time in her life with obvious joy. I asked her if she had ever played "patty cake" with them. When she replied that she had many times, I asked if she would play it with Matthew, who had never played it. When Betty played it with him, he became enthusiastically engaged without any self-consciousness. They both en-joyed themselves a great deal. I asked Matthew to show me how to play it and he did, with no reservation.

After that, at my request, Betty told us how hard it was at times raising her birth children because infants and toddlers are so dependent and require a great deal of time, supervision, patience, and emotional energy. We then discussed how important those first years were for her birth children. Betty's good parenting enabled them to learn to trust and love her, feel good about themselves and their development, learn to accept frustration and manage their fears, and be able to accept her discipline without feeling rejected. Betty turned to Matthew and told him that because he did not have many of the experiences that her birth children had, she could understand why it was often hard for him to trust her, feel close to her, and accept her directions and limits. She expressed sadness that she had not been able to raise him when he was an infant because she knew that he would be so much happier now and his life would not be so hard. Betty hugged Matthew and he was very receptive to her empathy and affection. Before he became anxious about this level of intimacy, I asked them to play "patty cake" one more time and they did so with a great deal of laughter. I asked Matthew if he would be willing to show Jack how to play "patty cake," with Betty supervising, and he agreed.

Over the next six sessions we explored in various ways Matthew's current behaviors with Betty and how those behaviors reflected his early years with Donna. Following my directions, Matthew told Betty that at times he did not trust her—he thought that she was being mean and did not care for him. He also told her that at times he thought that she was Donna and was not going to raise him well. I drew pictures of Matthew's self-concept at 32 months of age (i.e., bad, mad, lazy, selfish, dumb) and how his self-concept was slowly changing over the years with Betty. I made another drawing of how her discipline elicited shame within him which in turn triggered rage toward her. Together, Matthew and Betty drew an additional picture of her employing discipline. This time discipline was used to teach him to make good choices and to have a happier life. Betty wrote on a slip of paper her motive for wanting him to have a happier life (i.e., she loves him). Matthew had to guess what she wrote. If he guessed correctly on the first guess he would receive $1. He would receive 10¢ less for each guess until he got it right. He won 90¢.

At home during these two months, Betty noticed that although Matthew still became enraged often, his anger tended to be less intense and sometimes he seemed to have an element of self-control that he had never shown before. He also began to be somewhat more comfortable with initiating and receiving affection with her. I believe that Betty was now more confident in her interactions with him. She had a better understanding of the motives behind his responses and she also now knew the reasons why combining empathy with discipline was crucial for his progress. Finally, as she saw Matthew making some progress, it was easier for her to be patient and remain highly motivated to provide him with the level of care that he required.

During this time I held a separate meeting involving Betty, Matthew's caseworker, and his maternal grandmother. It was my impression from reading his record that Matthew's grandmother had been the one stable, nurturing, and consistent person in his first 32 months of life. Her value to his early development and ability to form an attachment to his caregiver now could not be underestimated. Because of her health problems and the distance from her home to his foster homes, she had seen him only a few times a year since he entered protective custody. We spoke with her about Matthew's life, his problems, and the progress that he had made. She knew that he was free to be adopted and she asked about that process. She also told us of Matthew's first few years of life. He clearly meant a great deal to her and she expressed intense sorrow over those years. She felt that she should have done more for him and kept him from her daughter. Her feelings for Donna were strong and mixed. She provided details of Donna's neglect of the children and her own efforts to provide for them what they did not receive from their mother.

We asked his grandmother if she would meet with Betty, Matthew, and me to help Matthew get on with his life. I told her that Matthew might be able to respond more fully to what she had to say than anything that the rest of us could tell him. I indicated that I would direct her to tell him some examples of the neglect and abuse that he experienced as well as her efforts to provide him with the care that he needed. She would be asked to tell him that she was not able to raise him although she did love him. He also needed to hear that she wanted him to have an adopted home so that he could have a good life with loving parents. She agreed to do so.

In the 17th session Matthew met with his grandmother. They had much to say to each other and Betty and I listened in silence. Betty sat near him when his grandmother spoke about the past and about what she hoped for his future. His central question for her was why Donna had failed him the way she had. This question brought tears to them both as she struggled to find an answer that made some sense. Matthew let Betty comfort him. He did, in fact, seem to be able to come to terms with his early life in a deeper way than we had seen before. It was evident in the interaction of Matthew and his grandmother that they had a bond that was strong and lasting. Matthew's fairly rapid response to the treatment interventions in large part was due to that relationship. Betty was now committed to making sure that Matthew and his grandmother would have monthly visits. I made sure to recommend to his adoption worker to include the value of maintaining this relationship in any discussions with prospective adoptive parents.

Betty had always been clear that she would not be applying to adopt Matthew. When his adoption worker had first met him a year before, he had given no sign that moving from Betty's home mattered to him. Betty had spoken with him about what his new family might be like and he showed little interest. Now Matthew told Roger, Betty's 17-year-old son, that he did not want to be adopted. The level of his aggression toward Betty and Jack increased. He became more resistant to engaging with her at home as well as in the next several therapy sessions. Matthew appeared to us to be struggling with the reality that someday he would have to leave Betty after he had finally begun to allow himself to become close to her. His grandmother's visit and her blessing for the future made him aware of adoption and loss in a deeper way.

In the 23rd therapy session I decided to focus very directly on his feelings about Betty and adoption. I briefly summarized our work, stressing his beginning to like himself better as well as his learning to trust and care about Betty. I directed Matthew to tell her that he wished that he could stay with her. He looked away so I quietly said that I would say what I thought that he felt. I asked Betty, "Why can't I stay with you?" Betty began her planned response and he interrupted, saying that he did not want to leave. She replied with empathy and he refused to look at her. I then spoke for him again and told her, "I'm angry with you for not letting me stay." She again responded with empathy. I followed by saying, "I'm sad, too, and think that you don't love me enough." Betty gave empathy and said that she loved him a lot and wanted him to have a good home. Matthew began crying and he allowed her to hold him. He again asked her why he could not stay and she briefly replied that she was a foster mom and she wanted to help Matthew and other children in years to come to be ready to learn to love their adoptive parents. Matthew continued to cry and Betty continued to rock him.

Betty had felt a great deal of guilt and ambivalence about the decision of her and her husband not to adopt Matthew. She was a very dedicated and committed foster mother who was being very truthful with him about her reasons. Still, she knew that her words would mean little to him. She and I discussed this topic quite a bit before we both felt that she would be able to present it to him—with sadness but with clarity and firmness. Matthew needed to see that he could not change her mind by being "good" and that he was not being "rejected" because he was "bad." He needed to feel her empathy, trust that he could speak with her about his feelings, and find a way to rely on her for the considerable support that he would need in order to make the transition into an adoptive home. Over the next few weeks, there were signs that he was beginning to do this. His anger began to decrease, he found various little "reasons" to go to her for comforting, and he was able to speak with his adoption worker openly about adoption and even to agree to have his picture taken for prospective parents.

By the 27th session we were beginning to see various indications that our interventions were likely to be successful. Matthew increasingly would surprise Betty with observations about situations that described well his thoughts and feelings. He showed empathy for difficulties that Jack was having. On a few occasions he acted like a "big brother" for Jack. His teachers commented that he appeared to be more relaxed and cooperative. He demonstrated more humor and he played with more enthusiasm and imagination.

Over the next two months, therapy was fairly uneventful. We revised our contract to include giving Matthew more choices in our discussions and activities. He and I walked to a store and brought back Betty's favorite soda. During one session he and Betty worked on a painting that he wanted to give to his foster father for his birthday. At times he showed surprising insight for a boy not yet 8 years old. Once he calmly said, "I used to be mad all the time." Another time he said, "If babies are loved, they don't have to learn how to love." We expressed happiness for the progress that he had made and for how he had learned to enjoy good times.

As his 8th birthday approached Matthew was told that an adoptive home had been selected for him. His emotional response was mixed initially, and then he asked numerous questions and seemed to be getting excited. His birthday was 2 weeks away and he told us that he did not want to meet them until after his party. We agreed. It was my impression that Matthew experienced his birthday as representing the successes that he and Betty had made over the past year. He needed to celebrate the year with Betty before he could meet and begin to engage his new family.

Matthew has now resided with his adoptive parents and two older siblings for about 6 months. He has had a number of phone calls and notes sent to Betty and his grandmother. His new parents have expressed confidence that he is making the transition into their home. His adopted mother has commented that she feels an emotional engagement with Matthew that seems genuine and mutually satisfying.

Matthew was somewhat unusual in that his progress had no major relapses and that it occurred fairly rapidly. The patient and accepting relationship that he had with his previous therapist may have had more benefits than was obvious in his behaviors at home. However, his lack of progress at home would undermine any hope for a more positive self-concept and for a mutually enjoyable attachment with Betty. This was the key, I believe. Betty proved to be quite responsive to my recommendations and to the reasons for them. She was committed, caring, and competent. Once she and I were able to help Matthew to respond to her interventions more positively and consistently, he relied on her for considerable psychological momentum. His history with his grandmother and her helpful intervention with him also helped him to move beyond his past and embrace the opportunities presented to him.

8

MELINDA

I first met Melinda when she was 11 years of age, though she did not look, feel, or act as if she were 11. Such a passive, compliant, and withdrawn child! So fearful and so sad! What did she feel, or want, or think, or imagine? How might I engage her when she habitually became tearful and intensely silent as efforts to explore her inner life were made? If asked what toy she wanted, or if she liked the cookie, Melinda might, or might not, give a brief response. She had spent a year in traditional nondirected, play therapy with little signs of change. How might one be directive with such a child, without traumatizing her or making her become even more passive and withdrawn?

Melinda had the good fortune to have entered an excellent therapeutic foster home 2 months after entering foster care, at the age of 8½. Her initial symptoms were profound. She spent much of her time in a fetal position, exhibiting constant soiling and wetting herself, masturbation, and stomach aches. Her personal hygiene and overall self-care were minimal. She was habitually withdrawn, passive, and submissive. Any stress brought tears. She ate in a slow and resistant manner. She had various compulsions—counting and repetitive writing. She often seemed "spacey," adopted different voices, and showed frequent amnesia. She could neither play appropriately nor engage in imaginary play. She showed little interest in stuffed animals or dolls. At school she was isolated and often teased. She demonstrated very little affection for her foster parents. Parties, holidays, and excitement generally elicited very regressed, unusual, or fragmented and frighted behavior.

Melinda's symptoms were not surprising. She had been physically and sexually abused by various members of her family. Her mother both infantilized her and gave her consent to the various instances of abuse. Much of the abuse involved parties as well as ritualistic baptism. She did not enter school until she was 7 years old. Those who abused her threatened to kill her with a knife if she told of the abuse. One perpetrator even told her that he blew a monster inside of her through her ear. This monster would come out of her and kill her if she ever told.

Finally, Melinda did tell her teacher. But she only told of abuse by her adolescent brother, hoping that he would be removed from the home. She was very upset and sad when she discovered that she had to leave her mother and that her brother did not.

Melinda had shown a gradual reduction in her symptoms over the 2½ years in her therapeutic home. Her symptoms of soiling, enuresis, masturbation, and poor hygiene were now intermittent—returning under circumstances of stress—and her compulsions were less. She was somewhat more active in her play, though she still demonstrated little imaginary play. Dolls or stuffed animals were not important to her. She still was very quiet and passive and would seldom either disagree or express any thoughts or feelings. She remained isolated and detached. She was a very fussy eater in her foster home, though she ate better elsewhere. She never spoke of her past abuse. She rarely seemed to have fun or to know what to do in those moments when she seemed relaxed. Her nightmares were less, but still present.

When Melinda entered my office and sat on the couch for the first time, she looked at Mary, her foster mother, and tears began rolling down her cheeks. This would occur often over the next several months. My responses were varied. Initially I gave her empathy for the fear and sadness that I thought her tears represented. I verbalized this empathy often over the months while not allowing the tears to drive me away or to prevent the hard work that awaited her. At times, I would carefully wipe each tear as it rolled down her cheek, hoping to catch it before it fell onto Melinda's pants or my couch. At times I counted the tears, since Melinda generally liked to count. I gave her a tissue, but she seldom used it. I accepted this choice as her desire to have me manage her tears, and so I did. Most often the tears were simply the context in which we worked. My message to Melinda was gentle but insistent: I did not feel sorry for her; I expected her to work hard with me to find ways to make a better life for herself.

With Melinda being tearful and choosing not to talk during the first session, I calmly explained her situation in life to her, the general source of her difficulties, as well as the tasks that lay ahead. I explained my role as well as the important role of her foster mom in treatment and in her life at home. It was important to elicit a contract with Melinda so I wrote a list of various goals and then asked her to write "yes" or "no" after each so that I would know which ones she wanted to work on first. Melinda signified "yes" to reducing her fears, her bad memories, her sad feelings, and her mad feelings. She also wanted help to deal with the "different people" that she felt inside. I recognized the wisdom of her choices, expressed confidence in our ability to do the work together, and finally, I expressed satisfaction with the good home in which she lived. During this session I often briefly and casually touched her arm, hand, shoulder, and hair. I wiped her tears while acknowledging how hard she was working already.

During the next several sessions I engaged Melinda by doing most of the talking, continuing to touch her and wipe her tears, and by showing gentle humor. I reflected her fear and sadness, showed understanding for her symptoms in her present life, and communicated patience and persistence in our efforts together. I provided some additional structure by developing a "Garbage Bag" (as described by Beverly James 1989) in which I wrote on separate strips of paper the various instances of abuse and neglect that she experienced, then I placed the strips in a paper bag, indicating that she would draw one during some of our future sessions and we would explore the incident together. This made clear to her that we would be dealing with those memories but at a slow, controlled pace.

I also wanted her to know that our work involved helping her to develop skills which would be of benefit to her life. Therefore, I added a "Garden Bag" in which I inserted strips of paper, each of which contained a skill that she, Mary, and/or I thought would help her in the future. Skills such as "learning how to have fun," "asking for help from Mary," "telling Mary when I disagree," and "making friends" were placed in a bag to be brought out at a later date.

By the fifth session I began to notice some playfulness and willingness to disagree with me. During this session I pointed out to her that when under stress she was beginning to pick at her thumbs more than usual rather than sucking them. I indicated that her thumbs needed my protection so I held them, gently rubbed them, and talked to them about the need for us to find ways to keep them safe. Melinda laughed, tried to pull them away, and maintained that they were her thumbs and I should leave them be. I offered to let her pick my thumbs for a while if that would give her thumbs time to heal. She refused, but smiled when I placed my thumb a number of times in her hand.

With the mild increase in animation in therapy came a significant regression in her functioning at home and at school. Her soiling and enuresis returned, she ate less, and her hygiene became worse. She began to resist her few chores and her performance of her schoolwork decreased. I gave her empathy for this regression, explaining how the work that she was doing in therapy was hard and it was natural for her to regress. Mary, too, was understanding and patient while calmly expecting more appropriate behaviors. Our attitude was based on empathy while at the same time communicating that her troubles were not an excuse to avoid trying to meet her responsibilities.

During this time of regression, from sessions five through 15, two highly significant therapeutic experiences occurred. During one session, Melinda drew from the Garbage Bag an incident of sexual abuse. She described it briefly, with little affect. She was talking somewhat more now, but slowly and with little animation. I asked her if during that experience of sexual abuse she had found a way to prevent it from hurting so much. When she did not respond, I suggested that some children, in such situations, manage to vividly imagine that they are in another part of the room so that they do not feel that the abuse is happening to them. Melinda immediately responded that she had often done that. She reported that she could imagine being by the opposite wall in the room and observing the abuse as if it were happening to someone else. During this session and the next I affirmed that she had protected herself in the best way that she had available. I recognized her resourcefulness. She indicated that she no longer had to use her imagination that way, though she acknowledged that she did become "spacey" under circumstances of stress, during which time she daydreamed and was able to ignore the stress. Mary and I explored these events with acceptance and gentle humor. Melinda actually remained engaged when we explored other ways to cope with stress rather than by using dissociative responses. We recalled these conversations in later sessions at some of the times when she became "spacey." Melinda began to demonstrate a deeper understanding and greater self-acceptance of her symptoms.

Because of the intensity of her regressive behaviors, I decided to focus during the sessions on the neglect that she experienced as a baby. By now,

I was often holding Melinda in my lap while we explored present and past events, using the papers from the bags or drawing sketches of experiences or thought-feeling-action sequences. Melinda accepted being held, at times with an attitude of mild resignation and she did not dissociate in spite of the contact. She was told that if she became frightened in any way from the contact, she should inform me and I would put her down. This was never necessary. Sometimes I held her in a calming, nurturing way, quietly talking with her about her past or present experiences. After particularly difficult discussions I would hug her briefly. At other times, I held her in a more playful way. I might tease her, make a fuss about her smiles and frowns, or check her fingernails. Increasingly she teased back, giving me a hard time about therapy itself or about something I asked or said. She would smile when I expressed shock or outrage about her criticism.

During one session Melinda was partially lying across my lap with her head on my arm. I began to speak quietly about how sad it was that when she was a baby, she often was not held, played with, fed, and kept warm and clean. Melinda then began to cry in a manner much deeper and more intense than was her frequent tearing. She then melded in my arms, as if she were an infant again. She seemed as if she would never move again. I talked to her quietly and mildly rocked her. After a time, I told her that she needed to have Mary hold her that way. I placed her in Mary's arms and Melinda maintained her deep emotional experience with Mary. She continued to resist turning to Mary for nurturance at home, but during a number of sessions, she allowed and responded to Mary's nuturance in my office.

There was a recurring sequence in our sessions. We would begin most sessions with some quiet talk and gentle mutual teasing. I would usually then alert her that I was about to discuss more difficult past or present issues so she might get ready to deal with this. I often then held her, explored an issue, and encouraged her response. I provided empathy for whatever she said or did not say. At times I would speak for her, using whatever emotion in my expression that I thought she might be feeling. I would again give empathy for her response to my speaking for her. At times Mary would comment on the issue as well, giving her impression of what Melinda thought and felt about a stressful issue. I then would return to some relaxed talking and laughter with her and her foster mother.

This sequence of establishing some engagement, inducing stress by focusing on a difficult theme, and reestablishing the engagement was important for Melinda. The stressful theme needed to be resolved and the intensity of her fear and resistance prevented her from taking the initiative to do so at home or in therapy. She learned that exploring either her abusive past or her misbehavior in the present did not interfere with her relationship with Mary. In fact, she discovered that the relationship became stronger since it could integrate these difficult themes. She also discovered that she could turn to Mary for comfort and support when she did experience stress. This support helped her to deal more effectively with the issues that she had previously avoided. Mary had always been available to her, but Melinda was just now realizing it. She had not often known this experience before since she had not often directly dealt with difficult thoughts, feelings, and behaviors, and she had less often asked for help in dealing with them.

Because of the intensity of her distress, I began to meet with Melinda twice each week. Significantly, along with her regression, Melinda began to show new behaviors that represented important developmental gains at home. During the week of the 12th session, Melinda had soiled and hidden her underwear. When Mary confronted her for the hiding, not for soiling, Melinda responded by maintaining eye contact with her, without crying and withdrawing as she had always done before. During the next 2 weeks Melinda began to express her inner life much more openly. For example, at dinner she stated loudly, "I don't like chicken; I don't want to eat chicken." Later, she said, "I don't want to do the dishes!" These assertions were a first for this 11-year-old child.

As she became more conscious of her own needs and felt more safe about expressing them, Melinda became verbal about the years that she had missed. During a quiet moment she turned to Mary and said: "I'd like to be 3, can I be 3 for one month?" Mary and I gave her empathy for this wish and for her willingness to express it. She showed an interest in playing with preschool toys. This was supported. She also demonstrated her wish to be younger by not keeping herself clean, not dressing herself properly, and not managing her few responsibilities. These choices were discussed with her in the light of her wish to be younger. Without Mary expressing any concern about Melinda's actions, Mary made choices for her and supervised her basic self-care activities. Melinda received some consequences for not managing certain responsibilities, but her choices to resist were understood and respected.

While Melinda was in considerable discord in her daily life, her therapeutic work continued without any letup. During the 18th session, Melinda again drew a sexual abuse incident from the Garbage Bag. She began to disclose the abuse in a manner that demonstrated much more appropriate affect, more details, and a significantly greater desire to communicate to someone more about what had happened than she had previously shown. She seemed to be more in control of herself. Her affect and cognition appeared to be more accessible and integrated than had been the case previously. She had taken an important step toward no longer experiencing herself as a helpless victim. It may be noteworthy that during the week prior to the 18th session, Melinda not only soiled but smeared the feces on herself. She had been told that her behavior reflected how her past traumas made her feel bad and disgusting. She was also told how her new experiences over the recent 4 months were making her feel better about herself and she was able to discover new skills within herself. She was asked to consider if this view of herself was the better guide for who she was and who she wanted to be.

During sessions 20 to 26, we were focusing increasingly on the turmoil in Melinda's present life. Mary and I would describe events, discuss what they might represent, and encourage Melinda to verbalize her thoughts and feelings about them. Often I would assist Melinda by guessing what she might think or feel and having her repeat what I said to Mary. We would then recognize Melinda's expression as if it came entirely from her. Yet, she was not simply parroting what I said without any thought. She increasingly would modify what I said or elaborate spontaneously. She also began to express her thoughts and feelings to us with less external help. This was occurring at home as well. To her foster father she said loudly: "I don't want to do that and you can't make me!" She began to cry more intensely at home in response to disappointments. She was asked to chart daily statements that she made at home expressing her "wants" and "not wants," which we would then discuss in therapy. This gave her more practice in becoming aware of and then indicating her thoughts and feelings to the significant adults in her life.

At this time, after various legal delays, Melinda's birth parents finally had their rights terminated. When told about this in therapy, she immediately cried. Her mourning seemed to represent both qualities in her original attachments to her birth parents and also a profound sadness over the terrible nature of those first years of her life. In the midst of this experience of loss, Melinda also realized that this would mean that she was now free to be adopted and so would be leaving her foster parents, who were not planning to adopt her but rather were committed to helping other foster children in the future. Melinda was able to acknowledge her intense sadness over the reality of moving someday in the future. She allowed Mary to nurture her and to provide her with empathy for her pain.

By the 28th session, summer vacation was beginning. Mary and I were convinced that Melinda, who was over 11½ years old, desperately needed the opportunity to learn to play. We successfully petitioned the Department of Human Services to hire a young woman who had just graduated from high school to spend the summer with Melinda and give Melinda the opportunity for extensive play. This woman engaged Melinda in arts and crafts, cooking, bike riding, swimming, and whatever else they felt like doing. Sometimes another child might be involved, but mostly it was just the two of them. Melinda could not completely control the interactions and activities. She needed to negotiate so that they both would have fun. During that summer we all observed a Melinda who was becoming more active, engaged, and enthusiastic with laughter and excitement that she managed quite well. We also saw her becoming more assertive. Not only could she express her "wants" more directly, but also she began to show some anger rather than tears when she was corrected. With her assertiveness, she also began to express some anxiety about whether or not others liked her. We explored her doubts in therapy and considered ways that might test how others really felt about her. She often was able to do so, with good results. Interestingly, at the beginning of this "summer of fun," Melinda made it clear in therapy that she did not want to explore her abusive background. I expressed delight in her ability to know and express her wish. I concurred with her. During the summer we would only focus on her present and future life.

In September, Melinda regressed with the return of school, the loss of her summer companion (although this woman still saw Melinda periodically throughout the next year), the continuing difficulties stemming from her abusive history, and the threat of adoption. However, along with a recurrence of many of her old regressive symptoms, Melinda maintained the progress that enabled her to show her anger much more directly. She yelled at her foster mom when limited, she defied her at times, and she refused to do her schoolwork. Through it all, Melinda continued to rely on Mary for comfort and nurturance. She now would call Mary when she awakened in fear in the middle of the night. She would allow Mary to hold her when she thought of having to move someday. When she regressed, Mary would again make choices for her, just as she had done in the past.

Melinda now began to ask to be baptized into her foster family's church. When given permission by her caseworker, she was expected to speak of her wishes to the pastor. Instead, she was rude to the pastor and refused to tell him of her desire for baptism. Mary and I understood this refusal as representing Melinda's reluctance to take an important step away from her past: to form a new life. It seemed to be important to again focus on the old abuse, with another technique.

Diane Davis is a woman who provided assistance to me at certain times in therapy, often through participating in psychodrama. We decided to create an interaction between Melinda and her "birth parents" where I would be her father and Diane would be her mother. Mary would provide support and some coaching to Melinda, who was being asked to confront these parents with Melinda's thoughts and feelings about their treatment of her in the past. In the 54th session, we employed psychodrama for the first time. After 5 minutes it was evident that Melinda was not ready to confront her "parents." Therefore, Diane played Melinda while I became first the father, then the mother, and finally the older brother. Melinda watched this interaction with interest. When we concluded, she asked to try it again. This time, she confronted her "parents" with animation and intensity. She spoke of her hurt, her fear, and her anger. She told them how wrong they were to have treated her the way they did. She was fully engaged; she was forceful and intent. At the conclusion, she showed great pride! She embraced Mary and beamed over her effort.

The next session involved a second act of psychodrama in which Melinda was also able to express some sadness along with her anger over how her mother had failed her and how much she had wanted a good relationship with her mother when she was younger. Again, Melinda was very expressive and left the sessions with considerable personal satisfaction. Two weeks later, Melinda very clearly and appropriately asked the pastor if she could be baptized. She was able to discuss her religious teachings and beliefs with him, and shortly thereafter, with joy and confidence, was successfully baptized.

Progress was evident in other ways over the next few months. The family dog died. Initially Melinda showed no emotion, but in the next therapy session she cried over the loss very acutely and asked Mary to comfort her. She also demonstrated a meaningful attachment to her doll, "Julie." She nurtured and cared for "Julie" quite well. With Diane's help, she used "Julie" to role play a mother and child. She sang to "Julie" and played with her just as a mother might. Diane went to Melinda's home for individual meetings for a few months to support Melinda's imaginary play and to help her to express her inner life. With some help from Diane, Melinda wrote a song about herself. Diane then put it to music and they taped it. During the 60th session, 14 months after Melinda began treatment, she brought the tape to the session for me to hear. The following was written by Melinda, when she was 12 years of age.

Melinda Ann

There's a little girl
deep inside of me,
never getting touched
the way she wanted to be.
This little girl only longed
for a little touch of love.
But this was something Melinda Ann
could only dream of.

(Chorus)   She longed for adventure
She longed for fun,
never wanting to be hurt
at the hands of another one.
But now Melinda Ann's
feelings she can share
with the people she calls "family."
She is learning how to care.

There's a little girl
longing to be free
and she can't wait
for her new family.
Leaving the past behind
choosing hope for tomorrow,
laughter and smiles
instead of tears and sorrow.

(Bridge)   Melinda me
Melinda now
Wants to live
and she is learning how.
(Chorus)

This song represents so well Melinda's struggles, wishes, and successes. Some of these words she had heard in therapy. They were now hers. She took pride in her song. She was pleased that other therapists, children, and caseworkers would listen to it and learn from her and her experiences.

Further progress was evident over the next 2 months. Her foster parents were gone for a week. When they returned, she expressed how much that she had missed them. At the same time she was able to openly express her anger at them. She also seemed to be coming to terms with adoption. She responded to stress generally with appropriate verbal expressions and assertiveness. Still, she wanted to be younger. This was evident in her expressed wishes, her play, and her interests. Melinda's peer relationships were improving. Other children wanted to be with her. She showed much better skills at playing with same age peers in a way that both had fun. At this time a younger foster girl entered the home. This child had significant emotional and behavioral problems. Melinda dealt with the stress of this child quite well. At times Melinda tried hard to be a "big sister" to her and she enjoyed her success. At other times she appropriately expressed her rage at this child's behavior toward her.

Melinda had by now made important progress in her work both in therapy and in her foster home. She was receptive to nurturance and she could ask her foster parents to attend to her wishes and needs. As she learned more appropriate behaviors, experiences of shame were no longer felt to be rejection and abuse. She learned to quickly reestablish the bond with her foster parents that had become so important to her. She could even initiate conflict with them, without fearing loss of love. Melinda had developed a secure base and was beginning to experience herself and the world with much more vitality and interest than she had shown before. She also had developed the inner strength to let her foster parents go so that she could have her own family; she began to actively desire adoption in spite of the loss of her foster parents.

Another summer came and again a young woman was assigned to spend much time with her. This appeared to be very fruitful, as Melinda's ability to have fun and to play like a child demonstrated further improvement. She was lively, assertive, active, and joyful. During the summer she had no therapy since she was doing so well and since she so much wanted to show that she did not "need" therapy. I saw her a few times in the fall. She did not regress when school began and she still appeared to be dealing well with adoption. We agreed to schedule no further sessions.

That winter, almost 2 years after I met Melinda, an appropriate adoptive family was found. I met with her and her adoptive parents a few times. She was ready to have her own family. She was now 13 years old. Since she had learned late how to enjoy being a child, she clearly did not want to be an adolescent. She wanted parents who would give her a family within which she could be a child and enjoy the love and care provided by them.

Melinda now is 14 years old. She has lived with her adopted family for 1 year. She still maintains contact with Mary. Mary played a crucial role in

Melinda's discovery of the meaning of attachment and her ability to establish such a bond with her adopted parents, "her new family." She is active and content within her family, school, and community. She has many interests and skills. She is an adolescent who is successfully becoming an adult.

9

BILL

Ten months after treatment had begun with Bill, he was demonstrating significant progress in all areas of his life. In fact, Bill decided that he wanted to write a book about his life, all 9 years of it. He did so, working independently for a number of hours over the course of a week. In his book, he briefly mentioned our work together; when I asked if I could write about him in my book, he readily agreed. He wanted to be able to help other children by telling his story.

After Bill allowed me to read his story, I shared with him the history of his life with his birth mother and father. I had previously read this to him earlier in his treatment, but this time Bill read the material from another perspective. Referrals had been made to the Department of Human Services (DHS) about the abuse and neglect that he had experienced at the hands of his parents and another adult almost continually from the time he was 6 months of age until he was 4 years old. During that 3½ years, a total of 35 referrals were made of significant neglect as well as physical, emotional, and sexual abuse. Many of the referrals were considered to be marginal or of questionable validity. But the overall pattern was horrific. Bill reacted to this information with shock. "Why didn't they take me away from them?" he asked again and again. He became aware that he could have died during that 3½ years. And he became enraged that no one had intervened to help him during that long period of countless acts of abuse and neglect that he had to experience. Bill asked to speak with his adoption worker about his early history. She reviewed his records with him in more detail than I was able to do. Bill needed to know. He then wrote to the Regional Manager of DHS and asked for a reason to help him to understand why he had been left in his abusive home so long. Bill was invited to meet with this man, who later commented that it was the most difficult meeting of his career. He apologized to Bill, although he realized that explanations about limited resources would provide little comfort to the child. He told Bill that the situation had not changed and he pointed to a stack of files of cases similar to Bill's that were not receiving an adequate response due to limited staff. Bill was shocked. There were many more children still experiencing trauma similar to what he had lived through. He cried over this discovery and he went on to save money and send it to the Commissioner of the DHS in order to help to protect children who were being abused. He also wrote to numerous elected officials, asking them to fund services for other abused children. Bill communicated well his sense of having been betrayed by DHS, and, in fact, by all of us. He spoke passionately for other children like himself.

For Bill to write about his life and to try intensely to understand his first 4 years demonstrates the significant progress that he had made over the prior 10 months. I began to treat Bill shortly after his eighth birthday. He had spent the past 4 years in foster care, living in his first home for 2½ years. For the most recent 16 months, he lived with Janet, a therapeutic foster parent, who had been given training regarding ways to raise a child with Bill's problems. He had also received traditional play therapy for 3 years. As part of the therapeutic program, he was also provided with a paraprofessional to work with him on skill development 12 hours each week. Bill had been diagnosed at times as manifesting attention deficit, hyperactive disorder, post-traumatic stress disorder, and oppositional-defiant disorder.

When I began treating Bill, Janet indicated that although he was somewhat less aggressive toward her than when he first came to her home, he demonstrated very little progress in other areas. She described him as being a very oppositional child who would argue about anything and everything. He was often destructive. He lied a great deal and he would strongly deny ever doing anything wrong. He avoided talking about all emotions. Anger was the only emotion that Bill would show. He needed to control everything from when he went to bed to what his foster parents talked to each other about. When under stress he would not seek assistance or support, and he was never comfortable with being touched. He had no special toys or other objects. Janet thought that she was beginning to be more important to Bill, though he would show this only briefly and only if he were in the right mood.

During the first session with Bill, I communicated empathy for how difficult his life had been over his first 8 years. I stressed that although he was no longer being abused, he was still experiencing many difficulties in his daily living. Since Janet had indicated that Bill had had very few privileges over the past 4 months, I communicated a desire to try to help him to earn his privileges again. At home he had demonstrated little motivation to do this. In fact Janet indicated that he would inevitably behave worse whenever he managed to earn a privilege. Having no privileges seemed to give Bill a sense of greater security. This suggested to me that he really did not like himself well enough to feel that he either deserved privileges or that he would have the ability to keep them. Thus, he might as well not try. When I shared his thought with Bill, we had the first of our many disagreements. He denied not liking himself and said that he really wanted his privileges. I suggested that he was bright and could certainly have them by now if he really wanted them. However, I was more than willing to teach him how to earn his privileges if he wanted them. I suggested that he might need to learn to like himself first. I smiled and touched Bill's arm while saying this. I did not ask for a reply and did not receive one. I then told him about therapy with me, giving him empathy for his disappointment that we would not be playing games.

After the first session, Bill told Janet that he would never be adopted because "no one wants me." He added that he needed "to get my behavior better." During the second session I agreed with Bill that his behavior was important but suggested that we needed to understand his past experiences of abuse and neglect in order to see how those experiences affected him now, including how he thought about himself and Janet. Bill had been very reluctant to explore his memories of abuse in his previous therapy. My matter-of-fact, "let's get going" approach seemed to catch him off guard and led him to explore this issue in greater detail than he had done before. I reviewed with him the documented history of his abuse and neglect. Without hesitation he then spoke of being sexually abused by his father and he was receptive to my empathy and support. I sat close to him with my hand on his shoulder. Whenever I anticipated that Bill was going to emotionally withdraw from me, I would engage Bill differently or introduce a different topic in order to maintain the engagement. Because of the intensity of his oppositional and avoidant behaviors, I thought that it was crucial to embed discussions that would elicit anger, sadness, or fear, all within a relaxed and playful atmosphere. We reviewed other events in his history as well. I paced his readiness to explore these traumas in any depth. I concluded this session with the illustrated story involving Bill putting a wall around his heart to avoid getting close to Janet.

After the second session Bill's oppositional behavior increased at home. He became aggressive toward Janet again, something that he had not done in a few months. Once, when angry, he exposed himself to Janet, something he had never done before. I decided that his behavior was escalating in part because of the difficult, but necessary, distress of his last therapy session. In my judgment, it was crucial to not ignore his behaviors with Janet. I needed to communicate to him that these resistant and angry behaviors were just the sort of behaviors that needed to be explored in therapy. At the same time, I also needed to communicate to him that in exploring such behaviors I would not be angry with him. He would not be yelled at or rejected nor would I give him the obvious advice that he had to learn to stop being aggressive toward Janet. Rather, my message to Bill was that we needed to understand his behaviors to help him to acknowledge the feelings associated with those behaviors. I suggested to him that he may have acted with aggression toward Janet to help himself to maintain the wall around his heart. He may have been telling her that he did not want to get close to her. I held Bill in my lap and told him to tell Janet that he did not want to be close to her. He did so after some hesitation. I then told him to tell her that he was afraid to get close to her. He refused. I gave him empathy for how hard it must be for him to express fear. I told him that I would say it for him since he was not ready to do so himself. When I spoke for Bill about his fear, he became angry at me. I had empathy for his anger and told him that at times I would have to speak for him about important issues in his life that were hard for him to put into words. I admitted that I was guessing and that I might be wrong at times. I assured him that when he learned how to express his emotions more easily, I would not speak for him.

It is important to note that in understanding his reasons for his aggression, I was not providing Bill with an excuse. He still received consequences for his behavior. The purpose of this work was to help him to be more likely to choose other behaviors in the future that would have more desirable consequences for him. Having a more enjoyable, trusting, and supportive relationship with his caregiver would be one such consequence.

During the above exchange with Bill about his aggression toward

Janet, I had held Bill. Listening to Janet and me talking about his aggression was hard for him and he screamed at us, tried to leave, and became angry at me for not letting him go. I showed empathy for his anger, and stressed how I needed to help him to remain involved with discussions about important experiences that he had. These conversations would include events and behaviors that were hard for him to acknowledge. I suggested that he tried desperately to avoid being aware of the part of himself that behaved aggressively. I also suggested that in spite of his efforts to avoid any realization of his angry outbursts, these behaviors contributed to his sense that he was bad. I again gave him empathy for how hard it must be to feel that he was bad. He again denied having such feelings.

Finally, during the third session, I suggested to Bill that if he wanted to reduce his oppositional behaviors, he could do so by practicing doing what he was told. Janet would tell him to do five things in sequence each day. If he did these five tasks, it would help him to reduce his oppositional behaviors and help me to know if he really wanted to do so. We practiced during the session, with Janet telling him to do five easy and somewhat funny tasks. Bill laughed, did what he was asked, and assured us both that this was easy and he certainly would do them all during the coming week.

Actually, during the fourth session I was informed that Bill was willing to do only about half of the five easy tasks asked of him each day. While he had not been aggressive toward Janet, he was as oppositional as ever. I thanked Bill for his honesty in showing us that he really did not want to do what Janet asked. I suggested that if he had a more cooperative and friendly relationship with Janet, then he certainly would have to like himself better. I acknowledged that being close to her was hard and that if he did what she told him to do, he would be taking down the wall around his heart and he was not quite ready to do that yet. I joked with him about my perception that I liked him better than he liked himself. After listing a few amusing "proofs" that I liked him better than he did (i.e., I enjoyed hugging him and I let him put his smelly socks on my couch), I spoke quietly and with empathy about how hard it must be for him to have to search for reasons to like himself. I briefly recalled his abusive history and wondered out loud how *we* would be able to convince him that his abusers were wrong when *they* had convinced him that he deserved the abuse and neglect that he received.

Between the fifth and eleventh sessions, with an exception of one week of fairly cooperative behavior, Bill was extremely oppositional and periodically aggressive toward Janet. Since in therapy we were focusing heavily on his relationship with her and his negative view of himself, this was not unexpected. Janet had managed to adopt a more accepting but firm manner with Bill and he was not often able to control her emotions through his behavior. He so wanted her to get angry with him that he tried much harder to get that result. When this was not successful, he lied about her, saying that she had knocked him down on the floor. He lied constantly and stole a number of items.

Bill also became very angry during the treatment sessions. He disagreed with my suggestions about his fears of attachment, his self-hatred, his inability to admit to poor choices, and his underlying sadness. I accepted his rage at me and encouraged him to express it more intensely if it would help him in any way. He would scream at me and Janet, blaming her for not treating him fairly and blaming me for being stupid. My encouragement of his anger only intensified it for a number of sessions. Then in the eleventh session, he seemed to develop a realization that I wanted him to be angry, so he decided to become passively resistant and not say anything. I immediately accepted this choice, encouraging him to show me how angry he was by being as quiet as possible. Later, I indicated that I would speak to Janet for him. I put my mouth behind his head and tried to imitate his voice. Janet pretended that she thought it was Bill speaking and she responded to "him." This infuriated Bill and he again screamed. We accepted this decision too.

During the sixth session I had introduced "Big Bill" and "Little Bill" to him. Big Bill represented the angry, controlling part of himself that did not want to trust Janet and to be vulnerable. Big Bill wanted to be the boss and rely only on himself. Little Bill was the part of himself that deeply wanted the childhood that Bill had never had. Little Bill wanted to trust, cooperate with, and feel close to Janet. Little Bill wanted Bill to take a chance and begin to trust Janet so that Little Bill would not feel so alone. Bill listened to this but would not respond. I spoke for Bill at times, saying that Big Bill would never trust Janet or anyone else. Bill had been hurt before and he would not be hurt again. Bill listened and did not disagree.

As I focused again and again on his relationship with Janet, Bill began to speak about his birth mother. He indicated that despite what she did and allowed to happen to him, he still loved her. He said that he could not love two mothers. I suggested that this was not so; his birth mother would in fact want him to love Janet, since she could not raise him. (Her parental rights had been terminated 9 months earlier.) I spoke to Bill's adoption worker, who was able to obtain a letter from his birth mother in which she very appropriately said that she knew that Bill's heart was big enough to love two mothers. During these sessions, we covered very significant material with Bill; his initial response was to increase his resistance and anger.

During the week prior to the twelfth session, there was the first hint that Bill was doing some constructive internal work on the themes that were developed during the treatment. At times he appeared to Janet to be sad over conflicts with her or limits on his behavior. His typical rage outbursts were not as evident. He appeared to be more subdued. I decided to continue to focus on his relationships with both Janet and his birth mother, supporting the option that he could love both of them. I imagined for Bill what his birth mother might say if she were to meet him when he was 18 years old and discover that Bill had continued to fight Janet and refuse to be close to anyone during his entire childhood. I suggested that she might say the following:

> Oh Bill, I am so sad that you were unhappy and angry during your whole childhood. I know that I was not able to provide you with a good childhood, but I so wished that you would let yourself get close to another mom who could have loved you, laughed with you, taught you, and kept you safe. I know that Janet could have been that mom; I'm sad that you did not let yourself get close to her. You could have loved her and me too your whole life.

Bill listened intently to this. He was so quiet and motionless. He did not disagree with what I imagined; for Bill, to *not* disagree might be taken as clear agreement. I added a discussion about Little Bill, again hoping that Bill might have a chance to be close to a mom. At that point Janet spoke of Bill's early days with her, during which he had allowed her to comfort him when he had recalled with her some of his early experiences of abuse. Again, Bill remained quiet. Janet then held Bill during the session and they laughed and talked and she read him a story.

From the thirteenth through the nineteenth sessions, there was evidence of a struggle within Bill. He was clearly ambivalent about reconsidering his relationship with Janet and risking greater intimacy. At times he became even more oppositional, destructive, and aggressive than he had been during the previous 2 difficult months. He would bite her without any sign of remorse. However he also would accept more physical contact and nurturance from her. After the sixteenth session Janet introduced the bottle at home. She gave him the bottle daily, with him lying in her arms. She would encourage eye contact, talk quietly, stroke his hair, and hum quietly. This was never forced; at this time Bill never refused. Bill would typically snuggle closely to Janet, relax deeply, and appear completely content. His only request was that Janet not give him the bottle before bedtime because if he had it then, "I think of my mom and her abusing me."

After the fourteenth session Janet left Bill in another foster home for a few days because she was traveling to the home of relatives, and Bill's behavior made it impossible to consider taking him with the rest of the family. We helped him to express his sadness and anger and Janet indicated that she was sad that he could not come too. When she returned, Bill made it clear to her that he did not miss her because he did not like her. Of course Janet accepted this and dealt well with his increased oppositional behavior during the next week.

During this time in Bill's treatment, he also demonstrated much ambivalence toward me. While at times he would be very angry with me and quite resistant, at other times he would joke with me, tease me, and engage in considerable mutual enjoyment. He might say that I had bad breath and he would threaten to eat garlic before the next session. (A year later, after Bill had made great progress, he did in fact come to a session after having eaten garlic. He greatly enjoyed my horror and my leaping up to open the windows.) I would respond that if he complained about my breath again, I would hug him. He would "forget" this consequence a number of times, and he would scream and laugh and moan as I hugged him and told him how much I liked him. At other times we talked quietly, and he was more responsive, emotionally and verbally. He was more ready to acknowledge that he often did not like himself. He expressed to Janet at home and to me during some sessions that he feared that when he got older he might abuse his children just as his mother and father had abused him. I created an illustrated story about a mad, bad, dirty, and lonely Bill in a desert, standing before a scary forest in which there were three paths. Two led in circles through fights and destruction back to the desert. One path led to Janet at a lake. There he could be warm, clean, well-fed, and having fun with Janet.

Before the nineteenth session Bill got sick, one of the few times he actually needed to stay in bed from sickness. He allowed Janet to nurture him. She brought him food, rubbed his back, talked and read stories, and rocked him for most of one afternoon. During this session Bill let Janet give him the bottle in front of me. He had been embarrassed to have anyone else see him before. This was clearly not the angry and controlling and tough child who I had met 19 weeks earlier.

During the 20th session and for each session through the 32nd, Bill was also not the child with whom we interacted during the 19th session.

During those 3 months Bill's ambivalence increased, but along with it he demonstrated significant regression in his psychological functioning. He urinated on himself, sometimes while being held by Janet. He often sucked his thumb, before and after taking the bottle. He had difficulty sleeping at night, complaining of nightmares. He would call for Janet and accept her support at night when he was afraid. He began to be very frightened and suspicious of what she was saying about him, and he resisted waiting in the waiting room while Janet and I talked. He aggressively interrupted her phone calls. He appeared to be convinced that she was laughing at him, saying that he was bad or stupid, and planning to send him away. During the first of these 3 months, his fears were very intense but his behavior was fairly stable. He accepted the rules and expectations most of the time and earned some of his privileges. During the following 2 months the aggressive and oppositional behaviors returned. He made intense demands and threats. He threatened to kill himself and Janet. He accused her of abusing him. He accused me of abusing him when I held him during the sessions. However, when he was aggressive toward Janet, he appeared to experience some genuine sorrow. He seemed to be angry with himself for his poor behavioral choices. At one point Janet's birth child was hurt and required a great deal of Janet's attention. Bill was very upset about this and hurt this child. Bill's criticism of Janet was intense, as was his fear that she was criticizing him to others.

For a number of months Bill's behavior required that Jack, the paraprofessional who worked with Bill weekly, come to the sessions. Jack needed to be in the car with Bill to insure that Janet could safely drive Bill to my office. He also kept Bill safe in the waiting room while Janet and I talked, and he also sat in on the sessions. He reinforced the work that happened in the sessions and he supported Janet at home. His continuing message to Bill, spoken and unspoken, was that Janet was a good mother and that he would work hard to help Janet to help Bill to learn to accept her authority and her nurturance. Jack performed this work quite well and he was very instrumental in the overall progress that Bill was able to attain.

During these turbulent 3 months, I tried to support Janet and assist her in believing that Bill's behavior reflected his intense fear of beginning to want and to trust her. She was becoming quite important to him; he needed to integrate some extreme feelings and gradually begin to regulate them. He needed to redefine himself as being a child worthy of love and capable of loving. He needed to resolve the past and create a new future. Janet wanted to believe that what I said was really happening. Had the earlier progress been an illusion? The work that she was doing was extremely hard. How could one continue to engage this child daily if there was no genuine hope for change? Janet remained stable. She was patient, empathic, firm, and noncompromising. She would not lower her expectations for Bill to learn how to relate to her with respect, cooperation, and affection. When Bill intensified his resistance, she did not "forgive" and "give him another chance" because he had demonstrated greater responsiveness to her for much of an earlier 6 to 8 week period of time. If she had expected less, I do not believe that he would have made the transition to the next level of psychological health and attachment. If Bill had had a less capable, caring, and committed foster mother, he would never have embarked on the journey toward well-being in the first place. Janet's high level of parenting, made it significantly easier for Bill to do the difficult work of learning how to form an attachment with her.

Bill was very oppositional, negative and aggressive during much of these initial 8 months of treatment. When he would not do a basic chore or follow a simple direction, he was told to sit in a chair near where Janet was so that she could supervise him until he felt ready to do what was expected. Bill would often choose to sit for hours before he decided to follow the simple request. At other times, he would choose to sit for days! Bill wanted to force Janet to comply with his need to control her and the family routines. He wanted her to feel guilty and he wanted to have an excuse to feel mistreated by "having" to sit for hours or days. Janet's habitual response was to accept Bill's decision about what was best for him. She did not try to coax him to change his decision. Nor did she become irritated and rejecting. Her attitude conveyed the message:

> Gee, Bill, if sitting is this important to you I imagine you'll probably decide to sit a while longer. I don't think I'd make this choice, but it's your life. If you change your mind just let me know.

Janet continued to go about her own activities. She interrupted Bill's sitting for mealtime, use of the bathroom, or for her own activities that required him to accompany her. She interrupted the sitting to give him the opportunity to exercise if he wanted. She also made it difficult for Bill to convince himself that she was mean and wanted him to sit. She would surprise him with a special fun activity, snack, game, or walk. She might sit with him and chat or laugh about something and then go about her business. She never rejected his choice to sit. At times Bill would experiment with following the direction after a few minutes of sitting. At other times, he refused to sit and was "escorted" to the chair. Sometimes he would sit on the chair, sing and talk to himself, and seem to be quite content. Or he would yell in anger for long periods. Many days, because of his cooperative behavior, he did not sit at all. Whatever he chose, Janet remained emotionally detached, empathic, and firm. Bill was learning an important lesson about himself, his choices, Janet, and his relationship with her.

I supported Bill's ambivalence, fears, doubts, and anger during much of the time between the 20th and 32nd session. I inquired about his choices. I showed empathy over his uncertainty about trusting Janet. I focused on the Big Bill/Little Bill conflict. During the 23rd session I introduced a stuffed bear to Bill and indicated that the bear represented Little Bill. Janet and I gave the bear empathy for how hard his life was. Bill joined in and was quite nurturing and genuine as he spoke quietly to the bear. I said that I would keep the bear safe with me until Bill could safely care for the bear in his home. Bill was so pleased that "Little Bill" could someday live with him. He never questioned the need for the bear to be safe first before leaving my office.

During many of the sessions I focused on Bill's conviction that he was bad, deserved to be abused, and certainly did not deserve to be loved by Janet. I was empathic about his fear of changing this view of himself. I gently teased him about his incredible efforts to convince Janet and me that he truly was bad and I wondered what it would take for him to "gradually or suddenly" realize that he was a good kid who made bad choices because of the mixed-up thoughts and feelings that arose during his abuse. At times I would do something silly or unexpected and ask anxiously if that helped him to like himself better. Bill needed to believe, as did Janet, that he could and would make significant progress. The question was when.

Prior to the 30th session, Bill was being quite oppositional and Janet indicated to him that she needed some space because she was feeling some anger over his behavior. Bill watched her quietly for a while and then approached her, asking: "Are you feeling friendly toward me now?" Janet indicated that she was, and their relationship proceeded as before. He was sick for a few days that week. As before, he allowed Janet to nurture him when sick and he intensified his opposition to her when he felt better.

During the 30th session there was some evidence of positive movement in Bill's functioning. I explored his feelings of being close to Janet when sick. He acknowledged that he was scared of the feeling and that he needed to "push her away again" when he felt better. He then sat for a moment and added that he also was mad at himself for loving Janet because he feared that now his birth mother would be hurt. He said that he could not love two "moms" at the same time. Janet and I were speechless for a moment. Though we had spoken to Bill, each of us using similar phrases in the past, we had not spoken about this theme recently and Bill spoke with strong emotion.

The week after the 30th session, Bill's behavior was more cooperative. He also decided to ask his foster father, Gabe, whom he had always called "uncle," if he could call him "dad." Gabe agreed and Bill seemed to be happy and relieved. During this period Gabe's father, who had been seriously ill for quite some time, was dying. We discussed this and Bill was able to acknowledge that he was sad and that Gabe and Janet also were sad. Bill seemed to identify with the emotion felt by the other members of the family. We again referred to Bill learning that he could love two moms and that he could be happy in his foster home. We imagined Bill, at age 18, telling his birth mom that he loved both her and Janet. We imagined further how pleased his birth mom would be over Bill's ability to do this and to have a happy childhood with his family. During this session, when Janet held Bill, as she had done a number of times before, he demonstrated more relaxed fun and engagement than we had previously seen from him. I then suggested that Janet give him a "hard time," and they laughed even more as she teased and tickled him.

During the following week Bill found excuses to be aggressive with Janet, and he screamed that she did not love him. I suggested to him that he might be feeling afraid because he was closer to her the previous week. I also suggested that the family sorrow over "grampy" dying was hard for him and Janet and that it was difficult for him to seek support from her. As we talked Janet cried and Bill engaged her with sensitive interest. He indicated that her sorrow made him sad. I sat quietly with Bill and Janet as we processed the experiences that he shared with her.

At the 33rd session Bill told me that his "grampy" had died. Bill had been at his side shortly before his death and he had spoken to grampy with concern. Later he told Janet that he wanted to cry but no tears would come. He allowed Janet to support him and he did not have to follow this with oppositional behaviors! He would say that he wanted to cry about other events a number of times over the next several weeks.

Two weeks later, Bill went on a family trip and handled the excitement and changes very well. Once, after he misbehaved, he expressed genuine sadness and said, "I do something good and then I mess it up!" Two weeks after that, before the 37th session, Bill again hit Janet, but this time he showed some tears and later he said that he was sorry! Once, when Janet was giving Bill a bottle, he appeared to be sad. She asked him what was happening and he replied: "I can't be close to you and tell you or I'll get mad!" Janet showed empathy for his fear and sadness and he did not get mad. During the next session I drew a picture of Bill and included his mad, sad, and scared feelings within him, showing how he was beginning to integrate these feelings into his overall view of himself. I suggested that he might not have to consider this part of himself as being "bad" much longer.

Prior to the 38th session, Bill demonstrated further psychological development. Janet told me with excitement how Bill wanted to ride a camel at a local circus but he was initially afraid. But, he eventually got on, calmed his fears, developed a big smile, and, after getting off, ran to Janet for a hug while manifesting "pure joy." Janet had never before seen Bill feeling so good about himself and life.

Over the next few weeks, Bill demonstrated a number of other emotions that he had not before shown. He actually cried in response to disappointments, and he allowed Janet to comfort him. At times, when corrected, he pouted briefly, as would a younger child, and then he appeared ready to get over it. He accidentally cut himself, and rather than his past hysteria, he let Janet attend to it. He had less interest in getting the bottle, as if he was receiving enough nurturance in more age-appropriate ways. He told the truth over some poor choices and he accepted the consequences. On two occasions Janet had to leave Bill at another foster home for a short time while she left town to attend to important matters. When she called him, he cried briefly about missing her and when she came for him, he greeted her with joy and affection.

At this time I indicated that the stuffed bear, Little Bill, would be able to go to Bill's home with him if he thought that he could care for him. He was so proud and parental when he took his bear home with him. He brought the bear back with him in subsequent sessions to show me how well Little Bill was being cared for. At about this time, Bill began to notice how other parents interacted with their children when out in public. He was quick to notice the parents who were unfair and emotionally cruel to their children. At this time Bill decided to write his autobiography and to learn more about his past from the Department of Human Services.

Truly, Bill had changed much over the previous 10 months. His body sense was more calm and comfortable with close interactions with Janet. His affect was better defined and integrated. His behavior was much better regulated. His cognitive abilities showed remarkable insight into his inner life. Most important, he came to trust Janet and to proceed with joy and interest in his life within his secure attachment to her.

Bill's treatment was relevant also because of the fact that Janet was his foster mother, not his adopted mom. We taught him to come to trust Janet only to prepare him to move away from her into an adopted home! I must note that early in his treatment, when Bill was very oppositional to Janet, he resisted any thought of moving into an adopted home. When his relationship with her became much more secure, he began to accept the idea of moving into an adopted home! I believe that this change in Bill reflected his discovery of the nature of parent–child love, as well as his confidence that he was capable of engaging in such a relationship with adoptive parents. Surely tears were involved in considering the possibility of moving away from Janet. But Bill demonstrated a degree of psychological well-being sufficient to make this difficult transition successfully.

Three months after Bill wrote his letter to the Commissioner and one month after I completed this chapter, Janet and Gabe applied to adopt Bill. They had never before been able to make such a commitment to him because of both the intensity of his emotional and behavioral problems and also his weak attachment to them. However, for 6 months his behavior remained very stable. His attachment to Janet and Gabe was strong. They were aware that they faced difficult times with him in the future but they had confidence that he had attained both the inner resources and the meaningful attachment with them which were necessary to successfully continue his journey into adulthood.

It has been 1 year since I wrote this chapter. Bill continues to do very well and the adoption will be finalized soon. I see Bill and Janet every 2 months.

10

JENNY

When she was 6 years of age, Jenny's kindergarten teacher became very concerned about how frequently she would take food or pencils or other small objects from the other children. When caught, she appeared to be sorry and she readily gave the taken object back. However, it happened again and again. Her teacher called her mother and was told angrily that she would "take care of it." Jenny would never talk with her teacher about what her mother said or did. In general Jenny tended to be passive and fairly submissive with both her teacher and peers. She smiled a lot and "fit in" with the rest of the class. She also seemed to be becoming more sad and withdrawn.

Once, when caught with another child's snack, Jenny mentioned to her teacher that she did not have dinner the night before. Her parents had not been home and must have "forgot" that she had nothing to eat. When asked what time her parents had returned home, Jenny replied that it was sometime after she went to bed. She had been home alone that evening. Her teacher called the Department of Human Services and that day a caseworker went to Jenny's home.

Her teacher's phone call had not been the first referral made about Jenny. There had been eight referrals, beginning in her infancy, about circumstances of medical and physical neglect and physical abuse. Jenny's parents, Ben and Linda, generally would minimize the problems but then agree to participate in some services or meet Jenny's needs more adequately and the case would be closed. On this most recent occasion, Jenny's parents were drunk when the caseworker came to their home. After they screamed at the caseworker to leave, she returned with the police and Jenny went to Cindy's foster home to live.

Cindy noted from the first day how easily Jenny adjusted to living in her new home. She called Cindy "mom" immediately, was quick to please, wanted a lot of attention, and presented many fewer behavioral problems than did Cindy's other three foster children. Jenny was referred to a therapist because of her history and her "lack of much feeling," and she was seen for about a year. Her treatment was unremarkable. She was described as being engaging, "probably too friendly," and unimaginative in her play. Nothing seemed to bother her about her past nor did she seem concerned about her future. After her treatment was discontinued, Cindy noted that Jenny continued to take things from the other children and hide the objects in her room. Jenny also seemed to be excessively friendly to neighbors and acquaintances and she could not "amuse" herself. She did not do any chores unless she was being supervised.

Jenny had to move to another foster home when she was 7½ years of age. Although her parents had made no progress toward reunification, she still visited with them one or two times each month. The Department of Human Services began to consider petitioning the court to cease efforts to reunify her with her parents and free her for adoption.

Her new foster mother, Susan, also noted that Jenny called her "mom" from the first hour in her home. Jenny appeared to have forgotten Cindy immediately even though she had lived with her for 18 months. Susan noted that Jenny wanted to be near her all the time and generally Jenny seemed to be content to sit passively and amuse herself with repetitive activities as long as she was not alone. She was quite content with a sitter when Susan had to leave the home and she was not disturbed at all by having to stay a few days in a respite home. Any caregiver would do, as long as the person was physically near.

Susan lived with her husband, Richard, and their 13-year-old birth daughter, Allison. She had been a foster parent for 7 years although she had no other foster children at that time. Susan's mother had "taken in" foster children and she felt that since she and her family had a good life, they should be willing to help children in need.

Over the first few months of Jenny's placement Susan became increasingly concerned about her for numerous reasons. She said that Jenny hoarded things in her room, lied when she did something wrong, showed no initiative, and manifested few interests. When she corrected her for something that she had done wrong, Jenny would seem to be sorry but then would do the same thing 30 minutes later. She did not seem to know how to relate to her peers, and she appeared to be the most comfortable with preschool children. She never talked about her own thoughts or feelings. Susan said that she did not feel that she knew Jenny at all and did not think that she really meant anything to Jenny. When Susan first spoke with me about her, she said, "She could move tomorrow and not care at all." This was after 4 months of living in her home.

I was asked to evaluate Jenny when she was almost 8 years old. Her parents, Ben and Linda, had decided not to contest having their parental rights terminated, and I was asked to comment on Jenny's readiness to form an attachment to prospective adoptive parents. After meeting with her and talking with Susan, it was my strong opinion that Jenny manifested a Reactive Attachment Disorder with a lack of any "selective attachments." Jenny was content with anyone. During my first meeting with her I was convinced that if Susan and I were to tell her that she was going to my home to live, she would have smiled and consented.

Just as she did not show a readiness for a selective attachment, she also did not manifest any cohesive sense of self. When with someone, she constantly sought direction and approval for her behavior, becoming what she thought the other person wanted her to be. She seemed to lack her own thoughts or feelings about events and, when alone, she had no sense of self to direct her activities. She did not appear to be particularly sad or anxious. She just seemed to be "empty" inside. Jenny made a favorable first impression. She would be an easy child to place for adoption but the stability of the adoption would be questionable.

I was asked to provide treatment for Jenny. I consented when the Department of Human Services agreed not to try to place her for adoption for at least 1 year. Before meeting with her for the first session I met with Susan to develop our treatment plan.

Jenny was fortunate in that she had a good foster mother who was committed to helping her and who had no other young children and no other foster children. Jenny would require a great amount of time and energy. She must have had very few experiences of emotional attunement during her infancy. Reciprocal enjoyment with a caregiver had been seldom felt. Jenny showed little energy for trying to understand and express what she thought and felt since her inner life had been of no interest to her parents and had not reduced her years of isolation and neglect. I assumed that because of the severity of her neglect, when she did get an adult's attention, her entire motivation was to do what she had to do to please the adult at that moment. Rarely had she ever felt special to someone and she had not had many socialization experiences offered with patience and empathy.

We could not expect her to have the inner resources of an 8-year-old child. If we expected her to have self-direction and age-appropriate judgment, she would constantly fail to meet our expectations. Behavioral modification would only work if she were being supervised and when supervised there would be no need for it. Expecting her to feel empathy for others, have wishes, and express her "feelings" would only create bewilderment when she sensed that she was disappointing her caregiver but had no idea of what to do about it.

Jenny needed much more than I could provide for her in my office. Traditional therapy is most successful in helping a child to resolve past traumas and inner conflicts and to find ways to express a troubled and confused inner life. The therapy that I employ in working with the child who has difficulty forming an attachment requires that the child live in a home which can be "therapeutic" hour after hour, day after day. Such a home is even more crucial for a child like Jenny who, rather than being insecure, anxious, and ambivalent in her attachment, is unable to experience any difference between an attachment and a relationship with any kindly adult.

Susan and I discussed the need for Jenny to have available to her the quantity and quality of interactions with Susan that one would expect if Jenny were 2 or 3 years of age. Susan easily remembered the emotional attunement that she had with her daughter when Allison was an infant and toddler. She described their playful and deeply meaningful daily interactions. She also recalled the amount of supervision and moment to moment socialization experiences that she provided for Allison. I asked her to provide a smaller range of experiences for Jenny. She wondered if Jenny might be self-conscious or feel that she was being treated like a "baby" if she engaged her in that manner and to that degree. It was my guess that Jenny would initially relish that degree of contact with her and that when she began to resent it, her resentment would be a sign of progress. I stressed the need to present it to her in a positive and matter-of-fact manner. Susan tentatively agreed to make this commitment although she first wanted to discuss it with her husband and daughter.

In a second meeting with Susan, I spoke with her about choices and consequences, discipline with empathy, and reciprocal enjoyment. We discussed the value of giving Jenny's teacher a general view of our impending work with Jenny and eliciting the teacher's aid by asking her to not emphasize independent work and homework. I also alerted Susan to the possibility of criticism from friends or relatives. Apart from school hours, Jenny would be with her almost constantly. Susan would not be likely to feel any moments of "connection" with her for months. This would be a difficult year for Susan, harder than Allison's infancy. It would be hard for Richard and Allison as well.

In the first session with Susan and Jenny together, I described for Jenny the work that would follow as well as the reasons for it. I knew that Jenny would comply with whatever we did, but it was important to give her a cognitive skeleton upon which she could organize her new experiences. She would hear the same concepts many times in the months ahead. We hoped that someday the words would have real meaning to her. I gently spoke to her about how important it is for an infant and toddler to feel special to her mom. A baby feels special by being held, rocked, touched, played with and fed. When she cries, she feels special when her mom takes care of whatever she was crying about. When she gets older and doesn't know what's best to do, she feels special when her mom shows her what to do without yelling at her. I told her that we knew that her mom and dad had not made her feel special very often. As a result, she did not often know what she wanted, thought or felt. She did not feel special and did not believe that she was special to Susan.

I told Jenny to look at Susan and tell her that she needed to learn to feel special to her. She did this, if only to please me. I told her to ask Susan if she would help her to feel special to her. This was harder for Jenny to do since asking for anything was difficult for her. She did what I asked and Susan replied, "I sure will, Jenny," and briefly hugged her. Susan and I then told her what they would be doing together. We talked of playing together, going for walks, cooking, and making things. We talked of Susan being with her a lot to tell her what were the best choices for her to make, since right now it was so hard for her to know what was best for herself. This would help her cut down on stealing things, not finishing chores, and lying. We told her that as she felt more special and learned to make better choices, she would have many chances to do things on her own. We asked Jenny if she agreed with our plan and, predictably, she did.

With obvious pleasure Susan said "Let's start now." She told her that she had always wanted to see how Jenny looked with her hair combed differently. She sat near her and began combing Jenny's hair while I held a small mirror so that Jenny could watch. Susan fixed Jenny's hair a few different ways; each time Susan showed her excitement. Susan finally decided that she liked it best one way and suggested that Jenny wear it that way the rest of the day. Jenny's delight in the activity was spontaneous and strong. There was no doubt that she enjoyed having Susan fuss over her hair. It was also clear that she also liked her hair the way Susan had it, although it was obvious that her preference was based entirely on Susan's. I then chose a book for Susan to read to her: *I Love You as Much.* Jenny sat quietly, looking intently at the pictures and smiled broadly when Susan gave her a hug.

For the next several sessions, I followed a similar pattern. We would talk briefly and I would review with them some of their activities. Jenny could not spontaneously recall much from their daily life but she was quick to remember incidents that Susan recalled. Susan communicated a good deal of pleasure in recalling their time together and Jenny showed a similar level of enthusiasm. I had Jenny express certain realities to Susan. For example, Jenny had managed to steal some of Susan's clothing and kitchen supplies despite the supervision. I told her to tell Susan that it was hard to stop taking things, that it was hard to ask for things, that she really did need to learn to make better choices, and that she wanted Susan's help to do so. After she complied, I told her that she must really be wanting something of Susan's to keep in her bedroom at night when she was alone. I expressed pleasure in her wish since it reflected that a small part of her was beginning to want to feel special to Susan. Susan agreed. I told Jenny to ask her to give Jenny something of Susan's to keep in her bedroom. Susan agreed to give her something but would not tell her what it was since she wanted it to be "special." That night Susan gave her a sweater which Jenny kept under her pillow. Her stealing was reduced but did not stop entirely until her anger emerged several months later.

The first crisis in our early work happened during the sixth week. Jenny became enuretic, wetting at night and periodically during the day. Generally she wet in her pants but on some occasions she urinated in a corner of her bedroom. Susan was finding it hard to remain nonjudgmental about this. We explored the behavior as reflecting Jenny's regression and Susan was generally more able to deal with it calmly. Jenny simply cleaned herself and helped to clean the sheets, rug, and clothes. However, the behavior increased in frequency.

One day Jenny asked if she could wear a diaper after school until the next morning! After considerable thought, discussion, and consultation with her caseworker, we bought diapers for her. This was one of Jenny's few requests and it had merit for that reason alone. She did not seem to feel humiliated by it and we told her that we would try it and she should tell us if she changed her mind. Jenny easily accepted diapers. She calmly told Susan whenever she was wet and she was directed to wash herself and change it. She seemed to be pleased with this arrangement. She may well have been testing us to see how serious we were about allowing her to feel like a very young child.

Jenny's daily routine began with Susan awakening her by sitting on the side of her bed, talking quietly while rubbing her back, and stroking her hair. She told Jenny what was for breakfast and she laid out her clothes for school. As Jenny dressed, Susan prepared breakfast, ate with her, and told her what she would be doing while Jenny was at school. She also told her what they would do first when Jenny returned home. She then waited with her for the school bus and gave her a brief hug as the bus was approaching.

After school Susan gave her a snack and talked with her about each other's day as she ate. Jenny changed into the clothes that were chosen for her and they played an activity such as working together on a craft, drawing, or putting together a puzzle. Sometimes they would hide things that the other would search for, practice a song to sing for Richard and Allison or me, or play word games. After their "fun" time, Jenny helped Susan with some chores and preparing dinner. As they ate dinner they would tell the rest of the family what they had done together. After dinner Allison and Jenny did the dishes while Susan and Richard relaxed. The four of them would do something together briefly and then Susan was on her own again with Jenny until bedtime. Susan had a very consistent bedtime routine for Jenny that included Susan reading or telling a story and quietly singing to her in a rocking chair. She would tuck Jenny in, talk quietly to her about that day and the next, and end the day with, "I was happy being with you today, Jenny-Penny." Jenny always replied, "Me, too, mommy."

These days were full with a great deal of attention focused on Jenny. Susan made almost all of the choices for her initially, from what she had for a snack to what she read at night. Jenny depended on Susan's judgment, attention, emotional tone, and direction for almost all of her waking moments outside of school.

Susan had noted that often Jenny had difficulty establishing eye contact with her for more than a few seconds. I told Jenny that we understood how she felt nervous with eye contact because she did not experience it often during her first few years of life. I indicated that having eye contact with Susan would help her to feel closer to her. I asked Susan if she would quietly remind Jenny to keep practicing to maintain her eye contact a little longer each day by holding her hand and gently squeezing it when she wanted her to look at her a little longer. Susan agreed to do this and they practiced during the session with Jenny laughing with mild anxiety.

By the tenth session I decided that Jenny might be ready to tolerate mild conflict with Susan and me so I told her to tell Susan that she did not want Susan to pick her breakfast anymore. "Tell her you'd rather pick it yourself!" Jenny said that she liked Susan picking her breakfast. I told her to say it anyway. Jenny became somewhat anxious and again said that she wanted Susan to pick her breakfast. I told Jenny to look at me and tell me that she did not want to do what I told her to do. She did what I told her, but very quietly, and I told her to say it again, but louder. She again said it quietly. I sat closer to her again told her to say it louder. She became more anxious and looked to Susan for assistance. Susan calmly told her to tell me loudly that she did not want to say what I told her to say. She turned to me, smiled, and yelled that she didn't want to do it. I told her that she did a good job and told her to say it again loudly, this time without smiling. She looked at Susan and, with Susan's encouragement, was able to do it. We both acknowledged how hard that sequence was for Jenny. We told her that she just did not have much practice telling others that she disagreed with them. I suggested that if she had told Ben and Linda that she did not want to do something that they had told her to do, they might have screamed at her and hit her. She agreed with me and appeared to be comfortable with the discussion.

Over the next five sessions we worked on Jenny's relationships with Ben and Linda. I drew pictures of them and hung them from my desk. I would tell Jenny something from her file regarding abuse and neglect and encourage Jenny to tell the drawings of Ben and Linda what she thought and felt about how they raised her. Jenny volunteered nothing so I gave her brief sentences to say, such as:

"You should have taken me to the doctor; I was very sick."
"I was very scared when you left me alone. Why did you do that?"
"Why did you spank me when I peed on the floor? I was very little."
"I'm sad that you didn't take better care of me."
"I'm mad at you for yelling at me and hitting me."
"Why didn't you want to play with me?"

Jenny generally complied and, whatever I directed her to say, she said, in a quiet and tentative voice. I did not challenge either what she said or how she said it. I also spoke to the drawings of Ben and Linda, expressing greater emotion than Jenny was able to do. She sat quietly with Susan while I did this. Once, I asked Susan to hold Jenny while Susan spoke to Ben and Linda about how they had raised Jenny. Susan began to cry as she spoke about how much Ben and Linda had hurt Jenny. Jenny looked at Susan with big eyes, showed a few tears, and then snuggled closely. I sat quietly as Susan rocked her and quietly said, "My Jenny-Penny."

During the 16th session I suggested that we review what Jenny had accomplished over the past 4 months. Susan and I stressed how well she was letting herself trust Susan to make choices for her. We recognized how she was following the rules better and lying less, without mentioning that she had little time on her own during which she could break the rules easily. Susan recounted the various things that Jenny had learned during their daily activities and mentioned how much fun they were having together and how they had come to love each other "a lot." I indicated that Jenny was doing well in telling "Ben and Linda" and me what she thought and felt, acknowledging how hard it was for her to tell people when she disagreed or was angry with them. We concluded this session with my making them both ice cream sundaes to recognize how much they had both done during the past 4 months. Jenny seemed to be very pleased with our enjoyment of her work and our affirmation of her relationship with Susan.

By coincidence or fate, 2 weeks after our celebration, Susan was sick for a few days and Jenny regressed. While Susan was in bed, Jenny took food and objects into her bedroom again. Richard tried to give Jenny things to do, but the moment she was unsupervised, she stopped doing what she had been told and did what she was not allowed to do, for example, watch TV, use craft supplies, and play with Allison's plastic horse collection. She cut some mail with the scissors and she "lost" a horse.

In the 19th session we reviewed the changes at home during the time that Susan was sick. Jenny would not say what she thought and felt during that time, so I directed her to say the following and she complied: "I was sad when you were sick. I missed being with you. I worried about you. I wanted you to get better. I was mad that you couldn't be with me." When she said that she was "mad," she became quiet and tense. I told her that she did well to tell Susan what she felt. Susan agreed, and she validated Jenny's feelings, including Jenny's anger at not having Susan with her. Susan also commented that she noticed that when she was feeling better,

Jenny seemed to be more distant. She did not laugh as much or seem to have the same enjoyment of activities with Susan. I suggested that Jenny may have wanted Susan to be aware of how upset she really was over her absence from their routine. Susan agreed and commented that one day Jenny would be able to tell her with words what she thought and felt more easily.

Susan and I anticipated that by supporting Jenny's experience of abandonment during Susan's illness, Jenny would resume her cheerful and compliant acceptance of their very structured and nurturing routine. However, this was not the case. Jenny's regressed and mildly oppositional behaviors continued. At the slightest opportunity she would do something without permission, seemingly to irritate. In school, Jenny did not appear to be oppositional but her teacher did say that she was more distractable and less motivated to do her work than usual. Susan and I thought that Jenny's behavior might reflect continuing anger over the disruption in their routine. We hoped that it also might represent a new stage in her treatment in which oppositional behaviors reflected a further development of "self."

At home Susan adopted a response to Jenny's behavior in which she acknowledged Jenny's choice to do something that she was not supposed to do and then gave her a mild consequence for the behavior. She was empathic about Jenny's desire to decide what she would do by herself and for her anger at the consequences for breaking the rule. Susan continued the usual routine, generally maintaining her friendly and accepting emotional tone. Even so, Jenny's oppositional behaviors increased. At times she would refuse to eat her breakfast and dress herself. Susan accepted her decision not to eat and she dressed Jenny so that she could go to school on time. Jenny sat passively as she allowed herself to be dressed.

During the second month of her oppositional behaviors, she finally told Susan that she did not want cereal and orange juice for breakfast, she wanted pancakes. Susan expressed pleasure that Jenny had told her what she wanted and indicated that she would consider her request for the next day's meal. Jenny chose not to eat her usual breakfast again. Susan called me to get ideas for the next day's breakfast. I indicated that while Jenny's verbalized wish was an important step in self-expression, her refusal to accept Susan's decision and eat the cereal was an act of defiance. I suggested that Jenny needed to know that expressing her wish did not mean that Susan would always grant it. It was not Jenny's role to decide when to change the routine. We wanted Jenny to tell Susan what she wanted and then Susan would decide what choices to give Jenny and when to do it. Jenny going from being totally submissive to being the "boss" would not help her development.

The next day, Jenny became even more angry with Susan for giving her cereal for breakfast. Susan expressed empathy for Jenny's wishes and she congratulated her for beginning to express herself. Jenny threw the cereal on the floor. Susan directed her to clean it up but she refused. When she returned from school Jenny had another chore waiting for her and, although annoyed, she did comply and did it.

In therapy the next day, I congratulated Jenny on discovering that she did have feelings and wishes and that she could express them without losing Susan's love for her. Jenny appeared to be frightened and withdrawn. I directed her to tell Susan that she was tired of Susan making all of the choices for her. She became agitated and screamed "No!" at me but would not express her anger toward Susan. I directed Susan to support her increasing ability to express her wishes at home. Susan did so but Jenny did not respond. Susan and I then assured Jenny that if she needed to continue to be oppositional at home, we would support her. However, Jenny would most likely have consequences for not following the rules because it was Susan's job as her mother to provide her with the appropriate consequences for both her good and her poor choices. Susan communicated empathy for how hard it was for Jenny now and hugged her. Jenny remained passive, although she was tearful.

Between sessions 30 and 45, Jenny struggled at home and in therapy with intense, sudden, volatile emotional expression. She would move rapidly from screaming to crying to withdrawal to arguing. Susan and I spoke frequently of our excitement over how seemingly real Jenny's expressions consistently were. Nevertheless, we were not seeing the emotions of an 8-year-old girl. Jenny reminded us of a 3-year-old at the height of her tantrums. She did not know what she wanted or felt but she knew that she was unhappy and she wanted all of us to know it. Susan was remarkable in her ability to communicate patience and understanding while remaining clear and firm with Jenny that her outbursts would not lead to submission by Susan. Neither Jenny's emotions nor her progress entitled her to be spared the consequences of her acts. To move into the next stage of the development and integration of her self, she needed to have these "socialization" experiences which did not humiliate or reject her.

During the therapy sessions I carefully but persistently worked to have Jenny express her ambivalence toward Susan. It was my judgment that if she could express herself verbally, she would be able to achieve a level of integration that would lead to a more stable and less volatile degree of functioning. I now had photographs of Ben and Linda that I used to encourage Jenny to express her rage at for the countless ways that Ben and Linda had not adequately cared for her, thus causing terrible pain and damage to her development. Jenny was able to direct her rage at the pictures more easily than at people who were physically present. During the 43rd session I directed her to tell them that because she could not trust them, she now had a very hard time being able to trust Susan. I directed her to tell Susan the same thing. Susan held her hands and Jenny was able to maintain eye contact and tell her that she wanted to trust her but she had a very hard time doing it. Susan simply replied that she would wait and Jenny fell into her arms and cried deeply.

Over the next 15 weeks, Susan and I noted a degree of consolidation in Jenny's functioning in all areas that always formed the basis of my confidence that a child has truly made sufficient internal progress to be able to achieve a secure attachment and a positive integration of the self. Jenny's anger outbursts decreased in frequency and intensity. They were more predictable and, although not yet age-appropriate, they were moving in that direction. She often expressed happiness over her life in a way that was contagious to all she encountered. She became emotionally more available to Susan, expressing her sadness and asking for help as well as expressing her love and seeking physical contact. She still liked to be with Susan but she also sometimes showed a desire to sit alone and play with her toys or read. She was now much less passive. She had her pancakes often since she asked for them frequently, but she was more able to accept those times when Susan said "no." One day she announced that she really did not want to wear a diaper anymore and she stopped, successfully. She often experimented with talking about her thoughts and feelings, observing and then commenting on routine situations as if they were new. Although she was often confused and easily hurt in her peer relationships, she nevertheless had developed an interest in her peers that suggested that she had only recently noticed them.

Jenny still lacked self-confidence. She often turned to Susan for a degree of reassurance that other 9-year-old girls do not need. She wanted to please Susan a great deal and she was clearly anxious when she expressed anger toward Susan. At times Jenny would withdraw and sit passively. Susan would initiate interaction with her at those times and would eventually begin to respond. We did not think that Jenny had developed the ability yet to comfort herself and regain her momentum without Susan's intervention.

As I have indicated, Susan's empathy and patience were necessary for Jenny's progress. Now that there were significant gains, Susan relaxed somewhat and at times was irritable with Jenny. This caused a short regression that may well have continued were it not for Susan's awareness of what had occurred. Susan was able to immediately reengage with Jenny and regain her trust. We discussed this in therapy and framed it for Jenny as being a sign of the strength of their relationship and an experience that would make it even stronger. Jenny laughed and hoped that it would soon be strong enough.

After about 15 months of treatment, Susan and I met with Jenny's caseworker and reviewed Jenny's considerable progress. Her caseworker thought that she should begin to work with Jenny on adoption. Susan anxiously said that she and Richard had talked about this and decided they wanted to adopt her. Susan indicated that she had not planned to adopt Jenny when she began to work with her, but now she could not imagine anything else. Susan said that the first 5 years of Allison's life was the only thing that she could compare with her involvement with Jenny over the past 15 months. Raising Jenny so far had been a high speed roller coaster ride. She was ready to ride on the merry-go-round with her.

A year after Susan requested to adopt her, Jenny's functioning became even more stable and her progress became taken for granted. She slipped briefly in one direction or another but she always immediately responded to Susan's direction and support. We became confident that she would do well as a member of her adoptive family and as a person in her own right.

Jenny's treatment did have the quality of being on a roller coaster ride. During her initial months of treatment, she absorbed the nurturing and affective attunement provided by Susan so intensely that it seemed that she would never get enough. Then, in the space of one week, Jenny had had enough and she began demonstrating primitive affect—rage, sadness, and fear—in an unpredictable and volatile manner. This lasted for months also until, just as suddenly, she seemed to find a way to reestablish a relationship with Susan that was more integrated and moderate. She appeared to discover a way to experience her ambivalence toward Susan that she could tolerate and gradually accept. She also seemed to be aware of who she was and of what she thought and felt.

Susan's daily interactions with Jenny over the first 10 months of Jenny's treatment were by far the most important reason for Jenny's development. Susan provided her with countless hours of early childhood, mother–daughter experiences through which Jenny was able to discover herself and the meaning of attachment. If Susan had not had that degree of time, parenting skills, and commitment, I am convinced that Jenny's progress would have been much less. Susan was a good parent for Jenny, yet I do not believe that Susan had remarkable or exceptional parenting skills. Rather she had a profound commitment to helping Jenny. She wanted to make a major difference in Jenny's life and so she was willing to place considerable demands on herself to achieve this goal.

My central role was to provide guidance and support for Susan. I also affirmed their relationship for Jenny and I assisted Jenny in becoming more able to accept the rage that emerged from the terrible abuse and neglect in her life and which found expression in her increasingly meaningful relationship with Susan.

One might say that the case of Jenny and Susan is not realistic because most foster children are not placed in homes that can provide them with such a high level of parental care. The reality is that many foster children who have psychological problems as severe as Jenny's will neither heal nor find their healthy developmental path without such a home. For these children our first obligation as professionals and as a society is to provide them with the opportunity to have an attachment with a "Susan." No other therapeutic or enrichment experiences will suffice. I am convinced that there are many "Susans" in every community who would be willing to take on the difficult task of enabling children like Jenny to learn to attach and to develop their autonomy. They need our specialized knowledge and our continuing support. Most of all they need to realize how much children like Jenny need them and how remarkably these children can benefit from their daily care.

11

PRINCIPLES OF
PARENTING

Just as there are basic principles for providing psychotherapy for the poorly attached child, so, too, are there principles for parenting him. What might be "Good-Enough Parenting" for many children is often insufficient for him. The poorly attached child has developmental gaps and deficiencies which resist spontaneous change. He perceives abuse and rejection when none is there. He thinks about and expects the worst from his new parents and from himself. He does not know how to relax with, enjoy, and rely on, his parents. Mutual enjoyment is replaced by opposition and isolation.

Parents of these children certainly need a great deal of understanding and support from the professionals who want to aid them. Since their poorly attached child has probably charmed most of their friends and relatives, the parents often receive insufficient understanding and support from friends and relatives and are criticized for being too strict. It is hoped that professionals will not give the parents similar responses. Beyond understanding and support, these parents need information about their child and about ways to intervene with him. They need a broad understanding of him and general principles for facilitating their child's attachment. Building on that foundation, they need specific suggestions regarding ways to interact with him in various circumstances and they need ongoing empathy for how hard the task is. Assuming that they are capable parents, they need to increase and develop confidence in their abilities if they are to be the *very* capable parents that their poorly attached child needs.

This chapter attempts to provide a framework for parenting these children. The next chapter will attempt to provide more specific interventions and situations. While these concepts and specific strategies have been developed from many sources over the years, I am most indebted to the skills developed and demonstrated in the therapeutic homes associated with The Attachment Center in Evergreen, Colorado.

FAMILY ATMOSPHERE AND INTERACTIONS

The central component of effective interventions to facilitate attachment in these children lies in the child's current home. Months and months of living within a safe and nurturing home are critical if the child is to have a realistic chance of making the profound changes needed to begin to live in a healthy manner. Excellent "60 minute" therapy cannot suffice when a child is living in a marginal home.

The child needs a home whose atmosphere is one of mutual enjoyment and respect, diverse interests and opportunities to develop, and clear, calm, firm expectations for the child's behavior. If the home is characterized by habitual anger, tension, and discouragement, then it will too closely resemble the original abusive home, and the child will be unable to make the differentiation needed for psychological change. The anger in the home will resemble rage and it will elicit rage, the tension will elicit general anxiety, guardedness and possible terror, and the discouragement will elicit pessimism and lack of hope for a new life. Usually the abusive home was not characterized by isolated traumatic acts, rather those traumatic acts were embedded in an atmosphere of hostility, defensiveness, selfish isolation, and fear. The new home must be remarkably different if the child is to become different. It is not simply acts of love, excitement, and enjoyment that enable the child to recover from past traumas and form an attachment. It is the habitual atmosphere that is most responsible for change. Note Figure 1, in which the necessary contrast between the abusive home and the new home is shown. The abusive home was the context for various abusive experiences (-), be they emotional, physical, and/or sexual. The atmosphere (significant tension, rage, isolation, and fear) in which these activities were embedded was often at least as destructive to the child's ability to form positive attachments to his caregivers as were the specific events themselves. In the same manner, isolated activities (+), no matter how positive, either at home or in therapy, will not by themselves facilitate significant change in the child. He needs an ongoing atmosphere (relaxed empathy, sharing, fun, and predictable security) that facilitates attachment. The parent needs a similar atmosphere to bond with her child. The parent needs, at all costs, to protect such an atmosphere from the compulsive, oppositional, or destructive behaviors of the child.

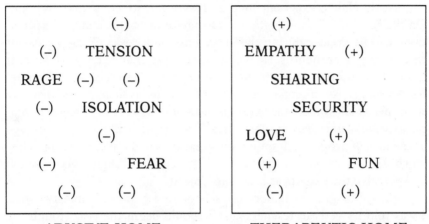

ABUSIVE HOME   THERAPEUTIC HOME

Figure 1. Contrasts between Abusive and Therapeutic Homes.

Parents need to have a clear idea of the type of family atmosphere that they want for themselves and for their children. They need to be fairly successful in maintaining this way of family living in day-to-day life before they should consider bringing a child with significant needs for psychological change into their home. The first goal when the child enters their home is to protect their atmosphere from the child's numerous efforts to change the family atmosphere to correspond to his own emotional life and to the atmosphere that he experienced in the abusive home. When the family atmosphere changes in significant ways to resemble the child rather than the child changing in significant ways to resemble the new family, the probability that the child will make significant internal changes is greatly reduced. When the family becomes more tense and less relaxed, more self-involved and less cooperative, the child is not likely to change. When the family has more repetitive conflicts and less laughter, more TV and less reciprocal interaction, the child is not likely to change. Also, if the family atmosphere in which the parents are the most comfortable and feel the most alive and "at home" is seen to be slipping away because of the pervasive influence of this child, the parents' commitment to the child will eventually decrease and the placement of the child in that home will be in jeopardy.

Clearly, if the poorly attached child is to make a healthy attachment to his new family, the child, not the parents, must make the most significant psychological changes. This reality must be made clear to the child with patience but with firmness and clear purpose. Parents must not "bend the rules" and lower their expectations for appropriate behavior in their home because the child is experiencing the stress of adjustment to his new home. On the contrary, his motivation to change to meet this family's expectations will be greater during the initial days and weeks of the placement than during later months. He will often work to change only insofar as it is firmly expected. If this child is seen to be "different" and "fragile" because of his past traumas and current stress and is then treated that way with special allowances made for his behavior, he will not change spontaneously and voluntarily at a later date. The parents will then feel betrayed at the lack of progress, despite their great love and understanding. They will become impatient and frustrated. Their child will experience rejection and perceive the parents as becoming "mean."

When I taught at a junior high school for a year in my mid-twenties, I was told by veteran teachers that I should begin the year "tough" by holding the students to high standards of academic and behavioral performance. I might later relax and allow myself to become somewhat "soft." In my youth, especially after having read Carl Rogers, I concluded that such advice was not necessary for me. I would engage the students with empathy and interest and so win their cooperation. I was foolish, and my year of teaching was not a success for me nor for many of my students. This advice holds just as well for new foster and adoptive parents. If they want to preserve their way of life in their home, which necessarily must be a better way of life than the child experienced in his abusive home, then they must not be ambiguous in making known to the child what is expected. He needs to learn quickly that it is in his best interest to change his functioning to meet the expectations of his parents. He needs to learn that it is not in his best interest and is obviously a waste of time to manipulate and tantrum in order to change his parents and the family atmosphere. Again, I must stress that the child will not change spontaneously; the child will change when it is the only viable choice.

While this advice may sound harsh to some parents and professionals, it is nevertheless valid and critically important. In my judgment, many placements have been greatly hindered and even lost in the first few months when the child was able to successfully bring his past way of functioning into his new home. The parents eventually discover that their family has changed—and not for the better—yet the child did not change. The parents say that they tried so much but that the child never seemed to "try." They conclude that the child will not or cannot change. Yet their expectations that he change were unclear, lacked conviction, and were inconsistent because of a desire to "go easy" initially to communicate "unconditional love" and to help him to adjust. They hoped that the initial resistant behaviors represented "testing behavior" and would decrease once the child trusted them. They did not see that these initial behaviors represented the child's early characterological adjustments to an abusive home and were now basic to his way of life. The child will not cheerfully give that up.

While working with one child and his preadoptive parents, the early progress was slow and there was some risk to the placement. I concluded one session by telling the parents that if they were uncertain how to respond to the child's misbehavior, they should err by being too strict rather than by being too lenient. The child quickly demonstrated more rapid progress and the parents had greater confidence in themselves and the stability of the placement. This was by no means the central therapeutic intervention but it was a critical piece of the comprehensive effort.

Being firm, and consistent does not imply that one needs to be harsh, critical, complaining, and negative. In fact, these latter qualities will undermine the success of the interventions. To be effective, the discipline of these children must be relaxed, engaging, matter-of-fact, and instructive. Discipline must reflect the overriding family atmosphere of mutual enjoyment and respect. Often parents think that to be firm one must be intense, quite serious, and at least mildly annoyed. On the contrary, one can be very firm while at the same time being supportive and empathic. In fact, the child is often able to better accept discipline when it contains these traits because he is less likely to see it as being mean and rejecting. A child is usually going to respond better to "Missing that TV show is going to be hard for you" than they are to "Turn off that TV!" as a consequence for misbehavior. I once gave this suggestion to an adoptive father and he complained that his kids would ignore him if he sounded like "Mr. Rogers." He agreed to try it for one week and he returned saying that to his surprise his children were bewildered at first but were clearly much more responsive.

Habitually showing mild annoyance in response to misbehavior elicits annoyance on the part of the child that is separate from his actual response to the discipline itself. This mutual annoyance interferes with the family atmosphere and becomes evidence to the child that he is disliked and that either he or the parent or both are "bad." Much better is a statement like the following: "You didn't put away the toys as we agreed. You're probably angry that you can't play with Billy now because you have to pick them all up. Maybe you'll remember next time." Such a statement, given in a matter-of-fact tone and with quiet empathy, can be quite effective in maintaining an atmosphere of mutual respect without compromising expectations or communicating rejection of the child. The child remains accepted, his distress over a consequence is given empathy, and the attachment is strengthened, not weakened.

Discipline is stressed initially because it serves as a basis for motivating a child with weak attachments to begin the difficult process of forming attachments. Discipline, given with empathy, can be more effective in the beginning stages of a developing attachment than signs of affection. When the child shows what to him is his "bad" side and the parent responds with clear consequences for the behavior, respect for the choice that led to the behavior, and empathy for his feelings about the consequences, he begins to sense a commitment on the parent's part to the whole child, not just to the manipulative "good" child. He begins to sense that the parent is competent and able to deal effectively with his behaviors. He notices that the parent is relaxed and undaunted by the behavior; only he, himself, is inconvenienced by the consequence of the behavior. He will begin to feel anxious over his inability to control the parents and the atmosphere of the home and he will begin to have an awareness that he may have to change to have a better life for himself. Slowly, he will begin to want to change.

Families who are able to facilitate attachment in the child do so also by offering a great deal of nurturance. It is fairly easy to provide nurturance to the child who is seeking affection appropriately or who is showing his vulnerability and following the rules. Providing nurturance to the child who is showing hostility and defiance is another matter. Nurturing the child who seems to "give nothing back" is a challenge. Providing nurturance when he does not seem to want to be a part of the family is very difficult, especially during the fifth month, and the fifteenth, and so forth. At those times, the parents are providing nurturance when they respond to his hostility with empathy rather than hostility. Nurturance means dealing with the child's rejection by not taking it personally, rather seeing it as his problem and burden. Nurturance means teaching the child hundreds of times how to ask for help, how to live with the consequences of one's choices, how to learn to trust someone who has the power to abuse but will never do so, and how to begin to feel intensely the range of emotions that occur within a healthy family.

Parents are not saints. At times they, too, become angry, defensive, and self-absorbed. Parents are not robots. That's the way life is and the child will cope and become stronger when he learns to accept that fact. He eventually will be able to do so if the *habitual* way that the parent responds is with the empathy, patience, and persistent consistency that is in the child's best interest. Actually, periodic anger and failure to respond to the child's wishes, done so with knowledge and intent, may be very therapeutic.

ATTUNEMENT AND EMPATHY

A new child needs attunement and empathy to become able to attach. This is true for the baby and this is true for the 12-year-old entering his adoptive home. Without attunement and empathy, the child will not experience a union with a new parent. Nor will he be free to experience mutual enjoyment. Nor will he feel understood. Nor will he realize that behavioral consequences are not punitive. Nor will he come to accept routine frustrations. And finally, the child will not discover his parents' love for him and, in fact, will not discover the meaning of love. The sense of autonomy that he does form will itself lack empathy for others.

In earlier chapters the central role of attunement and empathy in both the mother–infant dance and in psychotherapy was described. Affective attunement creates the felt union and guides the reciprocal movements of the mother and infant from moment to moment, day to day. The child in his new home relies on the parents' attunement and empathy to begin to feel that he is special to them. Empathy helps him to experience discipline rather than as abuse or rejection. He can tolerate shame and integrate the experience rather than responding with rage. Empathy helps him to have greater access to his inner life of thought and emotion and helps him to share his inner life with his parents. In this way, an attachment comes alive and begins to flourish.

In creating an affective attunement with her child, the parent matches the affect that he expresses in his behavior with complementary expressions of her own. When his behaviors demonstrate affects through their intensity, duration and shape, she matches his affect with complementary behaviors of similar intensity, duration, and shape. She interacts with her new child with a great deal of eye contact, smiles, and physical contact. She often touches and holds him since this makes it easier for her to match her child's affect and for him to experience attunement. She is very receptive to his affective expressions, matching their intensity and quality. Only by his having these frequent attunement experiences will feelings of attachment begin to emerge from this affective union.

In communicating empathy to her child, the parent needs to observe his movements, emotions, behaviors, gestures, and the current situation. Most often the child is nonverbal about what he is feeling. Using her observation, the parent verbalizes what she thinks the child is feeling, fully accepting whatever those feelings seem to be. She is always somewhat tentative about her observations since she cannot read her child's mind. If her child disagrees with her comments, the parent does not argue since there is no value to that even if she is "right." To communicate empathy, the parent's verbal observation must be nonjudgmental. If the parent is critical, the child will only experience criticism and not empathy. Even if the parent might hope that someday her child will not have that particular feeling in response to that situation, she accepts the feeling as being how the child is experiencing the situation now.

Here are some examples of statements that might communicate empathy, assuming that the parent has observed fairly accurately the child's inner life at the time:

You seem kind of sad now . . .
I think that you're mad at me now for not letting you . . .
You really look upset about what she said . . .
It's scary sometimes when you have to . . .
Boy, I bet that you really want to . . .
You seem so proud of the choice you just made . . .
Wow! Are you pleased with that!
You look like you're so mad at me. I wonder if you think I'm being mean
    about . . . ?
It seems to be so hard for you . . .
I see that you're happy about . . .

By making such statements, the parent is:

1) Communicating acceptance of her child's inner life;
2) Communicating understanding of her child's inner life;

3) Communicating that the parent thinks her child's inner life is important;

4) Differentiating between the thoughts/feelings and the behavior;

5) Communicating that talking about one's inner life is acceptable and even desirable;

6) Helping her child to increase his self-reflection and understanding;

7) Helping her child to develop a more complete and positive sense of self;

8) Fostering the attachment with her child;

9) Building important communication patterns with her child; and

10) Preserving a family atmosphere that facilitates attachment.

Empathy is usually given a central role in many parenting books and parent education courses. Parent Effectiveness Training (PET) and Systematic Training for Effective Parenting (STEP) are two notable examples. Empathy for the poorly attached child is especially crucial since this child has experienced a lack of empathy during his first several years of life. Empathy is also crucial for him if he is ever to experience trust of his parent and accept routine discipline.

CHOICES AND CONSEQUENCES

In teaching a child how his own behavior effects his own happiness, choices and consequences are very convincing. When these are routinely given with empathy, they are extremely effective because they provide a good response to the various problems that the child has. They work for the following reasons:

1. The child is often not aware that his behaviors represent the results of choices that he makes rather than being simply things that happen to him. It is to his advantage to be aware of these choices in order to act in the way that best meets his needs. He is responsible for making the choices that satisfy his needs. His impulsive and/or compulsive patterns require little thought and are not effective ways of responding to changing circumstances. Being aware that his behaviors represent choices that he makes facilitates thought and improves his ability to develop new behavioral patterns. It is in his best interest to do so.

2. Often the child's behaviors in the abusive home had no relationship to the actions directed toward him by the abusive/neglectful

parents. He needs to learn that he does have control of the significant consequences of his actions. Specific consequences follow specific behaviors. The poorly attached child is commonly shocked and feels unfairly treated by the consequences of his actions. He discovers that when you break your toys carelessly they are not replaced. He is enraged that he cannot play with his friends because he has not finished his chores. He needs to discover that losing permission to play with friends was not arbitrary, mean, and unpredictable, rather a predictable response to his choice not to complete the chore that he knew was his. If he "forgot" his chore, he learns that forgetfulness is not an excuse that enables him to avoid the consequence of losing his play time. Rather, it serves as a new choice that he might consider for the future, namely developing his cognitive powers sufficiently to remember his chores. His parents, if feeling kindly and judging his forgetfulness to be genuine, might offer to help him to develop his memory but never through "forgetting" the consequence.

3. **Choices and consequences communicate to the child that the best solution to the child's unhappiness over the consequences of his behavior lies within himself and within his own thinking capacities.** The solution does not come from learning to manipulate or control his parents sufficiently so that they give in to his wishes. Instead, the child needs to understand and accept the connection between his choices and their consequences. If he does not like the consequences, he must rethink the choices and develop alternative choices that have consequences closer to his liking.

4. **The child also learns that his parents have confidence in his thinking capacities.** They will not rescue him, choose, or think for him. His parents will neither constantly remind him of the consequences related to his choices nor will they coax him to make choices that connect with certain consequences. To do so only confuses the child as to who actually is benefiting from making specific choices. Instead, his parents communicate that it is his life. If he does not like the consequences, he is free to change the choices. If he requests assistance from them to find alternative choices, they will agree to help. However, they will never push their own solutions on him.

5. **It is harder for the child to remain angry at his parents for the consequences when he can see that he controls the consequences through his own behavioral choices.** His parents are not arbitrarily imposing consequences that he is stuck living with. If he wants other

consequences, he is always free to develop other choices that will better meet his wishes.

6. Because of the empathy that the parent shows in presenting to the child the consequences of his behavior, the child's relationship with the parent is not damaged by every act of discipline. Rather, the empathy helps the child to interpret the discipline as relating to his behavioral choices and not to any rejection or criticism of him as a person. This is crucial since when the parent does not communicate empathy while presenting the consequences of his choices, her child will often feel angry in response to his parent's apparent annoyance over the choice. A power struggle and resentment will usually follow. The poorly attached child habitually experiences pervasive shame that is intensified by discipline. When discipline is given without empathy, his shame is likely to intensify and trigger outbursts of rage.

7. Choices and consequences, with empathy, preserve the overall family atmosphere. Discipline is simply one component of a healthy family. There are no ongoing power struggles with escalating, reciprocal anger. The parents will not allow their child to manipulate their emotions in that manner. They will do the work necessary to maintain the atmosphere they want. Some days are difficult while other days are easy. The parents will remain fairly constant emotionally regardless of their child's choices.

8. Choices and consequences, with empathy, ensure that the parent does not reinforce her child's behavior through a negative emotional response to it. These children often seek negative emotions, both because they are familiar and because they make the child feel that he has control of his parents. They also seek negative responses to confirm their negative sense of self. Why wouldn't their parents hold them in contempt? They feel worthless and believe that they are worthless. The child may also want to hurt his parents because he feels hurt by the consequences of his acts. If he feels that he has made them tense and angry, and, hence, "unhappy," he begins to see this as a way of getting back at them. If he has success in controlling their emotion, he may begin to "blackmail" them by implying that if they let him avoid a consequence, he will not make them "unhappy" through his various oppositional behaviors.

9. When the parent responds with empathy to her child's anger or sadness about a consequence, she is showing that the child's feelings are valid and unconditionally accepted. The parent has not taken the child's behavior "personally." The child needs consequences to behavioral choices but these have nothing to do with his parents' love for him. His developing autonomy is respected and encouraged when his thoughts and feelings are accepted, and their expression is facilitated even if the specific behaviors are not permitted.

Maintaining a family atmosphere that provides choices and consequences for behavior is a very effective way to develop effective discipline while at the same time developing the parent–child bond. Too often, discipline interferes with the developing relationship. The poorly attached child is a master at using discipline situations as excuses for rage and mistrust as well as for thoughts that his parent is mean and he is worthless. Examples of choices and consequences will be presented in the next chapter.

ATTACHMENT SEQUENCES

Parents of poorly attached children need to be continually mindful of the fact that their child's very poor behavioral choices can best be understood and responded to within a larger context and over a longer sequence of interactions. If a parent can only see the present oppositional behavior, she loses sight of what it represents as well as what is needed if the behavioral incident is to be transformed into an opportunity for the child to develop a healthier autonomy and a more secure attachment.

In healthy parent–child relationships there are countless sequences during the child's second year of life in which the child briefly leaves the felt sense of being securely and joyfully attached with his parent to some behavioral choice that elicits parental disapproval and instigates the experience of personal shame. In healthy families each such sequence quickly leads back to reunion with the parent that affirms that such shameful experiences have no impact on the ongoing security of the attachment. Because of these experiences, the child manages to actively develop his sense of autonomy, including a healthy sense of shame, while continuing to be secure in a crucially important attachment. In fact, these sequences help to make the attachment more secure and complex.

The poorly attached child does not have this sense of positive self-worth or a history of a seemingly invulnerable and permanent attachment to rely on when he engages in misbehaviors. Such misbehaviors for this child elicit a profound sense of self-contempt and an overwhelming fear that they will cause his new parents to reject him. He cannot acknowledge such self-contempt and fear of loss either to himself or to his parents and he is left with only an intense sense of rage that masks his terror and self-disgust.

For parents to assist their poorly attached child to manage, integrate, and resolve these intense conflict situations, they need to:

1) Maintain a habitual positive family atmosphere that facilitates a sense of attachment preceding the incident;

2) Respond to the behavior and the underlying contempt, fear, and rage with empathy and matter-of-fact consequences; and

3) Reestablish the atmosphere and attachment quickly, thus reducing the child's fear and rage, making the shame an integrated aspect of a healthy sense of autonomy, and building trust in the attachment.

When the parent is able to incorporate the child's various resistant and oppositional behaviors into the structure of these attachment sequences, they become a natural part of family life and of a developing attachment. The child gradually comes to realize that his self-worth and his attachment with his parents are both of much greater significance than are his specific behaviors, no matter how outrageous. This developing attachment and sense of autonomy serve as the basic support for integrating both "good" and "bad" experiences. The child does not have to manipulate to seem "good" or lie to avoid seeming "bad." With time, he realizes that he has fundamental worth and that he is special to his parents. He and they can directly deal with his poor choices and then get on with the process of learning and loving as a family and as individuals.

When I stress the need to reestablish the reciprocal engagement quickly after the behavioral incident, I am not suggesting that the parent coax the child into being happy and affectionate with the parent. Such efforts would lead to failure. The child will think that the parent is afraid of conflict and needs to be close to the child. What an opportunity to manipulate the parents! He may quickly realize: "If I pout a little longer, they might be willing to buy me something so that I'll smile and forgive them for making me mad." Rather, I am suggesting that the parents refrain from maintaining a tense and annoyed attitude that hurts the family atmosphere and that communicates that the relationship will be used as a technique to punish the child for his misbehavior. The parents need to communicate a general acceptance of what just occurred and empathy for the child's response to the consequence. The parent might give the child a quick hug, pat on the back, or word of support and then accept his need to pout or remain annoyed if that is the case. The parent is communicating that the attachment is alive and well. If the child wants to reject it now, that's fine. The parent will not respond in kind.

At times, following a particularly difficult incident or during a particular difficult day, the parent may not be able to respond quickly to the child or may need some distance and time away from him for a while. Since parents are not saints or robots, that is quite understandable and needs to be accepted without guilt. At these times the parent should directly acknowledge this to the child and communicate the limited, temporary nature of the withdrawal. The parent might say:

> I don't have much energy now and I'm still upset over what you chose to do. That's my problem, not yours. I need some time alone to take care of myself. I'll let you know when I'm ready to be with you again.

When the parent does return to engage the child, she needs to relate with the empathy and availability as suggested above. These withdrawals from the child, if not the habitual response to conflict, are not likely to impede the child's developing attachment or sense of self. Rather, they serve to model a very good way of dealing with stress. They also demonstrate that such breaks are temporary and that the child is not being blamed for their occurrence. The parent is simply taking care of herself. All of us at times need to take care of ourselves in similar ways.

BEHAVIOR, EMOTION, AND THOUGHT

As we indicated in the discussion of choices and consequences, the child needs to learn that his behavior has consequences whether they be enjoyable or unpleasant. These behavioral consequences have nothing to do with his relationship with his parent. Also, his thoughts and emotions do not elicit consequences within the family. Parents need to accept the child's inner life and encourage its growth while focusing their efforts on influencing the child's behavior. Just the act of placing consequences on behavior will encourage the child to become aware of his emotions and to develop his thought processes so that his choices lead to more enjoyable consequences. It is a legacy of the abuse and neglect that these children usually do not have well-developed inner lives. They often have trouble identifying their immature feeling states and one state is poorly integrated with another. Rage may emerge suddenly and intensely and have little obvious connection to the immediate circumstances. This pattern is similar to that of the infant and reflects how little the child has come to modulate and integrate his emotional states. They lacked the affective attunement experiences that would have facilitated this developmental process. For this child, impulses often determine behavior. His sense of autonomy is poorly developed and does not serve to regulate and integrate his various affective states. There is little awareness of what he wants at a deeper level and little consideration of the consequences. When the child develops his emotion and cognition, he will become more aware of consequences and vice versa. From the differentiation and integration of all three aspects of self (behavior, emotion, and cognition), he will begin to become an autonomous individual.

Parents can facilitate the child's emotional life by helping him to identify his feelings, by accepting their validity, and by supporting him in his efforts to express them. The parent cannot read the child's mind, but the parent can say quite readily: "I wonder if you're mad because you can't go too. No? I probably would have been when I was your age." Or: "When you look that way, it makes me think you might be sad. Being sad is often hard for you." Or: "Sometimes when kids don't know how to fix something, they feel pretty discouraged. I wonder if you feel that way." Even when the child denies the feeling, his parent's comment might help him to recognize an emotion that was outside his awareness. The comment may help him to know that his parent is receptive and nonjudgmental about his emotional life. He may gradually discover that talking about his emotions really feels good and brings him closer to his parents.

Parents also help their child with his emotional life when they are able to model emotional expression for him. Parents have a variety of emotions too and the child benefits from seeing his parents struggle a bit with various feelings. He begins to have greater confidence that his parents will understand and accept his feelings because they experienced similar feelings themselves. I am not suggesting that the parent burden their child with their struggles. If they need to have someone listen to them to help them to work something through, then they go to someone else. They are simply showing him that they are human like he is. In observing this, the child learns more about his own inner life.

It should be noted that having a difficult feeling is never an excuse for inappropriate behavior. Parents offer empathy for the emotion and a consequence for the behavior. The child's statement, such as "I couldn't help it; I was angry," are met with responses such as

It sounds like you're going to have to learn how to deal with your anger differently (if you want to avoid this consequence in the future). You're a bright kid. You'll figure out a way. If you want to discuss your ideas with me, let me know.

Parents should also make efforts to encourage the child to think about himself and his life. They should make it obvious to him that his thoughts do not have to agree with their thoughts. "I think it might be a good idea to get your homework done so that you'll be free if your friend calls. What do you think?" This is a message that communicates respect for their child's thoughts and encourages their development.

At the same time, parents might raise questions about what their child seems to be thinking about an issue. If he reacts with extreme rage to what seems like a routine consequence to his behavior, the parent might wonder if the child thinks that she does not like him or is simply being mean. If the question is made in an open, curious way rather than as a way of justifying the parent's behavior, the child is likely to become aware of the underlying thought and his emotional response might become less extreme.

In my treatment interventions I often wonder out loud if the child thinks that the adopted parents have the same motives and feelings about him as did his abusive parents. Even when the child cannot verbalize such an association at the time, he often begins to think about such questions on his own in subsequent interactions with his parent.

RECIPROCAL ENJOYMENT

As was discussed in Chapter Two, the infant's attachment with his mother evolves out of affective attunement and countless mutually enjoyable activities between himself and her. The two are fully engaged in a dance that is both unique and universal. The same type of interaction, occurring again and again, must be the core reality for the foster or adopted child's developing attachment to his new family. Messing his hair, fixing a lamp, reading a book, shoveling snow, throwing snow, pushing snow inside his coat, finding the missing hat, laughing, hugging, sitting in front of the TV, singing, walking, preparing lunch and pancakes, all happening over and over, happening together, feeling fine together, are the realities of attachment.

These children often find ways to avoid, prevent, ruin, or minimize the value of these activities. Such activities are too unpredictable, too frightening, in their casual intimacy. In years past, during the early stages of abuse and neglect, the child had yearned for such activities but now is terrified of trusting that they are real. He is also terrified of giving his parent the power to elicit such wonderful, long-dreamed-for, moments. He is almost certain that these experiences will end; he cannot risk believing that they will last.

How must parents respond when the child tries to avoid or distort these mutually enjoyable experiences? First, the parent must be careful not to let the child determine the emotional tone of the interaction or else what began as a mutually enjoyable experience will quickly become a frustrating experience, at least for the parent. Rather, the parent should maintain her own enjoyment of the moment, patiently encouraging the child to enjoy it too while accepting that it is difficult. The child who is not comfortable with being touched still needs to be touched, though for shorter durations and in a lighter fashion than if he clearly enjoyed the experience. In fact, the tension around being touched should be acknowledged and accepted as an understandable response to past experiences. With gentle humor, brief quiet discussions, or knowing eye contact, the parent will communicate a commitment to help the child begin to feel comfortable with receiving a pat on the back, a quick caress, a scalp message, or an infrequent, loud, laughing bear hug.

Parents *will not* be rejected by their new child. The child's anger or aloofness is seen as a sign of the past and not as evidence of parental failure. These signs represent his efforts to control the situation and to be disengaged from the parent. However, the parent will not disengage. She may accept the anger and with good-natured humor communicate how impressed she is with its strength. The parent might encourage the anger to be expressed more loudly, with different words, or in a different setting. She might encourage the child to stand on the kitchen chair, call for attention by banging a pot with a spoon, and then proclaim for all to hear what a stupid family the child has had the bad luck of falling into. Should he refuse to be angry in this way, the parent might stand on another chair and proclaim loudly that the poor child has to put up with extremely dull, selfish, and foolish parents who waste too much time trying to enjoy themselves with their children. During that interaction the child will most certainly be engaged in spite of his efforts to disengage. The parent's task is to find creative, sensitive, relaxed, and often humorous or unusual ways to remain engaged with her child in spite of his roadblocks to the interaction. Even when he insists on his silence and isolation, he nevertheless is engaged with the parent when she acknowledges and accepts his hesitations or reluctance to be engaged more directly. She will again and again invite participation, talk about it, and work to have her child sense that no matter what he is doing or not doing, she is there with him in thought and emotion, if not actions, at this time. The message to him is that the parent will be engaged and will not be rejected. The child is special and the relationship is being nourished in whatever way it takes for the attachment to develop.

Deborah Hage, a very skilled therapeutic parent from Colorado, indicates that when she senses that the child's behavioral choices represent the child's efforts to push her away out of discomfort with the attachment, she may choose not to give the child a negative consequence to the behavior. Instead, she may cheerfully tell the child that his noisy or sloppy behavior indicates that he needs more "mom time!" She then showers the child with an enjoyable mutual activity, resulting in hugs and fun for both. By doing this, does she risk reinforcing misbehavior? Not really. The child was trying to control and limit the relationship. Deborah refused to allow the child to control his relationship with her. The behavior was not reinforced because its goal was not achieved. In actuality, the opposite effect occurred and he might be less likely to try it again with that goal in mind.

Reciprocal enjoyment needs to be the constant goal for parents to maintain when living with their poorly attached child. When they begin to have confidence that this goal is being achieved they will know that their child is learning to be attached to them.

REGRESSION

A child who has not attained the healthy developmental attachment patterns that are appropriate for his age may well need to be encouraged to regress as if he were considerably younger than his actual age. Such regression simply acknowledges that he lacks the body sense, affective integration, behavioral control, and cognitive reflective skills that he would have developed if he had progressed with healthy developmental patterns. Such regression also enables his parent to provide him with a greater degree of nurturance, involvement, supervision, and teaching, just as she would do for a younger child. Since he needs this more intense involvement if his parent is to effectively direct his healthy developmental movement, regression is often indicated in raising the poorly attached child.

For regression to have a significant effect on the child's functioning, it needs to be both comprehensive and of long duration. Simply encouraging him to use a bottle occasionally will have no meaningful results. Rather, the parent literally raises him *as if* he were much younger. Thus, if the 6-year-old boy is to be raised as if he were 2 years old, the parent will have to be prepared to provide him with the extensive supervision and involvement that she would actually give her 2-year-old. She assumes that his affective, behavioral, and cognitive skills are such that he needs to be watched closely for his safety and well-being. She assumes that many choices are beyond him, so she makes them for him. She schedules his day for him since he does not have that skill. He is not ready to choose his clothes or play with certain toys unsupervised nor can he select his food or play outdoors alone. He will have to be helped to dress or manage his hygiene.

She also assumes that for his development to proceed, he needs a large amount of one-to-one interaction with her. He needs to experience her attunement with him very frequently throughout the day. She needs to constantly chat with him, hug him, laugh over their activity together, sing to him, and hold him. He will accompany her during many of her daily activities so that she can both keep an eye on him and communicate enjoyment of him. His freedom to move around unsupervised is greatly limited. However this is not presented in a punitive manner. It is simply a matter-of-fact reality which reflects his parent's judgment that this form of child rearing is in his best interests for now.

If the parent is willing to allow her poorly attached child to regress, she will have to clear her schedule of many activities just as she would have to do for an infant or toddler. She will have to make other family members aware of her new commitments so that there are no misunderstandings and criticisms. She will have to make any baby sitters aware of his regression needs and elicit their cooperation. However, she will also have to realize that her child must not have baby sitters often now as this will reduce the effectiveness of regression as a means to facilitate attachment.

I have worked with a number of children whose foster or adoptive parents were willing and able to give them this gift of regression. Others have questioned this intervention, thinking that the child could feel humiliated and that the interventions could be experienced as punitive. I have been repeatedly surprised by the degree to which the poorly attached child relishes the opportunity to receive this high level of continuing care. Invariably, his reduced choices and his need to be constantly at his mother's side are not resented. He is neither embarrassed nor secretive about his being given a bottle, sung to, and rocked throughout the day. He often begins to talk "baby talk" with his mother and enjoy her attuned response of matching her speech to his. Moreover, I have never once seen a child want to remain regressed beyond the point where he no longer needed the experience for the sake of his attachment and development. I have seen children suddenly "lose interest" in a bottle or activity when they were ready to move on.

As stated before, regression requires a great deal of time and continuing awareness from the parent if it is to be effective. However, poorly attached children will inevitably demand a great deal of time and supervision anyway because of their unpredictable affect and actions. They are often constantly "in trouble" and their self-concept then remains very negative. By allowing them to regress, they are receiving an equally high level of involvement but it is now described and experienced as attunement and child care appropriate for their developmental level rather than as restrictions due to poor behavioral choices. The lack of maturation of the self is directly acknowledged and accepted. The child is provided with a home routine and parental relationship that conforms to his intense needs to experience a good parent who relates to him as if he were younger. This parent will assume many of his responsibilities to choose and act. She will also make him central in her daily life and she will do so with patience and pleasure.

PARENTAL SELF-CARE

Parents need to attend to their own psychological needs if they are to provide the high level of care that the poorly attached child requires. They need to maintain an inner calm and confidence while acknowledging and assertively pursuing what is important to them. If they neglect their own lives, they will not be able to maintain the positive family atmosphere that their poorly attached child needs. If they neglect their own intimate relationships, their child will undermine them. The following suggestions may help parents maintain their inner strength:

   1. **Recall often that you are not the source of your child's problems.** He came into your home with these profound difficulties that arose from his experiences of abuse and neglect at the hands of earlier parents. He now needs your aid in resolving these problems. You are not responsible for them. Rather, you are the primary source of their solution.

2. Acknowledge your own feelings of grief, rage, and despair. If you deny such feelings in yourself, you will lose the ability to have empathy for similar feelings in your child. Parenting a poorly attached child may not have been what you had in mind when your child entered your home. When he rejects your affection and overwhelming efforts on his behalf, you are likely to question your sanity, your abilities, and your future. You need to be honest about these realities if you are to find your own inner resources, which are necessary if you are to continue to make these overwhelming efforts.

3. Maintain a sense of humor. Humor helps to maintain your perspective and not take the child's behavior personally. It also protects your own self-esteem and enables you to feel stronger. Your poorly attached child loses much of his sense of control over you when you can maintain your inner peace through humor, despite his outrageous behaviors.

4. Maintain a central supportive relationship with another adult. You are not too old, and never will be, to benefit greatly from having your own significant attachment(s). Experiencing empathy and understanding from someone that you trust along with moments of considerable reciprocal enjoyment will go a long way toward assisting you to meet the profound needs of your child.

5. Maintain a support network with other parents of poorly attached children. Many parents and professionals will not be able to understand what you are experiencing. You will find a knowing look and an empathic comment from within the support network more often than anywhere else. These parents will serve as a lifeline for your sanity.

6. Maintain trust and openness with an assisting professional. A professional who understands poorly attached children will help greatly in maintaining perspective; considering ways to intervene in difficult situations; and learning to be optimistic when accepting small accomplishments. This professional will also be useful in validating your experiences in the face of skepticism and criticism from others.

7. Check out situations with other caregivers to avoid splitting. Your child will drive a battleship between you and your spouse or partner if your mutual communication is not a high priority. You must talk frequently with the other caregivers involved about what happened in a given situation, what your child's choices and consequences are, and what are the best ways of responding in future situations.

8. Be patient and maintain realistic day-to-day goals. Expectations of progress must incorporate expectations of periodic regression. If you are able to accept both progress and lack of progress as normal cycles in parenting your child, you will be more able to avoid disappointments and cycles of optimism and pessimism. If you become excited about progress, your child will be able to use your emotion to again take control of the situation. If you remain emotionally about the same whatever the child's degree of progress, you will be more able to provide for his care over the long haul.

9. Remember that if you become more like your child, you both lose; if your child becomes more like you, you both win. If you have a poorly attached child, your psychological well-being and your way of relating and living is superior to his. You must use yourself as a model both for him to incorporate and for you to maintain as your goal for his development.

10. Remember that if your child is able to form an attachment with you, you have participated in a psychological birth. This is not an overstatement. As has been stated repeatedly in this work, every aspect of your child's affective, behavioral, cognitive, social, and spiritual functioning is affected by his attachment with you. He will keep, within himself, this unique relationship with you for the rest of his life.

12

DAY-TO-DAY PARENTING

Often it is difficult to translate principles of change for the poorly attached child into the day-to-day struggles and strategies that make such principles real. Parents need to be aware of the tactics that others have tried in various situations with some success. However, parents always need to return to their unique child and their unique family in deciding whether a certain strategy would be effective for them. With poorly attached children, one is often surprised about what works and what does not work in a given situation. The surprise is even greater when just the opposite tactic works the next day. Parents should remind themselves of this point frequently while considering the following strategies.

Since poorly attached children are marvels at finding ways to avoid forming an attachment to their caregivers, the parents of one of these children need to be imaginative, resourceful, tenacious, and self-assured if they are to continually respond in ways that facilitate an attachment. On certain days, in certain situations, general guidelines for relating to their child are ineffective and parents must resort to other interventions, even when these are "illogical" and may in fact be the opposite of what the parents usually do. If parents become predictable in responding to the child who is resisting attachment, he eventually finds a way to circumvent the intervention and remain resistant and in control. In responding to their child, parents need to use their knowledge of their unique child, including his own strengths and weaknesses. They also use their awareness of the recent series of events that led to the current dilemma and their intuition about what creative response will keep the child off balance and facilitate some attachment with them. The following represent ideas, some of which may be helpful in a given situation. Some responses in these circumstances may be effective one time and never again. When they are not effective, parents need to discard them, take a breath, and try something else. I am indebted to Connell Watkins, Deborah Hage, Foster Cline (Cline and Fay 1990), and to the many parents with whom I have worked for many of these concepts.

MOVING IN

When a child moves into a new home, parents often assume that he will work hard to try to "fit in" with the family. As was stated before, children who are slow to attach are also slow to try to change themselves in any meaningful way to become more like their new caregivers. Rather, they search for ways to manipulate the new parents so that they can gain control of the new home. They search for "sympathy" for being new or for having been abused. Once received, sympathy is then experienced as an entitlement. The new parents are thought to be abusive, mean, or unfair for denying these entitlements. To the child, the new parents are certainly unfair for insisting on consequences for acting in certain ways. The child always has "excuses" for his behavior; a good excuse, in the child's thinking, prohibits any and all consequences.

Some parents state with pride that they will have no assumptions about the child when he comes into their home and they tell the child that he has a "clean slate." By this they mean that they will not hold his behavior in previous homes against him. That certainly seems reasonable. How can one give a child a consequence for a choice that he made in his last home? However, the parents often want to take the "clean slate" even further and not even consider the possibility that he will act the same way in their home. Having adopted such a fair, "up-front" approach, they are then surprised that the child reenacts the behavior which he manifested in his previous home. They become more strict, with fewer privileges and more supervision. The child then thinks that his parents have changed for the worse. He will report that his parents were nice to him "at first," but then became "mean." He feels betrayed; how can he trust these parents?

He has no awareness of the causal relationship between his behavior and the new "strictness."

For this reason, and others to be mentioned, parents need to "welcome" the poorly attached child to their home with very clear and comprehensive behavioral rules on the day he comes into their house. It is much easier for the child and the parents to loosen the rules than to tighten them once the child has lived in the home for a while. Besides this fact, and the reasonable assumption that more relaxed, ambiguous expectations are unlikely to be effective, the following reasons also warrant clear and comprehensive rules:

1. Such rules will help the child to avoid "failure" by presenting clearly what is, and what will be, expected. The child will then avoid feeling "bad" again. To do otherwise is to set him up for failure. Parents should not expect "miracles" from the simple act of the child moving into their home.

2. The child is going to be more receptive to their rules during the first days of the placement than later. He will be more motivated to comply initially, if only to give himself time while he "gets the lay of the land." It is easier to maintain initial compliance than it is to work for it after the child has "settled in."

3. During the "moving in" days, choices and consequences are more easily perceived as parental *teaching* rather than *punishment*. Rules can be framed as signposts that are considerate enough to provide their child with so that he can then make choices that are of benefit to him. Such rules will enable him to know what is expected of him in his new family. What is clearly implied is that he is expected to fit into the family's way of relating. His parents will not be changing their family atmosphere and interactions to fit him.

4. During the initial days, both parents and child are less likely to be angry at each other. By taking advantage of this time, parents will have more empathy for the child's behavioral choices and he will be more likely to comply. Power struggles are less likely to occur now than they might later.

5. The child is less likely initially to see the choices and consequences as being a rejection of self. Later, the child is more likely to personalize the consequence. It becomes a statement about him, rather than a result of the family's rules and his current behavioral choice.

6. The child is more likely to feel secure when he knows quite clearly what is expected of his behavior. Given such security, he will be somewhat more receptive to forming an attachment than if he needs to put a great deal of energy into keeping himself safe. He can learn quickly that his parents will relate to him in certain clear ways; they will not respond to him in a cruel and arbitrary manner.

How should parents present these "clear and comprehensive" rules when their child first comes into their home? As with any teaching, parents will be most effective by presenting their expectations in a matter-of-fact tone with empathy for their child's response. They can best present the rules as being a necessary means for him to be able to learn how people—adults and children—live in this home. For example, parents may say to their new child shortly after his arrival into their home:

> Well Johnny, you must have so many questions! I imagine it must be hard to move into a home with people you hardly know. You don't know how we act, what we think about things, and what we expect from you. You don't even know what we do with our dirty plates after dinner! Or what we say after we burp!
>
> We decided that the best way to help you to learn how we live in this family is to teach you over the next few days what we all, and that means you, too, do everyday, in many situations. We know this is a hard time for you and you're likely to make some mistakes. We don't mind mistakes. We don't mind doing this for you! And you're a bright kid; you'll learn pretty quickly!

This type of statement makes it clear to the child that his ignorance about the rules is to be expected and he is not blamed for not knowing them. At the same time, it is clear that he is expected to learn "how we live in this family" rather than the parents learning how the child lived in his previous families. It is also clear that the parents are very willing to teach him how to make any changes necessary and they will not resent him for not knowing or for making mistakes. Such teaching, or discipline, is an act of love. However, the child *is* expected to learn.

At the same time, such a statement does not threaten the child with punishment or rejection if he does not do what is expected. The statement must not be an initial power struggle in which the parents are trying to communicate that the child's opposition will be beaten. It is simply a statement that acknowledges how he now needs to learn "how we live in this family." The parents are simply doing their job and showing their love and commitment by teaching him.

What do the parents teach initially?

1. The parents teach the child what behaviors are expected in a

given situation. The parents indicate that when the child chooses to do the behavior that is expected, one consequence results. For example, when the child finishes playing with toys on the living room floor, he needs to pick them up. He then is free to do something else. This consequence is simply implied initially. If he chooses not to pick up the toys after playing with them, he quickly learns that he is not free to do something else. The consequence of being free to do something else only follows the consequence of not being free to do something else until the toys are picked up. If the child still chooses not to pick them up, his parents will comment on how hard this rule must seem to him, how angry he might be at living in such a home with such a rule, and how confident his parents are that he will make a choice, while sitting there by the toys, that is best for him. With further resistance, the child might discover the consequence of having a cold dinner alone, since the rule in this home is that consequences are successfully completed before one sits down to eat with the family. He might also discover that since it was so hard for him to choose to put the toys away, he probably is not ready yet for the fun of playing with them in the living room. Under no circumstances will his parents overlook his choice to break the rule because the child hasn't "settled in" yet. If they do, the child may never "settle in." It is very likely that he will pick up the toys during the first few days or weeks, especially if his parents clearly expect him to do so. But eventually the poorly attached child will begin to work, over and over again, to change these expectations for the worse. He will also want to know what his parents will do when he defies them so that he can use this knowledge to better manipulate them in the future.

2. **The child should be told that since his parents are likely to be unable to tell the child everything that is expected, the child needs to** *ask what the rules are* **before doing things that have never been discussed.** Thus, if the child does not know if he can watch TV at certain times, he will not turn it on but first find out if the behavior fits into the family rules for him. He will ask if he can turn on the TV. He will ask if he can go outside to play, take the cookie from the jar, play with the hammer and nails, or play with the cat. This prevents the child from breaking rules or getting into trouble in countless ways. More importantly, it emphasizes that the child needs to work hard at learning what is expected of him. Poorly attached children do not do this naturally. They assume that if they have not been specifically told not to do something, they can do it. They are then irate that their parents might question their judgment or suggest that they should have checked first before doing it. If asking about what is

expected before doing it is an initial rule, much is avoided and much is taught.

3. When the child first shows a reluctance to follow Rule 1 or Rule 2, his parents may have him *practice* the rule until he gets it right. Thus, the child who chooses, more than once, not to pick up his toys may need to practice picking them up 3 times a day for 3 days. This exercise consists of the child picking them up and then putting them on the floor again so that he has the chance to pick them up again. The child who forgets to ask what the rules are may have to ask permission to use the bathroom, enter the room, leave the room, sit on the couch, and so forth, for a period of time to help him to remember this important means of learning what is expected and how to avoid failure. But parents need to communicate empathy and possibly humor while insisting on practice. Thus, they might say: "This might drive you crazy, but . . ." Or: "I'm not sure if you're going to laugh or scream when I give you this practice . . ." Or: "While practicing, you might whisper to yourself what a dumb rule you think this is and it might go faster."

4. When the child first shows a reluctance to follow Rule 1 or Rule 2, his parents may have the child take some *"thinking time"* in order to help him to attend to these important rules and to be more aware of his choices and consequences. He will then report to his parents the results of his thinking—hopefully, with better insight into the choice that is in his best interest. Thus, the child who has taken a number of cookies without permission might sit at the kitchen table and think about how the cookies might be kept safe from his mouth and how he might win back the privilege of entering the kitchen unsupervised as well as the privilege of enjoying dessert with the family.

5. When the child has trouble with Rule 1 or Rule 2, his parents may choose to *supervise* him more closely. The child may have to be in the sight of his parents at certain times, or at all times if necessary, until he comes to realize the advantage of choosing to follow rules 1 and 2. When supervision becomes very comprehensive and long-lasting, it is considered to be a part of encouraging a child's regression.

6. When the child has trouble with Rule 1 or Rule 2, his parents may choose to *limit various activities* of the child. Life becomes dull for him since he needs to put more energy into following these basic rules of the family. If he does not follow them, his ability to attach is significantly reduced, and his future as a productive and content member of his family and society is compromised. The long-term consequences of such a choice are grave. The short-term consequences need to be sufficiently intense to get his attention and increase his motivation to work at it. Thus, the child who is repeatedly starting to take things without permission or refusing to do what he is told may have to sit and watch while the rest of the family has a pizza party and plays a game with prizes. His parents are not angry at the child while they refuse to allow him to participate in this activity; they simply express the hope that he will begin to choose to be a cooperative and friendly member of the family since he is now missed.

7. The child is shown that each member of the family needs to contribute to the good of the family. The child is expected to do this by:

a. *Chores.* These are concrete and immediate ways for the child to feel that he is a contributing, responsible member of the family. It also gives him some sense that "work" is necessary and that his parents do much of it which is of benefit to him. These children often do not do chores well. Initially, he should be given instructions on how to do the chore properly. He might be told that the chore is not complete until his parents have checked it. The child tells his parents when he is finished and he cannot do anything else until his parents have checked it. If done poorly, he will immediately do it again; this time he will wait longer for his parents to check it.

b. *Communication.* For a family to live and work and have fun together, communication must serve to build the family relationships, not to harm them. Therefore, communication needs to be clear, honest, appropriate, and respectful of one another. If the child does not communicate the way the parents do, he is choosing not to communicate and discussion must stop. If he needs to scream, he needs to do so away from the parents' ears. Once the basics of communication are assured, it can be used for playfulness, affection, sharing and helping one another.

c. *Work precedes play.* This is a fact of life for adults as well as for families that function well consistently over time. Poorly attached children habitually feel deprived and want to "play" constantly. The child needs to understand this basic concept and needs to be held to it or his resistance to responsible choices will be profound. If this rule is seen as a family pattern, which applies to all, the child's resistance may be less.

Some caseworkers and therapists may think that this emphasis on discipline is inappropriate during the initial days and weeks of the placement. They wish to emphasize the parents' affection, interest, and understanding and they hope that the child will come to feel secure and begin to trust the parents because of these positive experiences. This may well be true with children who have a positive self-concept, who have a history of successful attachments, and who genuinely want to please their new parents, identify with them, and return their love. However, with the poorly attached child, this sequence does not occur because he has little experience with trusting another to meet his needs. He will take the affection, interest, and understanding and use it to manipulate, control, and deceive his parents since he remains convinced that he alone will meet his own needs. With such a child, choices and consequences, given with empathy, are a necessary foundation for building an attachment. Choices and consequences are more effective initially than countless efforts to provide affectionate and joyful experiences. I am not suggesting that such experiences be ignored. Rather, the parent should not expect that they will create change. Joyful experiences are freely given, so there is a balance to the hard work involved in learning to accept the behavioral expectations. Also, during this period, the parent remains aware of the need to provide affective attunement experiences for him as these are the necessary building blocks of attachment.

DAY-TO-DAY DISCIPLINE

How are choices and consequences, with empathy, applied in daily life? First, the parents tell their child what his choices are, in a matter of fact way, communicating that *the parents can easily live with either choice that the child makes.* If the parents have a vested interest in their child making one particular choice, the child will sense that, and he may well choose the opposite.

Choosing the opposite makes him think that he has some control over his parents. It also confuses him as to why he is making this choice. The choice needs to be based on what the child wants, not on what the parents want. Our influence over what the child wants occurs in our choice of the consequence of his choice rather than in trying to control his choice. A parent might say to a young child having a tantrum in a store: "You can take my hand and we'll walk out of the store together or I'll carry you out. Which would you prefer?" To be effective, his parent really doesn't care which option the child chooses. If the child does not choose, his parent might simply add, "If you choose not to decide, I'll carry you, I don't mind." The parent then waits a few seconds, all the time smiling, and then picks up the child if his hand is not extended to his parent. There is no further discussion. It is now too late for the child to change his mind. But he had control of the sequence of events within the options that his parent chose for him. If he was embarrassed over being carried out, the next time he will probably choose to take his parent's hand. Better yet, if his parent becomes tired of this sequence in the store, she will add another choice: "You can choose to go to the store with me without tantrums or to stay home with Dad. Either choice is fine with me." If it is an inconvenience for dad to watch the child, his mother probably will add another consequence: "If you choose to stay home with dad, you'll be helping him to clean the car since that's what he's planning, and watching you will slow him down somewhat." Each choice and consequence sequence is presented in a relaxed manner, even the communication that his parent is curious as to what the child will decide. The choices and consequences provided to him need to incorporate his parents' values, obligations, and wishes, so that whatever choice he makes is truly acceptable to them. If his parents are angry at having to carry him from the store or having him stay home with dad, then this form of discipline will be much less effective. He will use their anger to justify his own rage, to confirm his worthlessness and their meanness, and to manipulate and pay them back in the future.

The best choice-consequence sequences are those that are *connected* in some manner so that the child is more able to see that the consequence is *not arbitrary*. When the child loses his parents' tools, the better consequence is to lose the right to use them, not to lose the right to watch TV. When the child makes a lot of noise while watching TV, he will leave the room so the rest of the family can watch it, rather than lose the right to have cookies after dinner.

It is important to stress that *choices and consequences* are *not commands and punishments.* For example, to say, with raised voice, "Pick up your toys or you're grounded!" communicates that I am annoyed with the child. Also, he has no choice, and if he does not obey me, I'll make him pay for his disobedience. The child is left with resentment and his only choice is whether or not to have a power struggle. Since he probably interprets my comment and emotion as a rejection of him, he may well choose the power struggle to hurt me back, or, at a deeper level, to plead with me not to reject him. Much more helpful would be a simple comment: "You can go out and play as soon as you pick up the toys." Or, if I cannot live with his choice to refrain from both playing outside and picking up the toys, I might say, "I'd like the toys picked up by 1:00 because the messy room is bothering me. If you don't do it by then, I will, but then you'll have to wash the car and cut the grass." In this situation, I would pick a consequence likely to be seen by the child as being worse than picking up the toys by 1:00. There is no need to remind him numerous times before 1:00 of his decreasing time because that communicates that I have little confidence in his memory or ability to choose what is best for him. Besides, it is a waste of my time.

One should also note that parents do not have to add a consequence for every choice that their child makes. Only choices that deviate in a significant degree from their standards for family living—or ones which are repetitive—necessitate a consequence. When we give the child the opportunity to decide for himself that the behavior represented a poor choice, he can then take pride in his choice to stop the behavior without our intervention. He is thinking! If he does not correct himself, simply giving him a friendly glance or calmly saying his name may well suffice. If he can accept this gentle feedback about his behavior, he is showing a receptivity to our guidance that suggests a deepening attachment! When that word or glance is not sufficient, the parents might be more explicit: "That's too noisy in the living room while I'm reading. If you want to be noisy now, you'll have to be so in another room." Only when these mild responses fail or have to be repeated often is it necessary to consider adding a consequence to the child's choice.

When a child becomes angry in response to the consequence of his choice, the anger can be used as an excellent opportunity to foster his attachment to the parents. Attachment is facilitated during times of emotional stress. If parents are able to *offer empathy* for the child's anger, he will feel closer to his parents, even if their decision to give a consequence is the original cause of the anger. He will feel a positive emotional engagement with his parents at that time. During the engagement, his parents are implying that he can manage, possibly with parental help, his emotional response. His parents are also communicating that the relationship is more important than any conflict and that the relationship is strong enough to incorporate anger and discord. Thus, when the child screams because he cannot play with his friend since his homework is not completed, his parents might comment: "You sure are angry at me. You must want to see your friend a lot! It's hard now that you can't." Usually there is no need to add: "Maybe next time you'll choose to finish your homework." The child should come to that conclusion on his own. If the parents point out how poor the choice was, he may experience it as gloating or preaching or trying to convince him to do what the parents think is best for him. The choice is the child's to make, the parents need to accept either one and to give the child empathy for the consequences that are not to the child's liking.

As has been discussed in previous chapters, the child's misbehavior and conflict with his parents elicits much more than a typical shame experience. The poorly attached child rightfully often felt abuse, contempt, and rejection when in conflict with his first parents. When we are able to maintain an emotional bond with the child during or immediately following a stressful conflict situation, we are helping him to reduce his pervasive shame and rage and to integrate such stress into his developing self and his deepening attachment to his parents.

Too often *time-out* is the immediate consequence for the angry child. By isolating him at that moment, the parents may be losing an opportunity for a stronger attachment. The child might also be getting a message that his parents reject or fear his emotion. He may also be learning that the only way to deal with an emotional situation is to withdraw from it. Often, it would be better to help him to work through conflict, integrate anger, and communicate directly with the person, on the spot. Using time-out routinely in response to parent–child conflict, is, at best, a temporary solution. Certainly there are specific times when separating until the parent or child calm down is necessary. However, the advantages to the relationship of dealing with intense emotion together should not be overlooked. If parents need a separation from their child to maintain their own peace of mind and emotional availability to him, then time-out can be helpful and even necessary. But if the child is the only one experiencing intense negative emotion, his parents might do better to try to stay near him, thus being available to assist him in integrating and resolving this experience and thereby facilitating the attachment.

Greatly limiting the child's activities can create a strong sense of security for the child who is repeatedly making poor choices across all settings. Although an outsider may see it as punitive when I direct parents to restrict their child's activities and give him constant supervision for a period of time, I have done this numerous times, often with an excellent response on the child's part. What is commonly obvious when he is so restricted is how happy and relieved he appears. He might sit for hours in a chair near his mother, laughing, humming, and singing to himself. His mother is temporarily making the choices for him. He need not put the energy into deciding what is the best choice for him. He need not become upset repeatedly with the consequences of his numerous poor choices. In such a restricted setting some children will regress and allow nurturance more easily than they usually do. His parents have removed from him the burden of making so many choices. They are making many of them for him, just as they would do for a much younger child.

When parents do become angry over their child's behavioral choice, they should admit it quite readily. Parents should accept responsibility for their own emotions ("I am angry at what you did") rather than blaming the emotion on the child ("You made me angry"). If there is danger that the parents will lose sight of an appropriate consequence and be tempted to impose a harsh punishment, they are wise to say "I'm angry now, I'll talk with you about it later." It is better to think about the situation after calming down and possibly discussing the situation with someone who is helpful before talking with the child. If they do impose a consequence that they later consider to be harsh, they have the option of changing it. Simply telling him that they reconsidered and now think that another consequence is more appropriate will suffice. They should not change the consequence in response to the child screaming about it. It is their judgment, not their child's anger, that is the guiding principle.

UNDERSTANDING THE CHILD'S REINFORCERS

Because the poorly attached child has had a tragic personal history, he most likely takes pleasure in, strives for, or strives to avoid, many things which have little or no value to another child. A closely attached child may take pleasure in pleasing his parents, while the poorly attached child may take pleasure in upsetting his parents. A closely attached child may work hard to get a gift; the poorly attached child may become anxious when given something and work to sabotage receiving the gift. We cannot assume that a privilege, gift, special time with a parent, or a compliment will serve as a means to reinforce a child's behavior. Common incentives for "good behavior" may have little impact on the poorly attached child. Also, a positive incentive may be mildly desirable to the child, but the act of opposing and frustrating his parents may have an even higher incentive value.

Here are some examples of what may actually be positive incentives for the poorly attached child. When he succeeds in attaining these goals, his functioning may well not change:

1) Being in control of the feelings and behaviors of others;
2) Engaging in and winning power struggles;
3) Saying "No!";
4) Causing emotional and physical pain to others;
5) Maintaining a negative self-concept;
6) Needing no one;
7) Avoiding emotional engagements with others;

8) Avoiding experiences of mutual fun and laughter;
9) Avoiding having to ask for favors and help;
10) Avoiding being praised for actions; and
11) Avoiding feeling loved and feeling special to someone.

If the above examples are relevant to the choices of the poorly attached child, one can understand why these children are often so resistant to "behavior management" systems structured to elicit behavior change. He may be experiencing significant pleasure in response to his misbehavior. The "benefits" of behaving well often cannot compete with these internal and historic reinforcers. Although at times the child may choose to go along with the "program" and attain a specific reward, one often notices that there is little carryover to other situations or even to other days for the same reward. The child, in those situations, is in control of the "behavior management" system. He is choosing when to reinforce his parents for establishing the system! Given his unique history, he may be experiencing great pleasure in the parent's frustration over the lack of reliable success. Many parents have expressed great disappointment over their awareness that their child will do what is expected of him "only when he wants something." They know that as soon as he gets what he wants, his behavior will take a turn for the worse. He is telling them that he is still in control of the situation. He will consider being "good" again only when they have some other reward for him that he wants. They had better think of something good!

I worked with one 8-year-old girl who vehemently resisted being praised when she made a good choice and accomplished something. Since most poorly attached children have this difficulty, I suggested to her foster mother that she calmly say "good job" or "I'll bet you like that" and then drop the subject. Most children can accept such a brief statement or a pat on the back if there is not too much emotion and attention given to the act. This girl, however, would not accept even such little recognition. She would quickly find something to do that her parents would object to. Not wanting to submit to her wish to avoid all positive recognition, we discussed this with her and gave her empathy for how hard it was to accept such praise. She understood, but her ability to do so did not increase. We then spoke with her about her and our dilemma. We told her that whenever her mother wanted to say "Good job" for something well done, instead she would say "It's a nice day." This proved to be very successful. No one else knew what it meant. Often she would smile or even laugh when her mother made that comment. She did not show any need to sabotage that recognition for what she had done.

With children who have difficulty with their reciprocal enjoyment or feeling close to their parents, we calmly discuss it in treatment in an atmosphere that itself is enjoyable for us all and which elicits feelings of acceptance and closeness. I often gently tease such children about how hard it is for them to have fun or accept a brief hug from their mom. This is done playfully but with empathy for not having had these experiences very often. One boy had to practice having fun with his mom during each session. She would pick an activity and he was asked to participate so that he might learn how to be with her in similar ways at home. I gave him some specific feedback on his level of having fun and modeled it a few times. He did participate well, if only to avoid some other activities in therapy that were hard for him. His mother indicated that he demonstrated a degree of enjoyment in being with her that he seldom, if ever, had showed at home. We then worked to transfer this behavior to his time at home. We picked a few activities, designated a time and place, and I instructed him that this was his homework. I assured him that I would not give him much to do because I knew that it was hard for him now. I then asked his mom not to "bug him" about having fun at any other times. He agreed, to his amusement. Gradually he came to be more able to accept mutual enjoyment with his mom and it began to occur more spontaneously and often.

What should parents do then if their child experiences a positive reinforcement from controlling the emotions and actions of the parents? Clearly it is important to prevent the child from gaining such control. That, of course, is easier said than done. Parents need to be aware of the circumstances in which it is happening and they need to consider alternative responses they might make that are not reinforcing to their child. Thus, if parents judge that their child really wants to get them angry, they need to identify what the child is most likely to do to provoke the anger and then to develop other responses. If parents can remain detached and express puzzlement, while showing empathy for him and his undesired consequence, he will be less likely to try it again.

If parents choose not to engage in power struggles, such struggles will not be reinforced, and their child's efforts to create them will be less. If parents do not react to his "No!" but instead respond to the behavior with an appropriate consequence, such exclamations will fall within the normal range. If parents do not "mirror" their child's negative self-concept, but instead communicate empathy and enjoyment rather than rejection and annoyance when administering a consequence, the self-concept will gradually change.

It is clearly crucial for parents to reflect on the meaning of the child's act before routinely responding to it. What effect is the child trying to attain by engaging in a certain behavior? If his parents do not think it best for that effect to occur, how might they respond so that a different effect occurs? The child is likely to be skilled in eliciting an angry and rejecting response. Parents need to develop skills to respond with an appropriate consequence to his action without confirming his negative perceptions of both self and parents.

PRIVILEGES AND PRACTICE

Because of their child's oppositional, impulsive, and disruptive behaviors, many family activities may need to become privileges. If the child becomes verbally or physically aggressive or destructive in a store, he might need to lose the right to go shopping. If the same occurs during family gatherings, he might have to stay home with a sitter. The consequence is quite reasonable, especially if the child is encouraged to learn the skills necessary to be able to go shopping again or go to the next reunion. His parents need to be willing to teach their child anger management, impulse control, or stress management skills as needed. He should be told that he can go shopping again as soon as his parents have confidence that he has learned some of these skills. Telling the child that he will miss the next shopping trip but can go on the following one, especially if he has shown no motivation to demonstrate more acceptable behavior, will probably end in a recurrence of the behavior. Waiting for some progress, whether it be for two days, weeks, months, or years, is more likely to lead to a genuine motivation to change.

Other examples of activities that may have to be privileges for the child who does not manage them well are:

Unsupervised time and places;
Unsupervised contact with animals or younger children;
Use of toys, TV, tools, crayons; and
Participation in social or sports activities.

Practice is the best way to learn most skills. If a child does not manage a certain activity well, the best consequence might be for him to practice the activity a given number of times. For example, if a child is repeatedly being corrected for running through the house, he might be instructed in how to walk quietly through the house for certain periods of time. The child who frequently lies might have daily practice sessions for telling the truth. In these examples and others, the best way to conduct such practice is with a matter-of-fact manner, possibly with some gentle humor rather than with annoyance. Other examples:

Screaming—practice assertive discussions or solitary screaming;
Poor public behaviors—practice with role playings, trial runs;
Poor chore completion—practice extra chores; and
Breaking rules—practice asking permission for routine activities.

PARADOXICAL INTERVENTIONS

For years now therapists have had paradoxical interventions in their treatment strategies. Therapists have discovered that often when they would tell the client to *increase* a symptom which the client wanted to decrease, it would actually *decrease.* This phenomenon of treatment has numerous explanations and has been adopted by various theoretical schools of therapy. Parents, too, can make good use of paradoxical responses to their child's behavior in their daily interactions. For example, when their child is *screaming* loudly in response to routine discipline and his parents want to decrease that behavior, the common response is to tell the child to stop it. A more effective response might be one of the following:

1) Praise the quality of the child's scream and encourage him to improve the quality further by varying the pitch, loudness, and so forth;

2) Recognize the child's need to scream and insist that he gratify that need for 5 minutes in the appropriately located "screaming chair";

3) Audio-tape the screaming to present to the therapist as evidence of how mean the parents are;

4) Suggest that the screaming lacks some quality so that the child needs to practice it 3 times each day and then chart his progress; and

5) Reward the scream, with enthusiasm, and give the child a cookie.

For those or other interventions to be effective, the parents need to communicate an overall acceptance of the symptom along with some mild enjoyment of the sequence. They also need to follow through with the paradoxical consequence. If parents use this intervention while communicating frustration and annoyance, their child will see through the "reverse psychology" and frustrate their parents further by increasing the symptom to win the "battle of wills."

These interventions also tend to be effective because they maintain the parents' emotional atmosphere and keep them from reacting in anger to their child's misbehavior. They deny the child's efforts to control the family atmosphere through his behavior and thus show him that his behavior has little merit in this regard and might as well be eliminated.

Other random examples of paradoxical responses are the following:

1) The child's *lying* is incorporated into a family game where members compete to see who can catch the most lies. Each family member then encourages the child to lie so that he might win the game;

2) The child who yells *"No, I won't do it"* is told to write those words, in large and well-designed and colored letters, on a banner to hang outside his bedroom door;

3) Parents imitate the child's "No, I won't do it" in their responses to each other;

4) The child who *destroys* his toys will spend his allowance at garage sales to find more toys to destroy. He will destroy them on Saturday mornings from 10 A.M. to 11 A.M.; and

5) The child who *steals* will be shown designated items to steal and rewarded if the items are not found by anyone in one week.

Again, to be effective, the parents must communicate a relaxed and serious response to the behavior without any evidence of frustration. A good description and explanation of paradoxical interventions for children can be found in *Troubled Transplants* (Delaney and Kunstal 1993)

REFRAMING

It is also the experience of many therapists that if they are able to help their clients to see the problem from another perspective, the problem often becomes more manageable or may, in fact, dissipate. The "silver lining" of the experience may be highlighted. The opportunity for growth or the chance to take another more successful approach is emphasized. If the client can see the problem as part of the ebb and flow of life, it also loses some of its dreaded qualities.

This approach is effective for both child and parents. A child misses playing with his friend because he did not complete his homework. His parents can help him increase his frustration tolerance if they calmly tell him that the consequence which prohibits him playing with his friend is actually an excellent opportunity for increasing frustration tolerance! The consequence is also an opportunity to learn how to avoid making such a choice again. The child might be told how fortunate he is to have that chance now, at his young age, so that he does not have to make countless more similar choices in years ahead. He might then be told to express gratitude to his parents for giving him such a fine consequence that will teach him so much. Such a response to the child's anger about the consequence often takes the intensity out of the anger as the child, somewhat bewildered and muttering to himself, says "thank you." At other times, he might grin and be able to quickly accept the consequence.

Regardless of the immediate behavioral or emotional response to this reframing, the child will think of the experience somewhat differently. Rather than simply focusing on the annoying aspect of the consequence, he will be more receptive to noticing the possible benefit of it. In therapy, I often will listen to a child complain about some consequence for a while and then say something such as: "Wow, you have such a great mom to notice how much you needed to do that chore in order to become closer to her. Way to go mom!" In doing this I am not denying the child's anger. I am interpreting the event differently than he is, and I am giving him this different interpretation.

Another child might be avoiding reciprocal enjoyment with his parents quite successfully. If the parents become frustrated, their child will be able to control his parents' emotion by preventing them from having fun too. At the very least the parents need to continue to have fun, even if their child will not participate. However, they might also reframe the child's resistant behavior so that he cannot so easily think of it as winning a control battle by holding his parents away. His parents might say, with some gentle sadness, that they realize that his behavior is a sign of how hard it is for him to "bond." They then calmly accept this "bonding" difficulty and tell the child that he could probably only tolerate having fun with them for 10 seconds. They then grab and tickle him for 10 seconds, say "That's enough," and calmly walk away for their own fun. The experience has been reframed to describe the child's problem, not the parents.' The result of this interaction may be that the child will reflect on his own resistant behavior somewhat differently; it may lose some of its value for him.

As a way to help a child to reframe his experiences, I often tell him that in his life most of his experiences can be understood as being like a glass that is half full. However, he is a master at seeing that his glass is half empty. Therefore, his task is to draw glasses on paper, each representing his various experiences, each half filled with water. He then uses words to describe the empty half, before working to find words to describe the full half. His parents and I serve as his coach for this process since he has had such little experience with the "full half" aspects of his life. This will be an opportunity for creative homework which encourages the child to begin to think about the full half, which pleases me, though I initially conceal my pleasure.

In a similar way it is often necessary and beneficial to help a poorly attached child to reframe his past experiences of abuse and neglect. He most likely has not benefited from past attempts to help him to "work through" his traumatic history. Instead he may well have incorporated them into a myth that involves him being "bad." He may also have begun to use them as excuses for his poor behavioral choices. In these situations his parents need to be aware of these tendencies and confront them. They may help him to reframe these experiences by first providing empathy for how difficult they must have been. The parents should also acknowledge that because of those experiences, he now has to "work hard" if he is to learn how to be a part of a good family and have a good life. He is offered help in his hard work. He may also be told that in some ways his traumas may have made him stronger than other children. He may have more stamina and resilience now in dealing with adversity. He may have a greater understanding of the value of love and responsibilities now than do other children. This reframing does not minimize his traumas; rather it accepts their reality and the fact that the past cannot be changed. The negative effects of the past can be reduced and turned into opportunities for growth.

DIFFERENTIATING THOUGHTS AND FEELINGS FROM BEHAVIOR

If the child is to acquire greater control of his behavior by making choices which are in his best interest, it is to his advantage to exert considerable effort in understanding what he thinks and feels about his behaviors and their consequences. It is often helpful for him to express his feeling and thought before doing something that he is being told to do. If parents notice that their child seems to be annoyed at having to sweep the floor for the third time, they might tell him to look them in the eye and say: "I am angry at having to do it again, because I think that it's good enough!" before adding "Now I'll go and do it again." The parents acknowledge the validity of what their child has said, even when they told him what to say. When he shows some skill at expressing honestly and clearly what he thinks and feels, he may be told to use his own words. This process has various purposes:

1) The child is learning to identify and express his inner life;
2) The child is learning that he can do things even when he does not "feel" like doing them;
3) The child is learning to analyze his choices and their emotional components;
4) The child knows that his parents understand what he thinks and feels, and even have some empathy for him, though the behavior still must be done;
5) The child is using words to communicate his angry thoughts rather than his usual devious or destructive behaviors; and
6) The child is tacitly acknowledging and accepting his parents' authority. Each time this happens some trust is developing and identification is occurring.

The "thinking chair" is also valuable in helping a child to reflect upon his behavioral choices and the feelings that were associated with them. Upon leaving the chair, he should summarize for his parents his conclusion about his choice as well as alternative choices he might consider the next time. Parents should not push on the child a "correct" choice or he will only resist it and frustrate them. Rather, if the choices appear to be poorly thought through, parents might simply comment: "I never would have suggested that option, I'm curious to see how it works."

Another purpose of thinking is to have a greater understanding of the emotion that is often associated with the poor choices that the child makes. Parents might at times guess why that particular emotion, with that degree of intensity, is there. For example, if their child is particularly angry that his parents insist that the chore be done before he sits down for dinner, they might say:

Since you had an hour to do the chore, I wonder why you are so angry about having to do it now and delaying your meal. Maybe you feel this angry that I won't feed you now, since you often did not get much to eat when you were little. I know eating is important to you. It must be hard to have to do the chore first. Maybe tomorrow will be different for you.

The value of helping a child to be aware of and express his inner life cannot be overemphasized. If he can learn to identify and verbalize his thoughts and feelings, he will have a much easier time making good choices, reducing the compulsive or impulsive quality of his behavior, and refraining from expressing his inner life in destructive or aggressive behaviors. As his "ownership" of his inner life increases, he will have a much easier time accepting responsibility for his behavior. He also will be more able to reflect on his life, his feelings, and his desires and so develop a more integrated and mature positive sense of self.

REGRESSION

When a child is demonstrating little if any developmental momentum in his affective, behavioral, and cognitive functioning, and his parent believes that he is experiencing little reciprocal enjoyment, she should consider structuring her home so that he has the opportunity to experience regression in a deep and comprehensive manner. This is a child who constantly manifests a lack of affect regulation, intense behavioral impulsivity, poor judgment with little awareness of the consequences of his actions, and various other symptoms reflecting a lack of trust and excessive shame.

Too often the parental and therapeutic response to this child is to repeatedly place him in situations in which he will make countless self-destructive and disruptive choices that lead to negative responses. Too often one thinks that to allow him to start "fresh" each day, without considering his compulsive maladaptive behaviors of the previous several days, weeks, and even months, is a gift to him. This tactic is considered to be a "positive" approach that will enable him to like himself better, trust his parents, and then try to improve. Such an approach often fails with the poorly attached child. His parents become increasingly frustrated and more often than not become increasingly emotionally reactive to his behaviors. While the approach, superficially, is "positive," the underlying atmosphere is often one of tension, anger, and discouragement.

Rather than react to each new poor behavioral choice, the parent might consider instead modifying her entire childrearing assumptions and routines to reflect the actual level of his developmental attachment patterns rather than his chronological age. She will treat her child as if he were much younger, since in fact he is living as if he were. By doing this, she will be providing him with a family environment that does match his developmental level and she will be fostering his regression to that level.

When the parent and therapist decide to facilitate this degree of regression, it is necessary to be realistic about the time demands that will be made on the parent. It is often exhausting to raise a 2- or 3-year-old child. So, too, will it be more demanding to raise a poorly attached child in this manner. The parent will be making her child the center of her waking day and he may well become a part of her sleeping hours also.

When the decision is made to raise the child as if he were much younger, it needs to be presented to him in a matter-of-fact, empathic manner. He should never be told, "Since you're acting like a baby we're going to treat you like a baby!" Such a statement would communicate an angry, punitive attitude that suggested that the parent were trying harder to win a power struggle. Rather the child should be informed with the decision in a manner similar to the following:

> I've noticed over the past several weeks (or months) how hard it is for you to be able to live in the family. So often you seem to make choices that leave you angry and sad because you have consequences that you don't like. Sometimes you don't seem to know what you want and you're sorry that you made the choice that you did.
>
> I've decided that I can help you more by spending a lot more time with you so that I can help you with your choices and also help you to have more fun in spite of how hard it gets for you at times. When you were little (younger) you probably didn't have enough time with your mom helping you in this way. That's why it is so hard to do it now. But that's OK. I want to do this for you because you need it now and you're special to me. What do you think?

When a parent makes a presentation similar to this one, her child often responds with some curiosity and general acceptance. The parent then gives examples of how the daily routine will be different for her child as well as new activities that will be added:

> At dinner I'll be selecting your food, cutting it, and feeding you. That's a special way for us to be together. It might seem a little strange at first but you'll enjoy it soon.

We'll have a lot of time to play together because that's so important for us to be closer. But I still have chores to do too so you can stay close to me while I'm working. I'll have things for you to do near me.

In encouraging regression the parent provides numerous experiences that can be considered as being either *nurturing* or *structuring*. Nurturing experiences will enable the child to have a variety of opportunities to relate more positively and closely with his parent. They are modeled on attunement between mother and child and they represent the primary need for him to experience attunement with his parent. Structuring experiences will provide an overall framework for greatly reducing his opportunities to make self-destructive, oppositional, or disruptive behaviors. They are modeled on the child's need to be safe and to be socialized in a manner that will provide a manageable shame with a quick reunion. No one experience is necessary or sufficient to achieve the developmental results that we are seeking. If a given experience does not seem suitable or appropriate for a particular child then it is simply not used. The following lists represent typical experiences that facilitate regression for the poorly attached child:

Nurturing Experiences

1) Feeding and giving a bottle;
2) Holding, rocking, hugging, and brief gentle tickling;
3) Songs and games for babies and toddlers;
4) Washing, dressing, and combing his hair;
5) Reading and telling stories;
6) Quiet, extended, bedtime routines;
7) Going for a walk and holding his hand; and
8) Supporting "baby talk." Engaging in much "small talk."

Structuring Experiences

1) Supervision: the parent (or substitute) is aware of the child at all times when he is not sleeping. If the parent is out of visual contact briefly, the child is confined to an area where he cannot harm himself or destroy anything important;
2) The home is "child-proof";

3) The child sits and plays or rests near the parent when she is busy;
4) There is a well-defined routine, alternating more active and quiet activities, as well as work and play;
5) The parent selects most food, clothes, toys, and activities, only gradually giving him an increasing number of choices; and
6) An audio monitor and/or door alarm is considered for the bedroom.

As I have indicated earlier, most poorly attached children are very receptive to both the nurturing and the structuring experiences. Many seem to be relieved that they no longer have to make so many choices and that they are therefore not making poor choices. Many also seem to feel safer with the parent's increased contact and involvement. Many show no embarrassment about being seen with a bottle or having to remain at their parent's side.

If a given nurturing experience is strongly resisted by a child, it should not be forced. Structuring experiences, however, are more directed toward safety and should be retained although the child's reservations should be heard and modified if it can be done and still be of benefit.

The minimum amount of time needed to have an impact on the functioning of the poorly attached child is a month. Often 3 or 4 months are necessary before the parent becomes aware of any changes of sufficient breadth and depth to reflect true development.

MORE IMAGINATIVE PARENTING AND PROBLEM SOLVING

Options for Consequences

A child may attempt to resist a consequence by doing it poorly in order to attempt to frustrate his parents. In this case they might choose to have him redo the consequence for a period of time. If the parents fear that their child might get some control of them by forcing them to impose a consequence that makes them feel uncomfortable, they might then give him a choice of consequences. For example, if he is not thinking in the "thinking chair" very well, his parents may not want to say "Sit there until you do it quietly and with good thinking." The child might then be sitting there longer than they want him to sit there. Instead, they might have more success by saying: "You can sit there for 10 minutes the way I told you to sit, or 20 minutes the way you want to sit. Either way is OK with me."

List of Wants and Needs

Often the poorly attached child will complain about most of what occurs to him or is provided for him in his home. This tendency may certainly represent his years of neglect, but it is a poor habit if he is to learn to get more satisfaction from his life. The child and his parents should sit down together and make two lists. The first involves things that the child wants and the second is for his needs. His parent will guarantee that their child's needs will always be met, although his wants may or may not be met. The lists should be hanging from a wall somewhere so that he can see if his parents are neglecting his needs. To inject some humor and to maintain the child's interest, the parents might add a "want" to the "needs" list each week and then be sure that the child has that, too. (A bag of M&M's can quickly become a high-priority need.)

Excuses

The poorly attached child is likely to have as many excuses as he has poor choices. Some of these excuses may involve his past traumas. Others involve being angry, forgetting, not hearing, or thinking that the rule was unfair in the first place. In response to such excuses, his parents might respond:

> You need to decide if you want to feel sorry for yourself and mess up your life or get strong from the pain. Let us help you if we can.

If he has hit another child and exclaims: "He took my ball and made me mad!" we might respond:

> Good thinking. You now know that your anger needs to be integrated better if you're going to avoid consequences like you're now going to get for hitting that kid. Good luck learning how to do it.
> Good job of realizing that you need to listen better if you don't want this consequence the next time too.

Rather than calling his "reason" for his poor choice an "excuse," accept it as a reason that should guide the work that he needs to do if he wants to avoid more consequences.

"Mom Time"

When parents observe that their child is in a negative cycle of numerous poor choices followed by consequences that he does not like, the parents might break this cycle by interpreting it as representing the child's fear of being close to them. He is then told that he could use some "mom time" to help him to become closer to his mom since he clearly needs it in spite of his fears. In this instance, the child is trying to control his parents by engaging in poor choices to "make" them give him unpleasant consequences. His parents respond by refusing to be so manipulated and by getting closer to him. Thus, if the child has just had a tantrum and refused to do his chore, his mother might say: "Gee, you're having a hard day. In fact, the whole week seems to be going poorly for you. I think that we need to have some fun together, and we need it right now! Get your jacket, we're out of here!" (This term, "Mom Time" is used by Deborah Hage, with much sensitivity and humor.)

Responsibility Training

Responsibility training, also a concept presented by Deborah Hage, involves parents allowing their child to be in a situation requiring some responsibility. They then *hope* that the child will make a poor choice and not be able to manage the responsibility. This provides them with an opportunity to give empathy for the choice and for its subsequent consequence, and it provides the child with an opportunity to be responsible for solving the problem of learning to make a better choice. The parents then allow another situation requiring responsibility. Such an approach to their child's poor choice allows both them and their child to reframe the action as a valuable growth experience.

Consequences, without Coaxing

Frequently, parents want so much for their child to make a good choice that they remind and warn him a number of times that if he makes the poor choice he will be given a consequence. By adopting this pattern, they are coaxing him to make a choice that should be in the child's best interest. The act of coaxing may confuse him into thinking that it is in the parents' best interest, and not his, for him to make the good choice. Coaxing also suggests that he cannot reason well enough to see that it is in his best interest. Finally, it suggests that he cannot remember very well since he needs to be reminded so often.

A much more effective approach, which conveys a healthier message to the child, is to present the consequences without any reminders, explanations, second chances, or discussions. Once the child has been informed of the choice-consequence connection, it is his responsibility to remember the connection and to make the best choice for himself. Presenting the sequence in this way communicates that his parents have confidence in him and will not tamper with the process. It also clearly demonstrates that his parents think he is strong enough to manage the consequences of poor choices and smart enough to make choices that are better for himself in the future.

GOOD TIMES: FUN AND LOVE

Bill, a 9-year-old with significant attachment problems, went to the local fair with his foster mom, Janet. The trip was a huge success and they were enjoying themselves enormously when Bill saw a sign for camel rides. He asked if he could ride a camel, and since he had been relating well and making good choices, Janet decided that he could. While waiting in line, Bill's excitement grew. As it got closer to his turn he began to be more and more anxious and had second thoughts about whether he should ride this very tall and strange looking animal. Janet told Bill that it was his choice. When it was his turn, he hesitated, but then shook his head "yes" and slowly walked to the camel. As the ride began, he gripped the saddle tightly until his hands were white. His eyes grew huge with fright and he looked straight in front of him, frozen in space. Some fun!

Slowly, however, as he rode, Bill began to relax his grip, smile and search for his foster mom. He made eye contact with Janet and his smile broadened. He began to notice the camel with pleasure rather than fear. Finally, at the end of the ride, Bill was helped off the camel and he went running to Janet, his arms wide, his smile even larger, and his whole self so alive. For the first time in her three years of being with Bill, Janet looked at him and saw joy! He ran into her arms and held her tightly; his tears flowed. The years of his screaming, fighting, and running from her had led to this moment. Bill could now experience joy! He had learned that he had her love. He was now free to find himself in the world.

Bill's experience with the camel was, in fact, new for him. Joy is a luxury for children who do not have the security of an attachment to a caregiver. It is beyond the grasp of children who truly doubt whether they even deserve to be fed and responded to with minimal respect. Pervasive loneliness and shame precludes joy as well as most other experiences of day-to-day fun. Poorly attached children have a great deal of difficulty accepting and functioning well within experiences that are fun. Just as they have difficulty dealing well with conflict and discipline, they have equal trouble managing the positive affect of shared fun within the family. Fun is hard to manage and control. If others are having fun, there is less for the poorly attached child. It will end, so it should be avoided in the first place. But most of all, the child feels he does not deserve it. If he does not deserve love, why should he expect to experience fun.

Often poorly attached children give the appearance of wanting to have fun. They oppose responsibilities because they would rather "play." Yet, the play which they choose usually involves activities such as passively watching TV, controlling, manipulating, and fighting with other children; hoarding and/or destroying toys and objects that they were so desperate to possess; and compulsively engaging in an activity or inducing others to engage in that activity. Games may be "fun" but only if the child wins and can brag about it. Cheating is an important skill used in order to maximize this "fun."

When the child is brought into family fun activities, he often becomes increasingly frantic, irritable, and controlling. When limits are placed on his behavior, they provide him with a reason to scream and be miserable. He then works to be sure that no one else has fun either. Many poorly attached children have attempted to ruin many family parties, picnics, birthdays, and holidays. One poorly attached boy that I was working with had a birthday party scheduled and his foster mom invited, at his request, five boys from school. Each boy accepted the invitation. However, the party was eventually canceled because in the next week at school, prior to the party, he proceeded to beat up each of the five boys. That will teach them for showing that they liked him and wanted to come to his party! That will teach him for initially hoping that he could be a normal kid who had a party. That will teach him for thinking that he lived in a family that would provide him with such a happy experience.

For poorly attached children, both fun and love are difficult experiences to manage well and to integrate into their self-concept and their interpersonal world. In healthy families, fun and love often are experienced together. While they may be unrelated at times, there is usually much overlap. Playfulness, gentle teasing, unexpected laughter, routine surprises, relaxing conversation, games, and festive occasions all communicate love in ways different than and as important as hugs-when-sad, encouragement, and words of love. These many experiences of fun nourish a deepening love relationship. Habitual love without mutual fun will not facilitate either the relationship or the selves of those in love. The commitment inherent in love will take it through hard times and such hard times will deepen love. But for it to flourish, frequent experiences of mutual fun must be present.

In assisting their child to be able to experience fun and love within the family, parents first need to be aware of the difficulties that such experiences entail for him. The following factors are often present:

1. The child truly does not see himself as deserving such experiences. He will work to negate their meaning in order to preserve his definition of self that says that he is not worthy. This is a *shameful* child. In his world there is no place for both shame and rage as well as love. It is easier to avoid or destroy these experiences than it is to build a positive self-concept.

2. If the child does begin to experience fun and love, he often does not know how to respond. He does not trust his feelings and he does not know how to communicate enjoyment and pleasure. He cannot forget himself long enough to become immersed in the activity and interaction. He cannot give up his need to control whatever happened and he cannot react spontaneously. Holding back, he watches with tension and distance. He feels uncomfortable, does not "fit in," and may actually experience shame again because he feels different and less than the other family members.

3. If he begins to experience these self-enhancing and attachment facilitating interactions, he immediately anticipates that they will end. He fears the loss that will come. Consequently, he might ruin the experience and so control the loss. He cannot trust that such experiences will be frequent and continuing. Rather than begin to hope that he will have many such experiences, he avoids them and returns to what he has lived with for so long, namely isolation, control, conflict, and so forth.

Facilitating Fun and Love

1. Experience fun and love yourself. It is hard, if not impossible, for parents to offer a resistant child experiences that are rare in the parents' own life. They need to take pleasure and pride in their day-to-day living, experiencing enjoyment in family life—including the challenges of raising this poorly attached child. Frequent fun and love with a spouse, companion, and/or close friend are also important. Interests and satisfactions from community, religious, and special group activities may be helpful. Solitary satisfactions to reestablish one's personal meaning and commitments may also help parents to maintain a positive and deeply enjoyable life. A habitually depressed, isolated, anxious, and resentful parent will have a great deal of difficulty inviting the poorly attached child into these experiences of fun and love.

2. Go slow, keep it short, but provide fun and love experiences. I recall a parent telling me that after three weeks she had not yet touched her foster child because she had been told that an abused child needs to feel in control of all touching of his body and only he should initiate all physical affection. My response was to encourage her to immediately go home and make her child aware that she does care for her child and that touching is an important way of communicating that caring. If her child is anxious about this touching, she should communicate empathy for the initial tension that he is likely to feel before getting used to it. A parent may also tell the very physically withdrawn child that she will not surprise him with quick touches during the next week or so. She is willing to schedule touches and hugs and negotiate their length and frequency. *But,* she will communicate, with caring, patience, and certainty, by word and deed: *"All kids* need to be touched and hugged and you do, too. I know it may be hard for a while, so you can tell me whenever it is. But I must, and I will, touch and hug you because I'm your mom and I care about you and you so need this."

Parents must initiate these fun and love experiences and not wait passively for their child to do so. Poorly attached children will make you wait a long time, often until it is too late to make a real difference in their lives. If we give a child complete control over whether or not he will be provided with these experiences, we will be neglecting that child's basic needs. If he is unable to choose these experiences, we must be sure that he has them anyway. We need to be attuned to his fears and so we may need to proceed more slowly and more briefly than we otherwise would. He may need some information to prepare himself if the experience might be stressful. But we must be persistent and be certain to give him some fun and love experiences daily if we want him to discover affect beyond shame and rage and to form an attachment.

3. Be direct and open about the child's need and difficulty. Just as one should communicate directly about the importance of the child learning to accept discipline, so, too, should one inform the child that fun and love experiences certainly may be hard for the child to have, given his past. Because of their importance and the child's difficulties with them, the parents are willing and able to assist him in learning how to incorporate these experiences into his life. The parents might do this in a number of ways:

1) Model such experiences among other family members.
2) Coach the child in beginning these interactions. ("The next time that you're bored, why not ask to go for a walk?" The child's shame may make this difficult for quite some time.).
3) Reframe experiences so that the child will recall qualities of an event for their fun and love components. ("You looked so proud when you blew out all the candles!").
4) When the child sabotages an interaction, interpret his action as reflecting his fear to be close, and so forth, and patiently speak of other, future opportunities. ("No problem. You'll have other chances to go swimming with us. You'll have fun with it yet!").
5) Make the family rituals and values explicit. ("Here we're sure that our kids have a chance to get pudding on themselves when they really like it. If you're too neat, I might stick some of mine on your nose!" or "When we like what you do, we tell you. You'll get used to it.").

4. Be playful when teaching fun and love. It most certainly is difficult to repeatedly speak seriously about the need for fun and love and then expect to get results. On the other hand, if parents approach this vital area of their child's life with a more light-hearted, relaxed, and playful attitude, the child is likely to experience fun and love without even expecting to do so. If he does not know it's coming, and if it is over quickly, it is much harder for him to avoid and then disengage from the interaction. At times, using paradoxical interventions may also help. Here are some examples of keeping this message light:

1) Give the child a quick, unexpected smile, touch, or hug for "no reason." If the child asks why, shrug your shoulders and smile.
2) Give the child an unexpected gift and then leave the room.
3) In the middle of his homework, take the child out for ice cream.
4) When the child is having fun or showing affection, acknowledge it briefly, without embarrassing the child.
5) When the child breaks a rule, give him a present or surprise activity.
6) Insist that the child must watch his favorite TV show, with ice cream, telling him that he will be sent to bed early if he refuses. But insist that he must not have "fun" while doing so.

Some Fun and Love Activities

Frequent eye contact and smiles;
Touch: long and short, tickles and hugs, loud and quiet, light and squeezes, rocking and snuggling, laughing and crying;
Feeding the child, nursing him with a bottle (Regression experiences);
Meals with conversation about family and self interests;
Walks and Talks: Memories and Plans;
Quiet bedtime rituals;
Joyful reunions;
Frequent "mom times";
Music;
Photographs;
Cooking, reading, group chores and activities;
Child has role in family rituals and celebrations;
Child is involved with extended family;
Family gifts, to supplement individual gifts;
Party on anniversary of child's arrival;
Helping the child with skill development;
One parent asking the child for help to surprise the other parent; and
Recall old conflicts with acceptance and humor.

In conclusion, poorly attached children fear and are very resistant to family activities that foster mutual enjoyment and affection. They habitually and unconsciously work to maintain experiences which are consistent with their early life of abuse, humiliation, and rejection. Parents of these children must have a well-developed appreciation for and ability to foster and maintain fun and love experiences within their personal and family life. Parents need to accept their child's fear and resistance, provide empathy, and then actively and persistently bring these experiences into their child's life. The child must not be able to prevent these experiences through his oppositional or avoidance behaviors. His behavior may necessitate restrictions from certain privileges or special treats, but it must never prevent his parents from daily introducing experiences of mutual playfulness, quiet talk, quick hugs and encouragement, and gentle teasing and laughter. Only in this way will their child know that his misbehaviors, although extreme and repetitive, will rightfully elicit shame but never contempt and rejection. He lives in a family where the members communicate and experience mutual love and enjoyment. He is a member of that family, in spite of his doubts and resistance. Love and enjoyment will be freely given to him again, and again, and again. At some point in time these experiences will be reciprocated.

13

CONCLUSIONS

Child rearing and therapy for the poorly attached child are very difficult work. It is difficult for the parents and the therapist. It is even more difficult for the child. In the family and in therapy we are asking this child to learn how to enter into a deeply engaging relationship with adults who care for him. We are asking this of a child who was ready to enter into such a relationship as an infant but who then met with abuse, neglect, rejection, and humiliation. We want him to believe that we are different. We want him to trust us and to try again.

Repeatedly I have read recommendations derived from evaluations of foster children that state that a child needs foster parents who will be both nurturing and firm. For the children described in this book, both parental qualities need to be multiplied by five. Children with attachment disorders need very high degrees of affection and empathy as well as clear and comprehensive behavioral expectations with unambiguous consequences. Poorly attached children want parents in their lives who will give them little affection and even less discipline. They are comfortable with parents who are often angry with them and who overlook their poor behavioral choices and so provide no consequences. They prefer anger as the only consequence for their behavior. Anger confirms their lack of self-worth, their mistrust of the relationship, and their feeling that they are being unfairly treated when they act in irresponsible ways. Only by responding to such behaviors with empathy and acceptance, along with the consequence, will the child acquire a better understanding of himself, his relationship with his caregiver, and the difficult job that faces him.

Nurturance is not provided to the poorly attached child through the application of one or more preselected experiences. Rather, this child can only truly begin to experience nurturance with his parent through countless interactions that involve emotional attunement. Just as this is necessary for the psychological development of the infant and toddler, so, too, is it needed by the poorly attached child.

If we do not insist that the poorly attached child work hard, he never will do so. Why should he? He does not know of the pleasure, comfort, joy, and excitement that will emerge from within an attachment with his parents. He has survived by relying only on himself. He will resist strongly our insistence that he turn away from his past and follow our view of himself and others.

If we do not insist that this child work hard, we will fail him. If we allow him to live on excuses, charm, and distortions by lowering our expectations and hoping that he will gradually begin to feel our love, he will fail.

In our insistence that he work hard, we—parents and therapist—must provide him with a great deal of empathy for how hard the task is. We must show him understanding for his pain and rage through our patient, firm, and accepting response to his behaviors. We still present him with whatever consequences his behaviors warrant. We will not allow him to define our discipline in a way that demonstrates rejection of him. We have empathy for him, for his emotions and thoughts, and for his distorted working model of himself and others that leads to his compulsive poor choices. We have affection for him, we play with him, we communicate our enjoyment of him. All the while we ask him to continue to work hard to discover what we are offering him.

Parents of poorly attached children exert a high level of behavioral interventions in their child's life because he is not able to make the behavioral choices that are in his best interests. The developmental attachment patterns developed poorly, and he does not have the inner resources to either deal well with the challenges of daily living or to turn to his parents for direction, guidance, or support. Once he has made significant progress in these areas, much of our task to facilitate his attachment is complete. His parents can then sit back and enjoy the healthy emergence of his "self" within the security that he experiences from becoming attached.

The children described in this book are our children. They were horribly mistreated by their original parents. They then were placed in the custody of the government. As citizens, we became responsible for providing them with a childhood that would meet their psychological needs. It is very challenging to do this well because the poorly attached children described in this book have not only been traumatized, they also have significant delays in the development of their affective, behavioral, and cognitive abilities. These delays can be addressed only by giving the child the means and skills to form an attachment to his new parents. Such is our responsibility.

Many of the children described in this book have, I believe, taken important steps toward achieving a positive, integrated identity and a strong attachment to their parents. Some children continue to have a great deal of hard work ahead of them. If their parents will continue to work hard with them, but not for them, I have confidence in their futures.

The children who lack such parents will not want to, nor will they be able to, do the work necessary to be able to attach, with or without therapy. For that reason, I continually salute the parents who facilitate the second birth of these children. These parents demonstrate a level of commitment and love for these children that is astonishing. Because of these qualities, along with the tools and support that they need and must receive, they are able to work the miracles that I have seen.

REFERENCES

Aber, J. L., Allen, J. P., Carlson, V., and Cicchetti, D. (1989). The effects of maltreatment on development during early childhood: recent studies and their theoretical, clinical, and policy implications. In *Child Maltreatment*, ed. D. Cicchetti and V. Carlson, pp. 579–619. New York: Cambridge University Press.

Bowlby, J. (1988). *A Secure Base.* New York: Basic Books.

Brody, V. (1994). Developmental Play Therapy. In *Handbook for Treatment of Attachment-Trauma Problems In Children*, ed. B. James, pp. 234–239. Lexington, MA: Lexington Books.

Brothers, D. (1995). *Falling Backwards.* New York: Norton.

Cicchetti, D. (1989). How research on child maltreatment has informed the study of child development: perspectives from developmental psychopathology. *Child Maltreatment*, ed. D. Cicchetti and V. Carlson, pp. 377–431. New York: Cambridge University Press.

Cicchetti, D., Cummings, E. M., Greenberg, M. T., and Marvin, R. (1990). An Organizational Perspective on Attachment Beyond Infancy: Implications for Theory, Measurement & Research. In *Attachment in the Preschool Years*, ed. M. T. Greenberg, D. Cicchetti, and E. M. Cummings, pp. 3–50. Chicago: The University of Chicago Press.

Cline, F. W. (1991). *Hope for High Risk and Rage Filled Children.* P. O. Box 2380, Evergreen, CO.

Cline, F. W., and Fay, J. (1990). *Parenting with Love and Logic.* Colorado Springs, CO: Pinon Press.

Crittenden, P. (1988). Relationships at Risk. In *Clinical Implications of Attachment,* ed. J. Belsky and T. Nezworski, pp. 136–176. Hillsdale, NJ: Lawrence Erlbaum.

——— (1995). Attachment and Risk for Psychopathology: The Early Years. *Developmental and Behavioral Pediatrics,* 16: S12–S16.

Crittenden, P., and Ainsworth, M. D. S. (1989). Child Maltreatment and Attachment Theory. In *Child Maltreatment,* ed. D. Cicchetti and V. Carlson, pp. 432–463. New York: Cambridge University Press.

Delaney, R. J., and Kunstal, F. R. (1993). *Troubled Transplants.* Ft. Collins, CO: Horsetooth Press.

Diagnostic and Statistical Manual of Mental Disorders (1994). 5th ed. Washington, DC: American Psychiatric Association.

Durrant, M. (1993). *Residential Treatment: A Cooperative, Competency-Based Approach to Therapy and Program Design.* New York: Norton.

Erickson, M. H. (1980). *The Collected Papers of Milton H. Erickson, Vol. IV: Innovative Hypnotherapy,* ed. E. L. Rossi. New York: Irvington.

Erickson, M. H., and Rossi, E. L. (1979). *Hypotherapy: An Exploratory Casebook.* New York: Irvington Publishers.

Field, T., Morrow, C., Valdeon, C., Larson, S., Kuhn, C., and Schanberg, S. (1992). Massage Reduces Anxiety in Child and Adolescent Psychiatric Patients. *Journal of the American Academy of Child and Adolescent Psychiatry* 31: 125–131.

Field, T., Schanberg, S., Scafidi, F., Bauer, C., Vega-Lahr, N., Garcia, R., Nystrom, J., and Kuhn, C. M. (1986). Tactile/Kinesthetic Stimulation Effects on Preterm Neonates. *Pediatrics* 77:654–658.

Finch, Jr., A. J., Nelson III, W. M., Ott, E. S., eds. (1993). *Cognitive-Behavioral Procedures with Children and Adolescents.* Needham Heights, MA: Allyn & Bacon.

Greenberg, M. T., Speltz, M. L., and DeKlyen, M. (1993). The role of attachment in the early development of disruptive behavior problems. *Development and Psychopathology* 5:191–313.

Greenspan, S. I., and Lieberman, A. F. (1988). A Clinical Approach to Attachment. In *Clinical Implications of Attachment,* ed. J. Belsky, J. and T. Nezworski, pp. 387–424. Hillsdale, NJ: Lawrence Erlbaum.

James, B. (1989). *Treating Traumatized Children.* Lexington, MA: Lexington Books.

————(1994). *Handbook for Treatment of Attachment-Trauma Problems in Children.* Lexington, MA: Lexington Books.

Jernberg, A. (1979). *Theraplay.* San Francisco: Jossey-Bass.

Jordan, J. V., Kaplan, A. G., Miller, J. B., Stiver, I. P., and Surrey, J. L. (1991). *Women's Growth In Connection.* New York: Guilford.

Kaplan, L. (1995). *No Voice Is Ever Wholly Lost.* New York: Simon & Schuster.

Karen, R. (1994). *Becoming Attached.* New York: Warner Books.

Kazdin, A. E. (1993). Psychotherapy for children and adolescents: Current progress and future research directions. *American Psychologist* 48:644–657.

Keck, G., and Kupecky, R. M. (1995). *Adopting the Hurt Child.* Colorado Springs, CO: Pinon Press.

Kobak, R. R. (1993). Attachment and the Problem of Coherence: Implications for Treating Disturbed Adolescents. In *Adolescent Psychiatry,* Vol. 19, ed. S. C. Feinstein and R. R. Marohn, pp. 137–149. Chicago, IL: The University of Chicago Press.

Lansky, V. (1993). *Games Babies Play.* Deephaven, MN: The Book Peddlers.

LeCroy, C. W. (1994). *Handbook of Child and Adolescent Treatment Manuals.* New York: Lexington Books.

Lieberman, A., and Pawl, J. (1988). Clinical Applications of Attachment Theory. In *Clinical Implications of Attachment.* Hillsdale, NJ: Lawrence Erlbaum.

Mahler, M., Pine, F., and Bergman, A. (1975). *The Psychological Birth of the Human Infant.* New York: Basic Books.

Perry, B. (1995). *Maltreated Children: Experience; Brain Development and the Next Generation.* New York: W. W. Norton.

Provence, S., and Lipton, R. (1962). *Infants in Institutions.* New York: International Universities Press.

Schore, A. N. (1994). *Affect Regulation and the Origin of the Self.* Hillsdale, NJ: Lawrence Erlbaum.

Silverstein, O., and Rashbaum, B. (1994). *The Courage to Raise Good Men.* New York: Viking Books.

Small, R., Kennedy, K., and Bender, B. (1991). Critical Issues for Practice in Residential Treatment: The View from Within. *American Journal of Orthopsychiatry* 61:327–337.

Speltz, M. L., DeKlyen, M., Greenberg, M. T., and Gryden, M. (1995). Clinic referral for oppositional defiant disorder: Relative significance of attachment and behavioral variables. *Journal of Abnormal Child Psychology* 23:487–507.

Stern, D. N. (1985). *The Interpersonal World of the Infant.* New York: Basic Books.

Surrey, J. L. (1991). The "self-in relation": a theory of women's development. In *Women's Growth in Connection*, ed. J. V. Jordan, A. G. Kaplan, J. B. Miller, et. al., pp. 51–66. New York: Guilford.

Thoman, E. B., and Browder, S. (1987). *Born Dancing.* New York: Harper & Row.

Welch, M. G. (1989). *Holding Time.* New York: Fireside Books.

INDEX